BLOOMSBURY CURRICULUM BASICS

Teaching Primary PE

By Jazz Rose

B L O O M S B U R Y

LONDON · OXFORD · NEW YORK · NEW DELHI · SYDNEY

Bloomsbury Education
An imprint of Bloomsbury Publishing Plc

50 Bedford Square   1305 Broadway
London   New York
WC1B 3DP   NY 10018
UK   USA

www.bloomsbury.com

Bloomsbury is a registered trademark of Bloomsbury Publishing Plc

First published in Great Britain 2017

A catalogue record for this book is available from the British Library.
Library of Congress Cataloguing-in-Publication data has been applied for.

ISBN:
PB 978-1-4729-2106-2
ePub 978-1-4729-2105-5
ePDF 978-1-4729-2107-9

2 4 6 8 10 9 7 5 3 1

Typeset by NewGen Knowledge Works (P) Ltd., Chennai, India
Printed and bound in Great Britain by CPI Group (UK) Ltd, Croydon CR0 4YY

This book is produced using paper that is made from wood grown in managed, sustainable
forests. It is natural, renewable and recyclable. The logging and manufacturing processes
conform to the environmental regulations of the country of origin.

To find out more about our authors and books visit www.bloomsbury.com. Here you will find extracts,
author interviews, details of forthcoming events and the option to sign up for our newsletters.

Other titles in the Bloomsbury Curriculum Basics series:

Teaching Primary History by Matthew Howorth

Teaching Primary Science by Peter Riley

Teaching Primary French by Amanda Barton and Angela McLachlan

Teaching Primary Spanish by Amanda Barton and Angela McLachlan

Teaching Primary Computing by Martin Burrett

Teaching Primary Geography by Stephen Scoffham and Paula Owens

Online resources accompany this book at: www.bloomsbury.com/BCB-Teaching-PE

Please type the URL into your web browser and follow the instructions to access the resources. If you experience any problems, please contact Bloomsbury at: companionwebsite@bloomsbury.com

Table of Contents

Introduction

The lesson plans in this book act as a guideline to teaching KS1 and KS2 PE in a primary school setting. The lessons are progressive, with each 'warm-up' and 'main lesson' being more challenging than the previous one.

With this in mind, it is important to progress lessons in accordance with how your pupils are advancing, as opposed to following the lesson plans too strictly. It is often a good idea to repeat the key teaching points from previous lessons, and to ensure your pupils develop a clear understanding and can perform the relevant skills to the desired standard before proceeding to the next lesson.

Transferable lesson plans

The lessons can be adapted to suit the needs of a specific group. Many lessons are also transferable to other physical education topics, e.g. teachers could use footballs in a hockey cool-down, or a basketball activity in a football lesson.

Teachers should scan the entire book looking for key games and ideas, so that they are fully aware of dozens of different variations to lessons, warm-ups and so on. This will also be useful to ensure adaptability when working with SEN schools, classes or groups.

Adapting to the learning environment

It is important to be adaptable, so on occasions the teacher may need to use a mixture of different lessons, warm-ups and main lessons in order to get the most out of each class and each child. For example, if a particular lesson requires a large outdoor space and it is raining, the teacher may need to deliver a different lesson from this book that can be successfully delivered indoors. *Teaching Primary PE* acts as a resource and guideline for teachers to work from in order to deliver outstanding PE lessons and school sport.

Demonstration

When teaching primary PE, it is important to explain each activity clearly and succinctly and to demonstrate each activity with precision. For new activities, games and topics, follow the formula opposite for best practice and effective pupil progress.

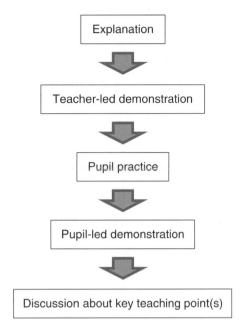

How to use this book

This book is divided into two parts: KS1 and KS2. For each part, there are three units:

- Unit 1: Invasion games
- Unit 2: Gymnastics and athletics
- Unit 3: Net/wall and striking/field games.

At the beginning of each unit, you will find a summary of what you should expect the pupils to be able to do by the end of the unit, including a key giving the attainment steps. Sentences or words wrapped in stars indicate what attainment step pupils are demonstrating if they can successfully complete the task:

KS1: Step 1 | *Step 2*
KS2: Step 3 | *Step 4* | **Step 5**

You will also find a list of the general equipment required for the unit. Any additional equipment needed for specific activities will be noted in the individual lesson plan.

Each unit comprises lesson plans for the different sports covered, e.g. Unit 1 in KS1 (Invasion games) comprises a sequence of lessons for ABCs (Agility, Balance, Co-ordination); basketball; tag rugby and football.

Each lesson plan provides the Lesson objectives and Key terms followed by a detailed five-part lesson.

Key terms

Key terms are listed under the Lesson objective for each lesson. These are some of the key words that you should continually refer to and check pupils' understanding of throughout the lesson. There are two key methods to help embed learning of key terms:

- call and response, e.g. 'I'm looking for an underarm bowl... I'm looking for an...' – open your arms to encourage a choral response from pupils, who say: 'underarm bowl'
- regular selected questioning, e.g. 'James, what type of bowl are we looking for?'

The five-part lesson

Each lesson plan is divided into sections. There are five possible sections in each lesson:

1. **Warm-up:** every lesson plan has a warm-up. This is designed to:
   - increase the heart rate
   - prepare pupils physically and mentally for further activity
   - introduce basic individual skills that will be further developed in the main lesson and throughout.

2. **Main lesson:** every lesson also has main lesson content, which allows pupils to make progress on the key learning objectives.

3. **Match play:** some lessons have match play scenarios, designed to develop the key skills and learning objectives further. Key skills must be emphasised by the teacher to help pupils ensure effective progress. Ensure pupils have developed the relevant core skills in the lesson before progressing to match play. Teachers may wish to skip match play sections for some lessons, e.g. if time is short or pupils' skills need to be developed further in order to minimise risk of injury. When doing match play, it is important to create lots of mini pitches or playing areas and ensure as many pupils as possible are playing at any one time, in order to maximise activity and learning time.

4. **Cool-down:** all lessons end with a cool-down. Cool-downs are designed to:
   - reduce the heart rate
   - reflect on the learning and discuss key ideas for progress
   - relax the mind and mentally prepare pupils for the next phase of their day.

5. **Plenary:** the cool-down should merge into a plenary. Ask pupils to sit still with their legs crossed and eyes closed (or lie down) and think about what they have learnt in the lesson. Ask them to discuss their thoughts with a partner, then ask the key questions listed; these will help to develop pupil understanding and will help you to assess pupil progress. These questions are given in the Plenary section at the end of each lesson, throughout this book.

   Effective plenaries act as a pupil and teacher evaluation of teaching and learning, whereby pupils are probed on what they have learned and have a distinctive opportunity to reflect on what went well and what could be improved next time. Plenaries are designed to enable pupils to reflect on the learning and think about/discuss ways in which they can use this knowledge to improve in the next lesson. You may wish to play calm classical music to help pupils reflect and feel calm in preparation for the next phase of the school day.

Other lesson features

Within each lesson, there are other important elements which include:

- Tips
- Differentiation
- Progression
- Variation
- Competition
- Key teaching points
- Additional lesson ideas and activities (KS2).

Tips
Key teaching skills and tips to help ensure effective pupil progress.

Differentiation
WT pupils: Pupils who are 'working towards' the relevant success criteria and require further support.
WB pupils: Pupils who are 'working beyond' the relevant success criteria and need to be challenged further.
WO pupils: Majority of pupils who are 'working on' the relevant success criteria in accordance with the required expectations.

Making an activity more challenging for WB pupils, or less challenging for WT pupils. Deliver regressions if and when the main criteria is too challenging, so that pupils are able to complete the tasks set before progressing to the next phase of the lesson. If most pupils have achieved the desired objectives within the main lesson, an extension activity provides an additional task that is slightly more challenging and/or develops further skills that have been practised in the main lesson.

Please note, different year groups will progress through the lessons at different paces. As such, it's not essential that a Year 3 or 4 class reaches lesson 6 in each section, as you may notice that more time needs to be spent repeating specific sections of past lessons and/or whole lessons to ensure pupils make steady progress.

Progression
This is the next phase of the activity, which increases the level of difficulty so that pupils are constantly challenged. Be sure to only deliver a progression once you are satisfied that the core objective has been achieved by most or almost all pupils to the required level.

Variation
If you do not have the required space, time or equipment available for a particular lesson, then a variation should be considered. In this book, if a variation is not shown and is required, you should use a suitable alternative activity from elsewhere in the book. All lessons should be delivered with best practice and in accordance with the 'STEP' principle, which increases or decreases the level of challenge according to pupils' needs:

- **Space:** Make the space smaller or larger.
- **Tasks:** Alter the main task or activity.
- **Equipment:** Change the equipment used.
- **People:** Arrange for pupils to work in larger or smaller groups, and/or with more advanced or less advanced peers. The lesson plans assume (in most cases) that there are 30 children in each lesson, so adjust the numbers or teams accordingly to suit the needs of your pupils or group.

Competition

Some lessons have a competition section. Once pupils have practised the key skills as individuals and/or as a team, competition helps pupils develop those skills under pressure, which prepares them for the next phase of learning.

Key teaching points

These provide clear points of advice on how to improve learning of specific skills during the part of the lesson. Key teaching points should be referred to throughout the lesson, and require pupils to:

- demonstrate best practice
- complete your sentences (e.g. 'I'm looking for good balance and. . .' – encourage pupils to reply 'control' by emphasising open hand gestures)
- discuss key ideas about the learning with a partner and/or the class.

Additional lesson ideas and activities (KS2)

These may be used at any time to vary a phase or section of a lesson, to help develop a core skill and/or extend learning. They also act as great ideas for pre-school, lunchtime and after-school clubs.

Transition

You may wish to use the **numbers game** to transition between the activities in these lesson plans. Call out a number (according to how many pupils per team you will require in the activity you are about to begin) and ask them to quickly get into a group of that number. Once they are sitting in these groups, give the class a clear demonstration of the next activity, with pupils observing, before they begin the new activity themselves.

Glossary of terms used in this book

You will find a glossary at the back of the book which provides a brief description or definition of key words or terms.

Part 1:
Key Stage 1

Purpose of study

A high-quality physical education curriculum inspires all pupils to succeed and excel in competitive sport and other physically-demanding activities. It should provide opportunities for pupils to become physically confident in a way which supports their health and fitness. Opportunities to compete in sport and other activities build character and help to embed values such as fairness and respect.

Aims

The National Curriculum for physical education aims to ensure that all pupils:

- develop competence to excel in a broad range of physical activities
- are physically active for sustained periods of time
- engage in competitive sports and activities
- lead healthy, active lives.

Attainment targets: by the end of each key stage, pupils are expected to know, apply and understand the matters, skills and processes specified in the relevant programme of study. Schools are not required by law to teach the example content in [square brackets].

Subject content

Key stage 1:
Pupils should develop fundamental movement skills, become increasingly competent and confident and access a broad range of opportunities to extend their agility, balance and co-ordination, individually and with others. They should be able to engage in competitive (both against self and against others) and co-operative physical activities, in a range of increasingly challenging situations.

Pupils should be taught to:

- master basic movements including running, jumping, throwing and catching, as well as developing balance, agility and co-ordination, and begin to apply these in a range of activities
- participate in team games, developing simple tactics for attacking and defending
- perform dances using simple movement patterns.

Unit 1: Invasion games

By the end of this unit, pupils should be able to:

a) Identify space and *use it effectively in pairs or small team games*.
b) Travel in a straight line (dribbling) with balls of various sizes (i.e. basketballs, tag rugby balls, footballs) *with control and accuracy*.
c) Send and receive the ball in a straight line to a partner (using various equipment including basketballs, footballs, tag rugby balls) *with control and accuracy*.
d) Have a basic understanding of how to work in a small team and encourage others to develop their skills.
e) Understand why it is important to warm up and cool down and *talk about why exercise is good for the body*.

Key: Step 1 | *Step 2*

Equipment required:

- stack of cones
- 30 bibs of at least two colours (15 of each)
- 30 beanbags
- 30 size 3 footballs
- 30 size 3 basketballs
- 15 size 3 rugby balls
- 30 tag rugby belts (desirable)

1 ABCs: Agility, Balance, Co-ordination

What do I need to know?

Agility, balance and co-ordination are commonly known as the ABCs of PE and sport as they form the foundation of all physical education and sporting activities. Loose definitions of each of these are listed below:

- **agility:** *the ability to move quickly and easily in a controlled movement, using a specific muscle or muscle group.*
- **balance:** *the even distribution of weight in order to remain upright and steady.*
- **co-ordination:** *the ability to smoothly and efficiently use different parts of the body together.*

Safety

While delivering all activities, it is important to follow the safety guidelines set out below to ensure a safe and effective learning environment.

- Ensure the playing area is always safe and free of any hazards such as sharp objects before use.
- Ensure pupils are wearing the appropriate attire and that any shoes with laces are sufficiently tightened.
- Check that equipment is not damaged or torn before each lesson.
- Inform and reinforce to pupils the importance of finding space and not bumping into others during warm-ups and other activities.
- Lay the equipment out before the start of the lesson, where possible, to ensure easy access to resources and a smoother transition between activities.
- Inform and remind pupils of the rules and expectations at the beginning of each lesson.
- When delivering line games or activities in which small queues exist, ensure pupils stand side by side so that you can always see them and they can see what is going on in front of them.
- Use verbal as well as visual signals to regain pupil focus and attention.

Rules

- No talking while the teacher is explaining something to the group or demonstrating a task.
- No talking whilst others are explaining something to the group or demonstrating a task.
- No touching other people or equipment without the teacher's permission.

Lesson 1 Exploring space

Lesson objective: Improve awareness of space

Key terms: "bent knees"; "space"; "change direction"

Warm-up: Exploring space (10 minutes)
Pupils walk around the playing area, listening and responding to the teacher's instructions, whilst also looking for space. Instructions could include 'walk', 'hop' and 'jog', progressing to quicker methods of travel such as bounding, bouncing (like a kangaroo), skipping and sidestepping.

After a few seconds, stop the class by calling 'freeze' or 'statues'. Give one point to the pupil who has found the most space.

Tip
Give pupils appropriate time, e.g. three seconds, to respond appropriately: 'Freeze!. . . 3, 2, 1'.

Differentiation
For WB pupils, when you call 'freeze', ask pupils to make a shape, e.g. a wide shape like a star (ensuring they are not touching anybody), or a straight shape, like a pencil.

Progression
Pupils jog around the playing area following the commands of the teacher. Give visual as well as verbal cues to start with, e.g. call out a cone colour and hold the corresponding cone up:
• red cone – stop, look and listen
• yellow cone – jog on the spot or change direction
• green cone – jog around the area.

Key teaching points
• Developing an awareness of space. Explain that 'space' means: 'being as far away from other people as possible, inside the playing area'. Ensure that pupils can repeat this definition.
• Changing direction quickly. Explain and demonstrate a bend of the knee to push off in a new direction.
• Developing confidence travelling in different directions.
• Using peripheral vision. Encourage pupils to keep their eyes ahead and look around or 'scan' for space, as well as looking out for changes in cone colour to indicate the different commands.
• Ask pupils why it is important to warm up before PE lessons and ask pupils why exercise is important. Briefly explain that a warm-up helps to get their muscles warm for exercise.

Main lesson: Sliding the beanbag (20 minutes)
Pupils stand in pairs five yards apart, appropriately spaced around the playing area. One of the pupils slides the beanbag to their partner, who should catch the beanbag with both hands

before rolling it back along the floor. Repeat this process. Look out for good sliding (passing) technique, and the 'cage' technique for catching the beanbag.

As the activity progresses, ask pupils on one side of the room to move one space to their left so that they change partners. This will help enable your pupils to learn to develop core skills with different pupils and develop team skills.

Competition
Set pupils the challenge of completing ten *successful* rolls back and forth. Pupils sit down and cross their arms to show that they have successfully completed the task; the first pair to finish wins.

Differentiation
Co-ordination for WB pupils: can pupils roll the ball to each other at a *similar speed*?

Communication between partners for WB pupils: can pupils inform their partners of when they are ready to receive the beanbag, by calling 'ready' or 'pass'?

Progression
1. Repeat the task, exchanging the beanbag for a tennis ball.
2. *Introduce a hockey stick. One pupil holds the stick and traps the ball before gently guiding it back to their partner. After a set amount of time, ask pupils to place the stick on the floor, before swapping places with their partner.*

Key teaching points
- Stay on the balls of the feet (on tiptoes).
- Keep eyes on the beanbag.
- Pupils start with the beanbag by their ankle, before bending the knee slightly and rolling the beanbag towards their partner.
- Pupils ensure their hand follows through *in a straight line* towards their partner.

Cool-down: Creep up on the teacher (10 minutes)
Pupils start at one end of the playing area standing shoulder to shoulder and attempt to jog towards the end line where you are standing, with your back turned so you are facing away from them.

In the style of the game *Grandmother's footsteps*, every so often turn and look at the pupils. When you do so, they must freeze in their current position, *demonstrating good balance and control*. If a child is moving when you turn around, they must take three large paces backwards.

Progression
Progress to pupils holding a beanbag in their hand while playing the game and completing mini throws (to the height of the nose) whilst creeping forwards.

Variation

If in a small space complete the classic cool down. Similar to the warm up but at a slower pace, reducing to a walk with pupils hands up above their heads and stretching their bodies.

Key teaching points

- Hold the stomach in to increase balance.
- Bend knees whilst travelling, to enhance balance.
- Keep eyes focused in one position, to maintain good balance.
- Travel forwards quickly and quietly on the balls of the feet. (Remind pupils of the skills learnt in the warm-up.)
- Ask pupils what they have learnt in the lesson and what they can improve upon for next time.

Plenary

- When we are waiting for the beanbag, do we stand completely still or do we stay on the balls of our feet?
- Do we stand up or kneel down when we are sliding the beanbag?
- Should our knees be a little bent or super straight?

Lesson 2 Improving ball and racquet control

Lesson objective: To improve ball control *and speed* when dribbling a ball with a racquet.

Key terms: "steady speed"; "control"; "space"

Warm-up: Travelling through the gates (10 minutes)
Phase 1: Mark out several gates using six different colours – one for each mode of travel (walking, skipping, jogging, hopping, sidestepping, bouncing). Each gate is represented by two cones of the same colour. Pupils travel in and out of various gates. Be sure to introduce one method of travelling at a time and clearly demonstrate each method. Make it clear which colour equates to which method of travelling, e.g. the red gate for walking, the blue for skipping, etc.

Phase 2: Pupils attempt to travel through as many gates as possible, avoiding other pupils within the area.

Phase 3: Pupils are asked to run to a gate and freeze. Demonstrate the activity below of picking up the racquet and dribbling the ball through the gates.

Progression

In Phase 2, pupils travel with a tennis racquet, rolling a ball through the gates. They continue looking for space so as not to bump into others, whilst ensuring close ball and racquet control.

Tip

Ask pupils to dribble the ball at a steady speed. Advise and remind them to keep the ball close to the racquet.

Key teaching points

a. Peripheral vision – look around to ensure you are in space and not about to bump into others
b. Keep your stomach muscles tight while travelling
c. Can you keep the racquet close to your ball? Imagine that you have a string attached to the ball and racquet strings, so the ball should never get far away from the racquet.

Main lesson: Tennis relay (20 minutes)

Before the end of the warm-up, play the 'numbers game' (see Introduction, pxii) to sort pupils into teams of three. Each team starts behind a different coloured cone, and each team has a coloured hoop to match the colour of the cone, placed 5–10 yards away. The pupil at the start of each line holds a small tennis ball or sponge ball.

One at a time, pupils dribble the ball with a tennis racquet to the hoop where they pick the ball up, gently place it in the hoop and return to their team. The pupil gives the racquet to the next person in the line and the next pupil repeats the task with a new ball.

Whilst waiting for their turn, pupils complete star jumps.

Competition

Once pupils have achieved the desired skill level, the game becomes a competition. The first team to get all of their balls into their hoop and sit down in a straight line, with their fingers on their lips, gains one point. Can they sensibly pick the ball up and place it accurately in their hoop, without the ball escaping?

Differentiation

If WT pupils are finding it difficult, ask pupils to complete the activity without racquets, and replace the balls with beanbags.

Health and safety

Ensure sufficient space is available to minimise risk of pupils bumping into each other.

Key teaching points

• Bend the knee and push off the back leg when changing direction whilst travelling.
• Use peripheral vision – keep eyes ahead whilst scanning for new gates to travel through.

- Keep the ball in close contact to the racquet *and demonstrate good ball control*.
- Dribble the ball *at a steady speed*.
- Dribble the ball *close to their racquet*.

Cool-down: Footwork ladders (10 minutes)
Phase 1: Ask sensible pupils to remove the cones and hoops from the playing area before asking pupils to travel in different ways using the whole playing area. Then ask pupils to: walk around the playing area looking for spaces; progress to a slow jog; hop around the playing area; walk sensibly around the playing area with their hands high above their heads and on the balls of their feet.

Ask pupils to quickly get into a group of three without talking or touching. To motivate the group to perform the actions quickly and sensibly, you may wish to inform them that the fastest and most sensible team to respond will be rewarded in accordance with the school reward system (e.g. house points).

Phase 2: In small teams of 3–5 pupils, children perform various footwork exercises on ladders to develop co-ordination: one foot placed quickly in between each space; bunny hops, keeping the knees and ankles together, swinging the arms for leverage.

Additional equipment
Ladders (if ladders are not available, use cones and space them accordingly).

Variation
Ask pupils to travel in the manner of various animals, e.g. frogs, birds, kangaroos... Can the pupils think of any other animals and how they might travel (in a safe way)?

Key teaching points
- Pupils travel in straight lines.
- Pupils identify suitable spaces.

Plenary
- Do we dribble super fast, super slow or at a steady speed?
- Why is it important to travel at a steady speed?

Lesson 3 Striking towards a target

Lesson objective: To improve accuracy of striking the ball in a straight line.

Key terms: "space"; "balance"; "weight"

Warm-up: Traffic lights (10 minutes)
Phase 1: Use question and answer to remind pupils what is meant by 'space' and how they can define it. Pupils travel around the playing area in different ways according to your instructions. When you call 'freeze', look for the pupil or pupils in the most space. One point is awarded to the pupil or pupils who are furthest away from their classmates, within the given playing area. Remind pupils of prior learning but increase the intensity of the warm-up from prior lessons, i.e. walking, jogging, skipping, sidestepping, walking backwards, hopping, running.

Phase 2: Quick feet: ask pupils to perform 'quick feet' – travelling with short fast steps – firstly pumping their arms as they travel; then with their arms behind their backs.

Phase 3: Introduce traffic lights one at a time:
• red cone – stop and stand still
• yellow cone – jog on the spot
• green cone – travel around the space using the method instructed, i.e. walking, jogging, skipping, sidestepping, walking backwards, hopping, running.

Tips
Ask pupils questions, such as:
• Can you look for spaces?
• Can you be light on your feet? Travel on the balls of your feet, so that you are able to *change direction quickly*.
• Can you be attentive?
• Can you keep *good balance* when I call 'freeze' by holding your body still?
• Which way is easier to travel – with their arms or without their arms? This forms a physical reminder that they should use their arms whilst travelling.

Progression
When you call the name of a shape, pupils perform that shape with their bodies as quickly as possible, e.g. 'star' or 'ball', or letters such as 'K', 'C', 'D', 'X'.

Variation
Encourage pupils' independence by asking them to come up with their own ideas as to how they can travel.

Main lesson: Striking the ball to a target (20 minutes)

For a class of 30 pupils, create ten teams with three pupils per team.

The first pupil dribbles the ball with their racquet to the red cone before passing the ball gently through the gate (goal) which is placed approximately five yards away/*eight yards away*. The next pupil in the group repeats the exercise.

Competition

Once the relevant skills have been taught, ask the first team to score 3–5 goals within their team to sit down to show that they have successfully completed the task. The quickest team wins. Asking pupils to put their hands on their heads to demonstrate completion is a good way to maintain a positive learning environment.

Progression

1. Create three small playing areas and six teams, to increase pupil activity time. Two balls are placed in the centre of the playing area. The red team takes the ball off the red cone and attempts to score, whilst the blue team takes the ball off the blue cone and attempts to score. Pupils gain one point for scoring successfully into their goal, and one bonus point if they are first (or fastest) to return their ball onto the cone.
2. Increase the number of goals that they need to score before the task is complete.
3. Pupils dribble in and out of two cones before striking the ball at a steady speed towards the goal. To extend the level of difficulty, replace the tennis racquet with a hockey stick.

Health and safety

Manage the teams effectively and ensure a quick turnover of movement so that pupils are not sitting still for too long. Ask observers to pay close attention to their teammates and see how they can support each other. If the lesson is taking place outside, encourage pupils to cheer their team on by repeating a chant.

Key teaching points

*   Keep *control* of the ball while dribbling – pupils to imagine that the racquet has glue on it.
*   Strike the ball *accurately at a steady speed* towards the goal. Remind pupils of prior learning and the technique for rolling the ball in a straight line.

Cool-down: Land and sea (10 minutes)

Pupils all stand behind a designated line. They must jump ahead of the line on your command, 'sea', and behind the line on your command, 'shore'. Pupil's feet must not touch the line and they must be encouraged to react quickly.

Variation

When you call, 'the waves are coming', pupils duck down and cover their heads. When you call, 'the sharks are coming', pupils quickly sprint to the opposite end of the playing area.

Health and safety

Ensure pupils are spaced appropriately across the line to avoid bumping heads or tripping over.

Key teaching points
- Improve balance and steadiness.
- Stretch different parts of the legs and develop an awareness of different muscles working in the legs, such as calf muscles (used in the spring upwards).
- Understand why it is important to exercise and the effect it has on their bodies.

Plenary
- Do we travel on the balls of our feet or on our heels?
- What can we do to help ensure the ball travels towards the target?

Cross-curricular links

Science: Explain how the amount of force behind the ball affects the speed at which the ball will travel.
Mathematics: Ask pupils to count how many gates they travel through before testing their arithmetic skills by asking pupils at random to add or subtract from the given numbers, e.g. 'How many gates did you travel through? 10 – excellent – and if you were to travel through three more gates, how many would you have to go through in total?'

2 Basketball

What do I need to know?

Children enjoy basketball lessons as they will get lots of time practising with the ball.
Basketball is a team game that requires tactile hand-eye co-ordination and individual skill.

Safety

While delivering all activities, it is important to follow the safety guidelines as set out below to ensure a safe and effective learning environment:

- Use size 3 basketballs for KS1 pupils and ensure the basketballs are adequately pumped.
- Ensure the playing area is safe and free of any hazards such as sharp objects before use.
- Ensure pupils are wearing the appropriate attire and that any shoes with laces and sufficiently tightened.
- Check that equipment is not damaged or torn before each lesson.
- Inform and reinforce to pupils the importance of finding space and not bumping into others during warm-ups and other activities.
- Lay the equipment out before the start of the lesson, where possible, to ensure easy access to resources and a smoother transition between activities.
- Inform and remind pupils of the rules and expectations at the beginning of each lesson.
- When delivering line games or activities where small queues exist, ensure pupils stand side by side so that you can always see them and they can see what is going on in front of them.
- Use verbal as well as visual signals to regain pupil focus and attention.

Rules

- No talking while the teacher is explaining something to the group or demonstrating a task.
- No talking whilst others are explaining something to the group or demonstrating a task.
- No touching other people or equipment without the teacher's permission.

Lesson 1 Improving basketball control

Lesson objective: To improve ball control whilst dribbling the basketball (a larger ball), and to develop an awareness of space, good footwork and changing direction.

Key terms: "steady speed"; "waist height"; "control"

Warm-up: Basketball traffic lights (10 minutes)
Phase 1: Introduce a light activity before delivering this warm-up, such as the classic warm-up in which pupils travel around the playing area following your instructions including skipping, jogging, hopping, jogging backwards, sidestepping, jumping, up, down, and so on.

Phase 2: Ask pupils if they remember the traffic lights from previous lessons. Remind pupils that they should remember to look for space as they travel around. All children are given a basketball to bounce around the playing area. When the teacher raises the red cone and calls 'red', all pupils must stop and stand still. When the teacher raises the yellow cone and calls 'yellow', all pupils bounce the ball on the spot. When the teacher raises the green cone and calls 'green', all pupils respond by dribbling the ball freely in the given playing area.

Tips
- Advise pupils not to dribble the ball too high or too low. Always get one pupil to demonstrate good practice whilst emphasising the key points.
- Can pupils respond to instructions appropriately and quickly?
- Can pupils dribble the ball at a *steady speed*?
- Can pupils dribble the ball at the *appropriate height* (i.e. waist high)?
- Encourage pupils to push the ball downwards *with control* and not slap the ball.

Differentiation
For WB pupils, pupils should be encouraged to dribble the ball:
a. using their weaker hand
b. at a quicker speed
c. completing dribbling skills as they travel.

Main lesson: Pick me up (20 minutes)
Children are separated into ten teams on the outside of the playing area. One at a time, pupils run into the central area and pick up one cone, before taking it back to their team. The pupil gives the next child in the group a high five and the next child then repeats the task.

Explain to pupils that they should try their best to:
- Travel in a straight line – ask pupils if they should travel on the balls of their feet or on their heels. Ask why and encourage pupils to explore their ideas – this is a good opportunity to introduce talk for learning, discussing it with the person next to them.

- Select which cone they will take quickly.
- Only travel one at a time (turn-taking) and only pick up one cone at a time (following the rules).

Competition
Turn this into a game: the game ends when all of the cones are cleared from the centre. The team with the most cones at the end of the game gets one point.

Progression
Pupils complete the following activity whilst bouncing a basketball:

Each team has an individual team colour. In the centre of the court or hall space is a selection of cones on the floor. There must be an equal number of cones of each colour. Pupils must dribble the ball to the centre of the court and pick up one cone of their colour and dribble the ball back to their team with the cone in their hand. The next person in the line cannot travel until their teammate has placed their cone on their team hoop on the floor, before joining the back of their line.

Differentiation
For WB pupils:
1. Complete this game with tennis balls instead of cones. Ask pupils to bounce the ball once before they return the ball to their team's hoop.
2. Increase the distance between the pupil stations and the cones in the middle.
3. Ask pupils to travel in different ways, e.g. forwards on the way in and backwards on return to their team, or by hopping.

Key teaching points
- Developing speed – how quickly can pupils travel to the centre?
- Decision-making – can pupils make an early decision as to which cone they will collect?
- Teamwork – can pupils work together as a team and high five the next person in the line?

Cool-down: Sharks and fishes (10 minutes)
This is a co-ordination activity. All children start by standing on a single line side by side; these children are the 'fish'. Select two children to be sharks, who then stand in the centre of the playing area.

The game begins when the sharks whisper, 'Fishy, fishy, fishy, swimming in the sea.' In turn the fishes reply, 'Sharky, sharky, sharky, can't catch me!' The 'fish' then proceed to run to the opposite end of the playing area without being tagged by the sharks.

If they are tagged by a shark, they then become 'seaweed'. Seaweed cannot move their feet but must try to tag oncoming fish in the next round by stretching their arms. The game ends when there are there are 15 remaining fish, or until space becomes too small for pupils to be able to travel to the other side safely.

Health and safety
This game involves gentle touching and therefore pupils must be reminded that no pulling, pushing or heavy touching is allowed. Anybody caught doing so may be asked to sit out and reflect for two minutes.

Key teaching points
- Dodging – development of agility.
- Making *controlled* changes of speed.
- Making *quick* changes of direction.
- Showing an awareness of space – can they avoid the sharks/taggers?
- Ask pupils what they learnt in the lesson and what they can do to improve their performances/skills in the next lesson. Encourage pupils to also keep active outside of lessons.

Plenary
- At what height should we aim to dribble the ball?
- What part of the body should we bend when changing direction?

Lesson 2 Sending and receiving the basketball

Lesson objective: To improve sending and receiving skills with a small basketball.

Key terms: "space"; "bounce pass"; "dribble"; "waist high"; "bent knees"

Warm-up: Classic warm-up (10 minutes)
Line the beanbags along the perimeter of the playing area.

Phase 1: Pupils jog around the playing area, listening and responding to your instructions and following key instructions: 'up' = jump; 'down' = crouch down; 'change' = change direction; 'jog backwards'; 'skip'; 'skip sideways'.

Phase 2: Ask pupils to each find and stand by one of the beanbags. At your instruction, pupils use or travel with the beanbag in the manner you call out (repeat some of the key instructions above), e.g. when you call 'up', pupils stand still, before throwing their beanbag upwards at about head height or just above the head and catching it.

Tips
Pupils should:
- show good listening skills
- jog on the balls of the feet

- look out for other pupils, dodging and weaving to find **space**
- use the arms as well as the feet when travelling to develop good practice in co-ordination and agility.

Progression
1. Pupils throw the ball upwards at head height. Once pupils have successfully caught the beanbag three times in a row they may progress to the next stage of progression.
2. *Throw the beanbag above head height.* Once pupils have successfully caught the beanbag three times in a row at this level they may progress to the next stage of progression.
3. *Continue jogging, whilst throwing and catching the beanbag at head height.*
4. *Continue jogging, whilst throwing and catching the beanbag above head height.*

Key teaching points
1. Throwing – Throw the ball upwards in a straight line, not forwards or backwards.
2. Keep your eyes on the prize, i.e. keep your eyes on the beanbag.
3. Catching – Make a cage by placing your baby fingers together and spreading your fingers.
4. Spatial awareness – Look around to ensure you are working in your own space and not in danger of bumping into others.

Main lesson: Gold star (20 minutes)
Set up a line of blue cones and a line of red cones opposite 6, 8 or *10* yards away and demonstrate the main activity as outlined below before sending pupils off in their pairs.

In twos, pupils roll the basketball back and forth to each other. After an appropriate amount of practice, move pupils along the blue line of cones across one space, so that pupils have opportunities to work with different children in the class.

Next, pupils bounce the ball to their partner, ensuring it bounces only once before their partner catches the ball (bounce pass). Remind pupils of prior learning and skills of sending and receiving from Lesson 1.

Differentiation
Adapt the resources used for WT and WB pupils respectively: WT pupils use a soft large ball; WB pupils use a tennis ball or a size 3 basketball.

Progression
Select sensible pupils and give them a set of single coloured cones each. Ask them to spread the cones out within the playing area.

All pupils are given a basketball to dribble within the playing area. When you say a colour, pupils must dribble the ball to a cone of that colour as quickly as they can before holding the ball steady and standing still.

Develop pupils' leadership skills by allowing members of the class to select and call out the colour cone that everyone should dribble to.

Key teaching points

Remind pupils of skills learnt in rolling the tennis ball/basketball, including:

- always be ready – jog on the spot
- bend your knees
- hold the ball near the ankle or between the legs
- keep your eyes on the ball
- make a cage with the hands to catch the ball.

Encourage and look out for:

- awareness of space
- *close ball control*
- *confidence in travelling with the ball*.

Cool-down: Target practice (10 minutes)

Pupils sit behind a cone. One at a time, pupils stand up, jog forwards and throw the beanbag into the hoop (which is placed in front of them), before collecting the beanbag and repeating the task.

Differentiation

Increase or decrease the distance from which pupils throw the beanbag for WB and WT pupils respectively.

By the end of the lesson:

- all pupils will be able to throw the beanbag in a forwards direction
- most pupils will be able to throw the beanbag into the hoop
- some more able pupils will be able to throw it in a hoop from a further distance.

Key teaching points

- Use the acronym below to help teach and improve pupil accuracy of throwing the beanbag:
  - o **B**end the knees
  - o **E**ye on the target
  - o **E**xtend the arms
  - o **F**ollow through towards the target.
- Ask pupils what they learnt in the lesson and what the key points were for them to remember when passing and throwing the beanbag.

Plenary

- How do we throw the ball to ensure it gets to our partner?
- What do we need to think about when catching the ball?

Ask pupils to sit down sensibly with their eyes closed and arms folded. When you tap a pupil on the shoulder, they may line up sensibly.

Lesson 3 Dribbling the basketball

Lesson objective: To improve control and movement; working with and without the ball.

Key terms: "control"; "speed"; "gate"

Warm-up: Explode and swap (10 minutes)

Lay the basketballs (an equal number to the number of children in your class) on an upside down cone placed around the perimeter of the playing area. Place a second cone on top of each basketball.

This is a dynamic warm-up game for warming up the muscles and raising the heart rate.

Pupils travel around each other in the playing area, avoiding each other by dodging and weaving. Ask them to perform 'quick feet' (short quick steps whilst pumping their arms) and various co-ordinated movement exercises.

When the teacher calls 'EXPLODE!', all pupils must sprint to a cone and place it on or above their head. Pupils who react quickly are awarded with one point.

Differentiation
For WB pupils, ask them to travel to the furthest cone away from them after they hear the word 'explode'. Spread the cones out further to increase the distance pupils have to travel to the outer cones. For WT pupils, ask them to travel to the cone nearest to them.

To extend this game further, ask pupils to combine other skills such as dribbling (close ball control) and running with the ball to develop close ball control with speed (see Progression below).

Progression
Introduce each progression one step at a time so pupils develop the key skills first before progressing to the next phase.
1. *Pupils stand by a basketball each and continue the game/repeat the activity above whilst dribbling the basketball.*
2. When the teacher calls 'down', pupils place their own ball on the floor. When the teacher calls 'swap', pupils quickly collect another ball from the floor.

Variation
When pupils arrive at the cone, they stand in a star shape or else balance the cone on one knee, on their back, between the legs, or in any creative but safe way they choose.

Now introduce one basketball per pupil and repeat the task, but this time pupils dribble the ball around the area.

Health and safety
Ensure pupils look around before taking a new ball and remind them of what to do if somebody else already has the ball, e.g. ask pupils 'What do you think you should do if you find a cone that somebody else has their hand on?' Pupils respond with: 'Look for another one'.

Key teaching points
- Increasing awareness of space – i.e 'where is the nearest cone'?
- Develop fundamental footwork skills: agility, balance, co-ordination, speed ABCs.
- Ask pupils why these skills may be important for basketball and other invasion games.
- Ask pupils why it is important to be healthy and to warm up their muscles. Pupils could discuss this briefly in pairs, before you ask various pupils what they discussed.

Main lesson: Gateway dribble (20 minutes)
Sit pupils down sensibly in their pairs. Ask two sensible children to collect two yellow cones, which have previously been set out neatly outside the playing area. Ask pupils to make a 'gate' of approximately 2 yards (2 big steps). Perform a demonstration of the task, dribbling the ball through the gates, before selecting more pupils who are sitting sensibly to collect their cones and create their own 'gate'.

Alternatively, you may choose to lay the gates out using a separate playing area in advance.

Differentiation
WT pupils walk. Ask WT pupils to travel through the gates whilst holding a beanbag. Each time they reach a gate, these pupils throw the beanbag up above their head and catch it, before moving to the next gate.

WO pupils jog.

WB pupils run.

Progression
1. Pupils say the colour of the gate that they are going to travel through to encourage quick thinking, co-ordination, communication and decision-making.
2. Pupils start the activity at walking pace. Once pupils have successfully dribbled through five gates whilst walking, progress to jogging.
3. Once they have successfully dribbled through five gates jogging with control, *progress to running with the ball*.
4. *More able performers may be asked to dribble with their non-writing hand*.

Key teaching points
1. Awareness of space – travelling through gates when they are free, and be sure not to queue behind others.
2. Dribbling skills – keep fingers spread out.
3. Bounce the ball at waist height.
4. Bounce the ball to the side of the foot at 2 o'clock so the ball does not bounce on your foot
5. Planning ahead – thinking about where you will travel before taking action.

Cool-down: Hot potato (10 minutes)

Divide the class into groups of six; each group makes a circle. Pupils bounce-pass the ball to different pupils around the circle. However, *pupils are not allowed to pass the ball to the person next to them*. Pupils should call the name of the person that they intend to pass the ball to.

Progression

Pupils are only allowed a maximum of 3–5 seconds with the ball. The teacher selects the appropriate amount of time, depending on the ability of the pupils. Label the ball as a hot potato that must be passed on quickly.

Key teaching points

- To pass the ball quickly. Each pupil has a maximum of three seconds to pass the ball.
- Can pupils *disguise the pass* using their eyes or a 'fake' pass? (Fake passing to one person, before passing the ball to another person.)
- Ask pupils why it is important to think about space when playing basketball.
- Ask pupils how they can get the ball from one space to another (rolling, dribbling, bouncing).
- Ask pupils what skills they use to dribble the ball successfully.

Plenary

- What part of the hand do we use to dribble the ball?
- Why is it important to look for space?

Cross-curricular links

Mathematics: Ask pupils how many gates they have travelled through before challenging pupils' mental arithmetic and numeracy skills.

3 Tag rugby

What do I need to know?

Tag rugby was developed to introduce the basic skills of rugby to children, whilst reducing the risk of injury and the physical contact side of the traditional game.

Safety

While delivering all activities, it is important to follow the safety guidelines set out below to ensure a safe and effective learning environment.

- Ensure the playing area is always safe and free of any hazards such as sharp objects, before use.
- Ensure pupils are wearing the appropriate attire and that any shoes with laces are sufficiently tightened.
- Check that equipment is not damaged or torn before each lesson.
- Inform and reinforce to pupils the importance of finding space and not bumping into others during warm-ups and other activities.
- Lay the equipment out before the start of the lesson, where possible, to ensure easy access to resources and a smoother transition between activities.
- Inform and remind pupils of the rules and expectations at the beginning of each lesson.
- When delivering line games or activities in which small queues exist, ensure pupils stand side by side so that you can always see them and they can see what is going on in front of them.
- Use verbal as well as visual signals to regain pupil focus and attention.
- The use of tags in tag rugby helps to separate tag rugby from rugby. It is important to place the tags on safely so as to minimise the risk of injury and ensure pupils feel safe.
- Advise and remind pupils to always place the tags on their hips, not on the front or back of their bodies.
- Ensure tag belts are tied safely and are not too tight or too loose.
- Advise and remind pupils not to overlap the tag belts or tie the tags underneath the main central belt. This is both an infringement of the laws of the game and is unsafe to themselves and others.

Rules

Some of the key rules teachers will need to know and understand in tag rugby include:

- No hands off – pupils are not allowed to 'defend' their tags by using their hands to guard, fend off or shield other players or pupils.

- If the tag is taken, the defensive team must retreat (five yards) before the game restarts with the attacking team. If more than a set number of tags (usually between three and seven, depending on the age and ability of the group) are taken from the attacking team within any given round, the ball is automatically transferred to the other team. It is useful to have the cones on the perimeter of the playing area spaced by five yards. This way, pupils know approximately what line to move back to.
- For a try to be successful, the player must hold the ball in two hands and place it on the floor in the end zone. If the ball is held in only one hand, in the legalities of the official game, this will not stand as a try.
- Pupils must call 'Tag' when they have successfully won a tag from an offending player. The referee shall then blow the whistle; the defensive players retreat (a set number of yards back) before play continues.
- A free pass – 'tap and pass' – is awarded for any infringement. In the official game, this happens in the centre of the pitch, where the defensive player passes it to the attacking player for the game to resume.
- If a player slides into the end zone or falls to the ground, the try is disallowed. It is therefore important to explain to children that they must stay on their feet and to hold the ball in two hands at all times.
- No forward passes are allowed. This is penalised by awarding a free pass to the non-offending team. Passing sideways (also known as a 'square pass') is accepted within the rules.
- Knock on: this is when a player attempts to catch the ball but fumbles it in a forward motion. Play continues as normal in this situation.
- There are no scrums and line outs.
- Ball away: this is when a ball carrier is tagged simultaneously in the act of passing and the referee has ruled in favour of the attacking team and not counted this as a proper tag. In this situation the referee should call 'Ball away, play on'.

Lesson 1 Evading opponents

Lesson objective: Develop sending and receiving skills and awareness of space development. Improve speed and decision-making to create space and evade opponents.

Key terms: "pop pass"; "balls of the feet"

Warm-up: Find the space (10 minutes)
Phase 1: Place tag rugby balls on the outside of the playing area next to the cones which set the perimeter of the playing area. Pupils begin by travelling around the playing area as instructed by the teacher: walking, jogging, hopping, bounding, sidestepping, etc.

Ask each pupil to get a ball and hold it safely whilst repeating the activity above. When the teacher calls 'freeze', pupils must stop and stand still. Pupils in the most space are praised.

Phase 2: Introduce some other commands:
- 'Up' – pupils must throw the ball up and catch the ball or *clap once before catching the ball*.
- 'Change' – pupils respond by calling 'Direction', before shaping to travel in one direction then sprinting in another direction. (Advise and remind pupils to bend the back knee and push off in the direction they wish to travel.)
- 'Switch' – pupils must place their ball on the floor and quickly find another ball. (Remind pupils that they have done this with the basketballs – what key skills do they remember?)

Key teaching points
- Stay on the balls of the feet.
- Look for spaces and try to be as far away from any other person as possible.
- Use dodging skills and change direction.
- Practise good ball familiarisation skills – keeping two hands on the ball.
- ABCs – agility, balance, co-ordination, speed.

Main lesson: Pop passing and line games (10 minutes)
For a class of 30 pupils, create ten teams of three pupils per team. The first pupil in each team must sprint to the cone 15–20 yards ahead with the ball in their hands. They sprint around the cone and return, before handing the ball to the next person in their team.

Ask pupils to also complete a relevant SAQ (Speed, Agility, Quickness) footwork exercise between the start and end cone, e.g.
- sidestep between three small cones
- bunny hop over three small cones
- using 3 or more small cones, pupils place one foot between each space as quickly as they can.

Competition
For each round, one team is awarded ten points for being the quickest team to have applied the relevant skill correctly. The team with the most points after a set period of time is praised or rewarded.

Differentiation

To differentiate this activity, adjust the space: make the gap between the cones larger for WT pupils and smaller for WB pupils.

Progression

In addition to the SAQ exercises in between the start and end cone of each line, ask pupils to form a variety of ball handling skills at the end cone before sprinting back towards their team, e.g.

- *throw the ball slightly above the head before catching it*
- rotate the ball around the waist three times
- pass the ball between their own legs in a figure of eight
- *complete all three of the above tasks in a sequence*.

Key teaching points

- SAQ development (Speed Agility Quickness) – SAQ activities help develop the mental-neuro system, which triggers the brain to act quickly and respond.
- Ball familiarisation – can pupils spread their fingertips for more *tactile ball control*?
- Developing the basic 'pop pass' technique: throw the ball from the hips, with fingers spread and thumbs up; follow the hands towards the direction of the pass, *snapping the wrist for extra ball rotation*. (Remind pupils of prior learning, e.g. follow through towards the target with the hands.)
- Developing teamwork – through passing and receiving the ball and developing team skills of working together.

Match play: One vs one tag (10 minutes)

Set up a series of mini pitches and assign two teams to each pitch (around four pitches works well, with 3–4 pupils per team, so around 8 pupils per mini pitch). Each pupil should have two tags, one on each hip. One team (e.g. the blue team) is seated inside a square of blue cones. The opposing team (e.g. the red team) is seated at the opposite end of the playing area, inside a square of red cones.

The first person in each team stands up and both players aim to pass each other and sprint around the square of cones at the opposite end before returning to their home square. They should each attempt to use evasive skills to get back to where they started without being tagged by the opposing team member, and should also try to tag their opponent, thus practising their attacking skills.

After being tagged or a home run being made, the next pupil in each team takes their turn. Pupils sitting in the squares of cones should be watching and observing to identify key skills being performed.

Key teaching points

- Developing dodging and weaving skills:
    - pretending to go one way, then travelling the other
    - showing a change of speed, e.g. go from slow-fast *to successfully evade opponents*
    - *using eyes to trick opponents*.

- Bending knees low, for a low centre of gravity and to increase agility.
- Taggers: 'Defenders; can you. . .
  - keep your eyes on the tag?'
  - bend your knees?'
  - ensure your hands travels from low to high when attempting to win the tag?'

Cool-down: Snake train (10 minutes)

Organise the pupils in groups of two or three, with one ball per group.

The leader can run in any direction, and the others must follow like a snake with their hands on the shoulders of the person in front of them.

When the teacher calls 'Pop pass', the leader must stop and hold the ball out to the side so the next person can take the ball and continue running. The 'leader' then joins the back of the 'snake'.

Variation

- Pupils travel around the playing area, following the instructions of the teacher, including: 'Touch left' (pupils touch the floor with their left hand); 'Touch right' (pupils touch the floor with their right hand).
- Side shuffle only.
- When the teacher says 'Change' pupils repeat 'Change' and change direction.

Key learning points

1. Quick responses and reactions.
2. Staying on the balls of the feet (commonly referred to as 'staying on your toes').

Plenary

- What can we do with our bodies to get away from the taggers?
- What do we do with our knees when attempting to win the tag?
- *Does anybody know why we bend our knees?*

Lesson 2 Passing the rugby ball

Learning objectives: To improve co-ordination and passing skills.

Key terms: "tag", "pop pass"

Warm-up: Scarecrow tag (10 minutes)
Select some sensible pupils to be taggers. All children jog freely around the grid with tag belts in their waist, responding to the instructions of the teacher by repeating the instruction and performing the appropriate action, e.g.
• 'Up' – jump
• 'Down' – lunge or touch the floor
• 'Change' – change direction
• 'Shuffle' – move the feet sideways quickly.

When the teacher calls 'tag', the taggers begin ripping tags from the other pupils or touching pupils gently to 'freeze' them.

If a pupils tag has been taken (or they've been touched), they must stand with their hands and legs apart. Pupils may be freed by another pupil who successfully runs underneath one *or both* of their arms.

Health and safety
Explain to pupils how to win the tag safely. Tell children that they are not allowed to hold onto their tag to keep it away from a tagger. Remind pupils to follow the rules sensibly.

Key teaching points
Pupils should:
• show good awareness and stay clear of taggers
• demonstrate quick changes of direction
• bend low to win the tags by having a 'low centre of gravity'.

Main lesson: Pop passing and line games (10 minutes)
Set up the lesson, the same as in the previous lessons, with 3 pupils starting behind each starter cone, facing 3 cones placed one foot space away from each other. Pupils jog with the tag rugby ball to the three cones in the middle of their line before performing the following footwork tasks:
• approach the cones facing sideways, then move forwards between the first and second and backwards between the second and third cone
• diagonal sprints around three cones
• sprint to the first cone, jog to second cone, walk to the third cone and then sprint to the end line again.

When pupils arrive at the end cone towards the opposite end of the playing area, pupils perform various tasks as learnt in the previous lesson, including:
• throwing the ball up and catching it
• rotating the ball around the waist
• rotating the ball between the legs.

Pupils run back to their team and hand the ball to the next person in the line.

Differentiation
Increase or decrease the distance between the central cones where pupils perform their footwork tasks for WT and WB pupils respectively.

Ask each of the WT pupils to perform a pop pass as they approach the next person in their team.

Progression
Pupils progress to pop passing the ball to the next person in line from a few paces away.

Key teaching points
- Changing speed of travel – can pupils travel slow, then fast then slow?
- Whilst travelling through the cones, bend the knees slightly.
- Travel on the balls of your feet to avoid touching any of the cones.
- Keep eyes focusing forwards.

Match play: One vs one tag (10 minutes)
Create several mini playing areas of an appropriate width and length (approximately 10 x 5 yards). On the long end of each playing area there will be a starting cone for each team (e.g. a red cone for the red team and a blue cone for the blue team). Place a large yellow cone in the corner of each playing area. The first pupil behind the red cone passes to the first pupil behind the blue cone who catches the ball, turns and runs around the large yellow cone before attempting to score a try on the opposite end line without being tagged by the opponent. After throwing the ball to the blue player, the red team pupil turns and runs around the large yellow cone on the opposite end before attempting to tag the opponent.

After a set time, or number of turns, pupils reverse roles so that the blue team defends, and the red team attacks.

Progression

To progress the activity, ask pupils to go two at a time – two reds and two blues travel at the same time. They may pass the ball sideways or backwards to their partner in the same team in order to score in the end zone. If a tag is taken, the defending pupil takes three steps back, before allowing the attacking pupil/s a second attempt at completing the try.

Key teaching points
* Developing dodging and weaving skills:
  ○ pretending to go one way then travelling the other
  ○ showing a change of speed, moving from slow to fast
  ○ using eyes and hip movements to move away from opponents
  ○ bending knees low, for a low centre of gravity and to increase agility.

Cool-down: Snake train (10 minutes)

Organise the pupils in groups of two or three with one ball per group.

The leader can run in any direction, and the others must follow like a snake with their hands on the shoulders of the person in front of them.

When the teacher calls 'Pop pass', the leader must stop and hold the ball out to the side so the next person can take the ball and continue running. The 'leader' then joins the back of the group.

Variation
* Touch left (touch the floor with the left hand)/right (touch the floor with the right hand)
* Side shuffle only

Key teaching points
1. Keep your eyes focused ahead and over the person in front's shoulder.
2. Travel on the balls of your feet.
3. Open hands to the side of your body and spread your fingers, ready to receive the ball when the teacher says 'pop pass'.

Plenary
* What skills can we use to evade an opponent?
* Where do we pass the ball from – is it our hips or our chest?

Lesson 3 Passing the rugby ball on the move

Learning objective: To develop ball handling skills, co-ordination and agility.

Key terms: "pop pass"; "communication"; "speed"

Warm-up: Scarecrow tag (10 minutes)

Select five children as taggers and ensure all other pupils have tag belts on.

Pupils jog freely around the playing area with tag belts in their waist.

When the teacher calls 'tag', the taggers begin ripping tags from the other pupils. If tag belts are not available, use a soft ball that pupils can use as for 'tagging' other pupils.

If a pupil's tag has been taken, they must stand with their hands and legs apart. Pupils may be freed by another pupil who successfully runs underneath both of their arms and calls 'freed'.

Tips
- Show good awareness and stay clear of taggers.
- Demonstrate quick changes of direction.
- Bend low to win the tags – 'low centre of gravity'.

Main lesson: pop and go (20 minutes)
Place two cones of the same colour a suitable distance apart. In between the cones and off to a slight angle, place a hoop: this is where the 'passer' will stand. Set up ten teams, each comprising three pupils: a runner, a pop passer and an observer.

The runner runs towards the pop passer and calls 'Pass'. The passer hands the ball to the runner who carries the ball to the end try line. The watcher then becomes the runner and repeats the activity. Change the pop passer every few turns.

Competition
Once pupils are confident with the activity and performing it to a good standard, introduce a competitive element to the game whereby the first team to make each try gains one point. Change the passer every so often so that pupils have the opportunity to play different roles.

Differentiation
WT pupils can use a beanbag as opposed to a tag rugby ball.

For WB pupils, the ball is pop passed as opposed to being handed to the oncoming person.

Progression
Play this as a speed game: two teams are at opposite ends of the playing area; two balls are placed in the centre. On the teacher's instruction, one pupil from each team sprints into the middle, picks up the ball and scores in the opposing end zone (the end line on the opposite end of the playing area). The point is gained only by the first pupil who returns their ball to the middle after scoring their try.

Key teaching points
Pupils should focus on:
- the timing of the pass (pass into the path of the attacking runner)
- speed development and *confidence* running with the ball
- carrying the ball in two hands – advise and remind pupils of this rule
- passing the ball from the waist upwards; ensuring that the hands travel in the direction they want the ball to go
- communication – calling for the pass.

Cool-down: Pass the buck and go (10 minutes)

Demonstrate the activity first before dividing the class into teams of five.

In their teams, ask pupils to link hands in a circle before taking a step back. This should ensure pupils are appropriately spaced for the passing activity.

Pupils must pass the ball around their circle as fast as possible. When the ball is returned to the pupil who started the game, the team sits down, places the ball in the lap and places their hands on their heads to demonstrate that they have completed the task.

The fastest team to have all of their players sitting in their circle, with their hands on their heads after completing the task is the winning team.

Progression

When the pupils who made the first pass receives the final pass, they sprint to a designated end line, place the ball down to make a try before returning to their team.

Key teaching points

1. Use of correct catching skills - Make a 'W shape' with the hands to prepare to catch the ball.
2. Keep your eyes on the ball.
3. Pass the ball from the waist and follow through towards the target person. Often referred to as throwing the ball from 'hips to lips' as the hands start at the height of the hips and end up at the height of the lips straight ahead of the body when the ball is released.

Plenary

- What do we need to do before we receive the ball?
- What shape do we make with our hands to receive the ball?

Cross-curricular links

Science: Ask pupils why it is important to get low when changing direction. Briefly explain that a low centre of gravity helps them to move their bodies quicker.

4 Football

What do I need to know?

During this section, teachers should introduce pupils to the basic skills required in invasion games through football. Skills that pupils will learn include: sending and receiving, dribbling, and striking the ball towards a target.

Safety

While delivering all activities, it is important to follow the safety guidelines set out below to ensure a safe and effective learning environment.

- Ensure the playing area is safe and free of any hazards such as sharp objects before use.
- Ensure pupils are wearing the appropriate attire and that any shoes with laces are sufficiently tightened.
- Check that footballs are not flat or worn.
- Inform and reinforce to pupils the importance of finding space and not bumping into others during warm-ups and other activities.
- Lay the equipment out before the start of the lesson where possible, to ensure easy access to resources and a smoother transition between activities.
- Inform and remind pupils of the rules and expectations at the beginning of each lesson.
- When delivering line games or activities in which small queues exist, ensure pupils stand side by side so that you can always see them and they can see what is going on in front of them.
- Use verbal as well as visual signals to regain pupil focus and attention.

Rules

- No talking while the teacher is explaining something to the group or demonstrating a task.
- No talking whilst others are explaining something to the group or demonstrating a task.
- No touching other people or equipment without the teacher's permission.

Pupils in KS1 do not play to offside rules. Some KS1 tournament rules will require pupils to roll the ball into play as opposed to throw the ball into play, as demonstrated in the 11-a-side game.

Lesson 1 Dribbling the football

Lesson objective: To move the ball with different parts of the foot, and in various directions.

Key terms: "balance"; "control"

Warm-up: Numbers game (10 minutes)
Pupils travel around the playing area as directed by the teacher, e.g. jogging, hopping, skipping, bounding, and jogging backwards. When the teacher says a number, pupils get into a group of that number as quickly as possible.

Pupils demonstrate effective completion of the task by:
• placing their hand(s) on the shoulders of their partner/group
• making a star shape with their legs and arms apart whilst touching the shoulder of their partner/group
• *balancing on one leg, whilst placing their hand(s) on the shoulders of their partner/ group*
• balancing on their bottoms *whilst placing their hand(s) on the shoulders of their partner/ group*.

Differentiation
Ask WB pupils if they can think of any other balances or shapes that they can make with their partner. Following a clear explanation and demonstration, ask pupils to perform the appropriate shape or balance.

Progression
Pupils perform the above activity whilst steadily dribbling a football at their feet. When the teacher calls a part of the body, e.g. knee, hand, elbow, back, bottom, pupils respond by stopping the ball and making contact with it using that part of the body.

Key teaching points
• Ensure pupils adopt the right posture.
• Communication.
• Awareness of body parts.
• Listening skills.

Main lesson: Traffic lights football (20 minutes)
Place a football on each cone on the perimeter of the playing area.

Phase 1: Pupils start by standing behind a football. Inform and demonstrate to pupils what they should do when the teacher shows a green, red or yellow cone:
- green cone – pupils will dribble the ball by tapping it steadily in between their feet
- red cone – pupils must respond by placing their foot on top of the ball, demonstrating good ball control
- yellow cone – pupils respond by placing alternate feet on top of the ball quickly whilst counting 1, 2, 3 *4, 5, 6*.

Phase 2: The teacher places several cones of various colours on the floor within the playing area. Pupils dribble around as many cones as possible whilst avoiding touching the cones, another pupil's football or other children.

Key teaching points
- Develop awareness of various body parts.
- Speed of movement and reaction to instructions – how quickly can pupils group up and perform the shape or balance?
- Inform and remind pupils to keep a 'soft motion' at all times and not to 'lock out' any joints.
- Develop agility, balance and co-ordination.

Cool-down: Classic cool-down (10 minutes)
Pupils travel around the playing area by:
- skipping
- jogging
- jogging backwards
- hopping
- star jumping or sidestepping.

Key teaching points
1. Awareness of space – stay away from other pupils.
2. Travel on the balls of the feet.
3. Practice steady breathing.

Plenary
- What skills did we practice today?
- Do we keep the ball close to our feet or far away?
- Why is it important to keep the ball close to our feet?

Lesson 2 Sending and receiving the football

Lesson objective: To improve close ball control with both feet whilst developing an awareness of space.

Key terms: "communication"; "sole"; "inside of the foot"

Warm-up: Swap (10 minutes)

Set up a cones of the same colour around the perimeter of the playing area. Children must dribble the ball using only the insides of the toes and avoiding other pupils within the coned area.

Pupils dribble the ball taking three short touches with the right foot, before stopping the ball. Children then repeat the skill using their left foot.

When the teacher calls, 'Foot on', pupils must place their foot on their football to stop it, then leave it where it is and walk or jog around the playing area. When the teacher is satisfied that all pupils have stopped their ball, the teacher calls 'Swap' and all pupils find a new football to dribble.

Tip
Suggest pupils imagine that there is a string attached to the ball that they are holding, and that the ball cannot leave the space between their feet.

Differentiation
Pupils can work at their own progressive pace in which they feel confident dribbling the ball in various directions avoiding others:
- WT pupils – walk
- WO pupils – jog
- WB pupils – *jog faster or run with the ball*.

Progression
Once pupils have reached the desired level, progress to pupils immediately searching for a new football when the teacher calls 'Swap'.

Health and safety
Advise and remind pupils that if someone else already has a ball near their feet, they should look for another football, and not take it off them.

Key teaching points
- Find lots of space whilst dribbling the ball – develops an awareness of space.
- Dribble the ball using the insides of the feet – 'penguin steps'.
- *Think and react quickly* – try to find a different ball as soon as possible.
- Dribble with close ball control – *eyes ahead and chin up*.
- Improve awareness *and control using different parts of the foot* – advise and remind pupils that it is not a race and that close ball control is much more important at this stage than speed.

Main lesson: Gold star passing (20 minutes)
In pairs, pupils stand facing each other in between two cones. They then take three steps back each.

Pupils begin by passing the ball to their partner. The receiving pupil controls the ball before passing it back using the inside of the foot.

Remind pupils of prior learning of sending and receiving the ball in tag rugby. Ask pupils if they can identify any similarities or differences compared with sending and receiving the ball in football?

Differentiation
Pupils progress to passing the ball through the gate. Increase/decrease the size of the gate for WT and WB pupils respectively.

Layered differentiation: Once pupils have completed six successful passes back and forth, pupils initiate their own progress by making the gate a little bit smaller.

Progression
Pupils control the ball with the left foot before passing it with the right foot and vice versa.

Key teaching points
- Always be on your toes ready to receive the ball.
- Trap the ball using the sole of the foot (heel down toe up – so that the ball does not slide under the foot).
- Pass with the inside of the foot *and follow through towards your partner (using the appropriate speed and weight of pass)*.
- Communication in pairs – can pupils call for the pass?

Cool-down: Quick feet (10 minutes)
Set up a series of ladders (or set of cones) in the centre with a red cone 5–10 yards away from one end of the ladder and a different coloured cone 5–10 yards away from the opposite side of the ladder. Pupils group up into teams of 3 and stand side by side facing the opposite group. Pupils complete fast feet drills on the ladders before tagging the next pupil, e.g.
- place one foot in each space on the ladder
- place both feet one after the other in each space (right foot leading/left foot leading)
- perform bunny hops in each space (bent knees; feet and ankles together)
- place both feet one after the other in each space facing left/right.

Key teaching points
- Bend knees for balance.
- Focus on good co-ordination with the arms as well as the feet.
- Travel on the balls of the feet.
- Keep eyes in a fixed position and ahead of the feet.

Plenary
- What parts of the foot can we use to dribble the ball?
- How do we ensure the ball doesn't travel under our foot when controlling the ball with the sole of the foot?

Lesson 3 Striking the football to a target

Lesson objective: To improve sending and receiving skills, and aiming towards a target.

Key terms: balance ; control ; pass

Warm-up: Dribble to the cone (10 minutes)
Phase 1: Using a selection of different coloured cones, give each pupil a cone and ask them to find a space before placing the cone safely on the floor.

Pupils jog around the playing area. When the teacher calls a colour, e.g. 'Red' or 'Blue', pupils respond by dribbling safely and *quickly* to a cone of that colour.

Phase 2: When pupils arrive at the cone, they perform a balance, e.g.
• balance on one leg
• balance on one leg and two hands
• balance on one leg and one hand
• balance on the back with feet and hands off the floor.

Tip
Progression
Ask pupils to perform various skills according to their ability and confidence of dribbling the ball, e.g. stop, turn; step over, foot on, etc.

Variation
Label the cone colours as various fruits and water, e.g
• blue – water
• yellow – bananas
• green – apples
• orange – oranges.

Ask pupils if they can think of any other fruits. What colour are they? Ask pupils about healthy eating and why they think it is important.

Key teaching points
• Encourage pupils to identify spaces *quickly*.
• Demonstrate good reactions.
• Travel to the cone quickly.
• Perform good balances by bending the knee a little bit.

Main lesson: Through the gates (20 minutes)
Ask pupils to clear the cones up before sitting down sensibly. Ask a sensible pupil to make a 'gate' with two cones spaced two yards apart. Demonstrate the activity with one pupil, control and pass the ball safely through the gate, controlling the ball with the 'heel down, toe up' technique, and passing the ball with the inside of the foot.

Repeat the previous lesson's main activity (Gold star passing, p35). However, this time pupils must perform three foot-ons before passing the ball to their partner.

Introduce a competitive element: the first pair to complete a set number of successful passes through the gate sits down and gains one point. Once pupils show competence in the above task, introduce the progression.

Progression
After passing the ball, pupils search for a new space and a new gate to pass through. Pupils must only pass the ball through the coloured gates.

Key teaching points
- Passing in pairs – *quality of pass = weight and accuracy*.
- Communication in pairs – ask pupils to think about *where to pass (between which colour cones) and when to pass* (e.g. not when there is another person in the way).
- Ask pupils whether they think the ball will travel slower or faster on concrete in comparison to grass.

Competition: Skittles/football bowling
Create 7–10 teams, with three pupils per team. Set out 'u' skittles (three large cones in a triangle shape) for each team.

One at a time, pupils dribble five yards to a red cone before stopping the ball and attempting to pass the ball accurately, so it hits the skittles. Pupils get one point for each time they hit the skittles (the skittles do not need to be knocked over – encourage pupils to demonstrate accuracy as opposed to power). Once a pupil has taken their shot, they must quickly collect their ball and return to their line, before the next pupil set off.

Differentiation
WB pupils – if pupils show competence in striking the ball whilst on the move, this should be encouraged (rather than discouraged).

Ask pupils what part of the foot they should use to help them hit the ball accurately?

WT pupils – bring the skittles closer to the red cone, so the distance between the striking cone and the cones is shorter.

WB pupils – move the skittles further away.

Key teaching points
1. Keep the ball close to your feet whilst dribbling tapping the ball between the feet as you travel or *dribbling the ball with the laces*.
2. Pass the ball towards the target using the inside of the foot.
3. Arm out for balance.
4. Follow through towards the target.

Cool-down: Go for goal (10 minutes)
Split the class into three groups of 10. Pupils have six seconds to dribble the ball to the opposite end of the playing area or hall space and strike the ball into an empty goal (the goal may be represented by a 'gate', which is cones spaced two–three yards apart).

Note: This game is about achieving success through scoring goals in a simple manner. The pupils simply dribble, score, pick up their ball and return to the end of their line. The teacher should use positive encouragement words, such as 'success', 'excellent goal', 'good control' 'outstanding effort', and so on. This will help ensure pupils go to their next lesson or part of their day, with a smile on their faces, knowing that they have achieved something positive. Ensure there is enough time left for every pupil to have a turn, and to sit down and reflect on their learning.

Refrain from using the term 'unlucky'. Inform pupils of the appropriate step to make progress, e.g. 'Good effort. Next time, try to follow through towards the target.'

The team that scores the most goals within 60 seconds wins.

Development phase: Alternatively all pupils can count down from a number, e.g. '10' or *'6'* (the amount of time allocated by the teacher will depend on how far away the goal is and how quickly most of the pupils can dribble to the other end. The idea is that you want as many children to be successful as possible, but also to provide a degree challenge to urge the dribbling player in their team to score.

Key teaching points
- Running with the ball *confidently*.
- Striking the ball on the move *with accuracy and precision*.
- Improving confidence.

Plenary
- What can we do with our knees to dribble the ball safely?
- Which part of the foot did we use to strike the ball accurately?

Cross-curricular links

Science: The more force placed behind the ball, the quicker it will travel. The amount of friction on the floor will also be a determining factor as to how fast or slow the ball travels.
Science: Briefly explain that the side of the foot has a *larger area than the toes, so gives more accuracy when kicking the ball*.

Unit 2: Gymnastics and athletics

By the end of this unit, pupils should be able to:

- Travel safely around the gym area and practise various shapes required for gymnastics *with control*.
- Travel safely across a mat performing a basic roll *with a degree of confidence and accuracy*.
- Jump off low-level apparatus *showing understanding that performances should have a beginning, middle and end*.
- Display confidence in jumping, running, and throwing and be able to briefly explain what helps them *perform them confidently in athletic activities*.

Key: Step 1 | *Step 2*

Equipment required:

- 6 gymnastics vaults or boxes
- set of 50 spots or cones
- 15 large gymnastics mats
- 10 foam javelins
- 30 beanbags

5 Gymnastics

What do I need to know?

Gymnastics is a core element of the National Curriculum for PE as it focuses on fundamentals of movement which develop the ABCs of all sports: Agility, Balance & Co-ordination.

Teachers should be trained by a gymnastics professional so as to ensure that all lessons and techniques are taught, supported and delivered safely.

Safety

While delivering all activities, it is important to follow the safety guidelines set out below to ensure a safe and effective learning environment.

- Ensure the playing area is always safe and free of any hazards such as sharp objects, before use.
- Ensure pupils are wearing the appropriate attire and that any shoes with laces are sufficiently tightened.
- Check that equipment is not damaged or torn before each lesson.
- Inform and reinforce to pupils the importance of finding space and not bumping into others during warm-up and other activities.
- Lay the equipment out before the start of the lesson, where possible, to ensure easy access to resources and a smoother transition between activities.
- Inform and remind pupils of the rules and expectations at the beginning of each lesson.
- When delivering line games or activities in which small queues exist, ensure pupils stand side by side so that you can always see them and they can see what is going on in front of them.
- Use verbal as well as visual signals to regain pupil focus and attention.
- Pupils should only perform moves of which they are confident and capable and skills should be taught in a segmented manner, so that pupils build skills and confidence before completing the full move or skill e.g. forward roll.

Rules

- Demonstrate good posture during all activities by holding the stomach in controlling breathing patterns.
- When the teacher raises the hand above the head, all pupils must stop, look and listen.
- When using apparatus children will be given a set time to return to their stations and sit down sensibly, allowing time to complete a move, before re-focusing. Once the countdown has begun, children should not attempt to start a new move, skill or action.

Lesson 1 Low-level gymnastics shapes

Lesson objective: To choose and apply skills complementing gymnastics shapes and balances.

Key terms: "tuck shape"; "pike shape"; "dish shape"; "arch shape"; "posture"

Warm-up: Mr Men game (10 minutes)
Say the name of one of the Mr Men characters; pupils have to move like him, following a brief demonstration from the teacher, a pupil or both, e.g.

- Mr Slow – move slowly
- Mr Muddle – travel backwards
- Mr Bounce – bounce
- Mr Small – crouch and move
- Mr Strong – flex/stretch muscles on the move
- Mr Tall – reach up on the balls of the feet
- Mr Short – crouch as low as possible
- Mr Rush – move fast.

Introduce other examples that you or the pupils can think of.

Progression
Ask pupils to come up with some of their own ideas for creative development.

Health and safety
When doing Mr Rush, remind pupils not to cross the boundary lines and not to go too fast so as to avoid bumping into others.

Key teaching points
- Awareness of space – praise or award the pupil/pupils in the most space.
- Changing direction quickly.
- Developing confidence using their body to form shapes and in safe manner, and to experiment creatively.
- Ask pupils why it is important to warm up before PE lessons.
- Ask pupils why exercise is important and briefly explain physical, mental, social benefits.

Main lesson: Low-level shapes (20 minutes)
Phase 1: Ask the pupils to practise the following shapes after a clear demonstration of each by the teacher: pike shape, tuck shape, dish shape, arch shape.

Ask pupils to hold each position for three seconds initially, increasing the length of time required for the hold, the stronger and more able your pupils are.

The teacher announces and demonstrates all the shapes listed above, ensuring that pupils adjust the shape according to the commands, e.g. 'Can you show me the dish shape, now hold your position, and hold your tummy in. Well done, now show me the arch shape.'

Phase 2 – paired work: Ask pupils to repeat the shapes above in pairs (two per mat). Introduce 'linking' – this is where pupils make contact with their partner whilst changing shapes. Explain to the pupils that you are looking for two or three of the following (based on outcomes):
- good posture
- good timing
- good balance
- good co-ordination with their partner/good sequencing (adjusting from one position to another)
- good fluency of movement.

Tips
Ask pupils to demonstrate to the class before asking about what was good and what could be improved.

Differentiation
Pupils will be able to perform the shapes with various degrees of quality. Be aware of children who require support and provide support and guidance accordingly.

Progression
Ask pupils to practise all four shapes with their partner and practise moving *fluently* from one shape to the other. If pupils have reached the desired expectations and show good demonstrations of each shape, introduce basic *linking* – pupils perform the same shapes but they must make contact with their partner within the performance.

Key teaching points
- Learn the four shapes.
- Balance and control – pupils keep their stomachs tucked in, whilst holding their shape.

- Posture – pupils point their toes and hands during the demonstration of each shape.
- Linking (working in pairs) – pupils to make positive contact with their partner during the performance.
- Improving core strength that pupils will need for future activities.
- Fluency of movement – pupils to move *fluently* from one shape to the other.

Cool-down: Teacher says shapes (10 minutes)
Pupils walk around the gym area. When the teacher calls a shape, pupils safely sit down on a mat before performing the shape and holding the shape for three seconds.

Progression
1. Ask pupils to travel in various ways around the gym area, e.g. crawl, jog, hop, skip, listening carefully for the commands of the teacher who will then call out a shape.
2. Develop pupils' leadership skills by selecting one sensible pupil to act as the teacher and call the name of the next shape.

Variation
Pupils jog on the spot following the teachers' instructions, e.g.
- 'Down' – sit down
- 'Up' – jump
- 'Cross' – cross feet over
- 'Walk' – walk
- 'Hop' – hop.

Finish off with a deep breath and simple stretching exercises. Tell pupils to rise up on the balls of your feet and reach up really tall; breathe in on the way up and breathe out on the way down. Repeat this three or four times to develop pupils' basic breathing and relaxation techniques.

Key teaching points
- Balance and control:
  - Hold stomach in to increase balance.
  - Bend knees whilst travelling to enhance balance.
  - Keep eyes focused on one position to maintain good balance.
  - Travel forwards quickly and quietly on the balls of the feet (tiptoes).
- Ask pupils what they have learnt in the lesson and what they can improve upon for next time.

Plenary
- What are the four gymnastics shapes we have been practising today?
- What part of the body should we keep strong when performing our shapes?

Lesson 2 Preparation for the forward roll

Lesson objective: To increase strength and confidence travelling on various body parts in preparation for the forward roll.

Key terms:
"linking"; "posture"; "front support"; "front crawl"; *"tension"*

Warm-up: Animals (10 minutes)
The teacher explains to pupils that for the purposes of this exercise, they are in the jungle. Ask pupils what animals they may find in a jungle. Begin the activity by asking pupils to move like those animals, e.g.
- snake – low and slow
- giraffe – tall
- elephant – big
- kangaroo – jumping
- frog – large bounds
- bird – flapping arms
- lion – fast
- snail – slow
- human – jogging.

Inform and reinforce that pupils are not to make sounds so as to not to wake up the lions.

Tips
Always ask one pupil who is performing well to demonstrate good practice to the class.

Progression
1. When the teacher says the number 'two', pupils must quickly find a partner and stand side by side linking wrists. Pupils stand facing each other whilst linking wrists. Ensure pupils find a new partner for each round of activity. (This provides good preparation for future activities which involve rolling and linking.)
2. Ask pupils to create new ideas to add to the game.
3. Ask pupils to raise their hand if they wish to instruct the class of the next movement command.
4. The first pupil who adopts the correct position gains a point.

Variation
Play the 'Tape deck game': the teacher gives various commands to do with operating a DVD player and pupils follow the commands accordingly, e.g.
- 'play' – walk
- 'fast forward' – jog
- 'fast fast forward' – run faster
- 'pause' – static balance in your position
- 'stop' – legs together, arms by your side (or above the head), neck and back straight
- 'rewind' – jog backwards
- 'eject' – jump up and down
- 'fast rewind' – run backwards

- 'skip' – skip
- 'change (tape)' – change direction.

Key teaching points
- Good listening skills – encourage instant and correct decision-making.
- Applying *good technique and posture* – build on what pupils can remember from previous lessons.
- Learning to work under pressure.
- Good and appropriate *co-ordination, balance and speed* skills.

Main lesson: Preparation for the forward roll (20 minutes)
Phase 1: Pupils travel around the playing area listening to the teacher's instructions. The teacher instructs pupils to travel on four parts of their body:
- two feet and two hands – hands in front of the body
- two feet and two hands – hands behind the body.

Phase 2: Call the number 'two'. Pupils pair up and show good linking skills. The teacher demonstrates the next activity before sending pupils to their mats accordingly.

Phase 3: Each pair has a mat and teacher explains and demonstrated best practice in the following activities:
- front crawl – hands in front of the body
- front crawl – hands behind the body
- frog jumps across the mat (travelling from low to high)
- burpees across the mat – pupils lie flat on the stomach and press both hands firmly into the floor; they bring the knees forward into a tuck position, before jumping up as high as they can.
- log roll – rolling across the mat like a log.

Pupils finish at the end of the mat by adopting the 'finish position' – arms straight out in front of the body, knees and ankles together, and perform a hold for three seconds.

Differentiation
For WT pupils who find it difficult to achieve the movements, the ability to verbally describe the motions involved and working with a partner is crucial to develop their core learning outcomes. Where possible, allow for plenty of practice time with these games and provide support where appropriate.

If WB pupils have demonstrated the tasks above effectively, ask them to travel across their mats by starting in the front support (front crawl) position (with hands in front of the body) and then move their hands one at a time in a clockwise motion so they complete a full circle. They should complete three to four rotations across the mat.

WB pupils could then practise the forward roll: feet together, bent knees (from the tuck position), hands and elbows slightly in front shoulder-width apart, chin tucked in – push forward come up in the tuck position, stand up and perform a straight jump to finish.

Have two WB pupils sharing a mat; they perform the forward roll, one at a time, with the other pupil supporting at the other end of the mat at the finish point. The supporting pupil offers their wrist (facing upwards), so that on completing the roll, pupils are offered support to move into a standing position.

Health and safety
Pupils travel one at a time.

Key teaching points
- Hand position – press hands firmly into the floor with fingers widely spaced.
- Remind pupils to go as low as they can and jump as high as they can (frog jumps).
- Core strength – pupils should hold stomachs in and follow a smooth breathing pattern throughout each activity.
- Look ahead at where you are travelling.
- Breathe in slowly in through the nose and out through the mouth whilst travelling.
- Keep your stomach in towards the spine for the development of good posture.
- *Tension – after each activity, ask pupils where they can feel most tension/pressure. Help pupils develop an awareness of various body parts.*

Cool-down: Seed to flower (10 minutes)
Ask pupils to make the smallest shape they can make with their bodies. Ask pupils to grow from small to big, like a seed growing into a flower. Repeat this exercise three or four times to improve breathing technique, control of the body and balance.

Variation
Pupils stand facing the teacher with their legs shoulder width apart. They start with their hands between their legs, wiggling their fingers. The teacher and pupils continue to wiggle the fingers, whilst making a circular motion with their hands, so that hands move left, up, right and back to the starting point like a clock. When the hands reach the top, above the head, the teacher whispers, 'Hi Class' and pupils respond by whispering 'Hi Sir/Miss'.

Key teaching points
- Pupils develop good breathing patterns, reduce their heart rates and cool down for the next lesson.
- Ask/remind pupils of why it is important to establish regular breathing patterns during physical activity.

Plenary
- Which parts of the body were we using and strengthening today?
- Why do you think we need to make these muscles strong for gymnastics?

Lesson 3 Learning the forward roll

Lesson objective: To develop *accuracy* in forward rolls and to introduce skills of jumping and landing safely.

Key terms: "forward roll"; "entrances and exits"; "teamwork"; "control"; "smooth"

Warm-up: Tape deck game (10 minutes)
The teacher gives various commands to do with operating a DVD player and pupils follow the commands accordingly, e.g.
- 'play' – walk
- 'fast forward' – jog
- 'fast fast forward' – run faster
- 'pause' – static balance in your position
- 'stop' – legs together, arms by your side (or above the head), neck and back straight
- 'rewind' – jog backwards
- 'eject' – jump up and down
- 'fast rewind' – run backwards
- 'skip' – skip
- 'change (tape)' – change direction.

Progression
Add a competitive element to the game, e.g. the first pupil who adopts position gains a point.

Key teaching points
- Good listening skills – instant and correct decision-making.
- Applying good technique and posture – pupils build on what they can remember from previous lessons.
- Working under pressure.
- Good and appropriate co-ordination, balance and speed skills.
- Bending knees and using arms.
- Link the jumping activity to jumping as learnt in previous lessons, and ask pupils how they can jump higher and with increased balance.

Main lesson: Accurate forward rolls (20 minutes)
Phase 1: log roll – with two pupils per mat, pupils lie on their backs and travel by rolling from one end of the mat to the other end, whilst keeping their arms straight above their head and fingers semi-locked together. Inform and remind pupils that their thumbs should be locked in a comfortable position.

After practising this skill; pairs can compete to see who can travel one complete log roll and return to the start position quickest.

Important note: Although it is a race, emphasise that pupils should not reduce the quality of their skill to gain speed, as this can cause overbalancing and increase the risk of injury.

Pupils then travel from one end of the mat to the other without allowing their torso to touch the floor. One by one, pupils travel across the mat using only their arms and legs, travelling in the front support position.

Phase 3: forward roll – pupils work in pairs, one on either end of the mat. One pupil raises their hands above their head and smoothly moves into the forward roll; their partner must 'offer their hands' for their partner to come up smoothly. Repeat the activity three or four times before pupils change roles.

Tips
How to do a forward roll: feet together, bent knees (tuck position), hands and elbows slightly in front, shoulder-width apart, chin tucked in – push yourself forward, come up in the tuck position, stand up and perform a straight jump to finish.

Start with two pupils per mat allowing pairs to go one a time or one supporting at the other end of the mat at the finish point.

Differentiation
For WT pupils who find the forward roll difficult, adapt the task in one of the following ways, depending on which part of the forward roll the pupil finds most challenging:
• roll downwards from a height, e.g. a triangular shaped box or stacked mats
• travel across the mats on all fours (to develop confidence with placing the weight on the hands)
• bunny hops across the mat (to develop strength in the hip flexors)
• perform the log roll (to develop core stability)
• revise the exercises in previous lesson.

For WB pupils who can complete the forward roll with ease, encourage them to:
• Complete the forward roll without support to stand up at the end.
• Introduce a short run-up before delivering the forward roll.
• Perform one complete forward roll *without support*. (Ensure pupils strive to improve their performance by completing the skills in one complete motion, and coming up into a standing position, from a tuck position. This involves lots of flexibility, leg strength in the hips and practice.)
• *Take a three step run-up (three long strides)*
• Practise *different entrances and exits to the forward roll*, e.g.
  o entrance and exit in star shape
  o entrance and exit by balancing on one leg in front
  o entrance and exit by balancing on one leg to the side
  o entrance and exit by balancing on one leg, straight and behind the torso (known as 'Arabesque')
  o a combination of different sequences as above.

Progression
As pupils' performance improves – the teacher should help them to accelerate their progress by asking them to *travel faster through the motions* of the forward roll, developing good momentum. If pupils can perform the skills well, they can be shown the *'run-up'* before they do the forward roll.

Health and safety

Explain and demonstrate to pupils how to lift their partner safely with their palms outstretched, facing upwards towards the ceiling.

Remind pupils to always keep their head on the mats so as not to roll off and bump their head. Ensure pupils are taught all steps of the forward roll safely before attempting the exercise.

The teacher must demonstrate the ways in which pupils can/cannot travel on the apparatus and stipulate key conditions to ensure that the safety rules are followed accordingly.

Key teaching points

Phases 1 and 2

- Balance and control – knees and ankles together.
- Good balance – hand position: press hands firmly into the floor.
- Good posture: stomachs tucked in – ensure a good smooth breathing pattern.
- Teamwork – pupils to produce *symmetrical or contrasting balances with their partner*.

Forward roll

- Develop good breathing patterns.
- Improve core strength, and strength in the biceps, triceps (arms), quadriceps and hamstrings (legs).
- Supported positions – developing linking and co-ordination skills.
- Improve the performance of the forward roll (from tuck position to tuck position).

Cool-down: Classic cool-down (10 minutes)

Pupils travel around the gym area following the teacher's instructions, e.g.

- 'Down' – sit down.
- 'Up' – jump in the air with feet together, finishing with arms straight out in front of their bodies.
- 'Star' – jump into a star shape.
- 'Pencil' – jump into a pencil shape (straight back, straight legs, with arms by the side).

Key teaching points

- Emphasise the need for safety – pupils should walk in the gym area and not run and take careful decisions not to use equipment whilst someone else is using it.

Plenary

- What parts of the body do we use to perform the forward roll?
- What shapes can we see in a complete forward roll?
- What do we do with our stomach muscles to keep good posture?

6 Athletics

What do I need to know?

Athletics is a core part of the National Curriculum for PE. Children should be taught fundamental skills of running, jumping and throwing to improve health and fitness, whilst developing a basic cognitive understanding of how their bodies function and perform.

Safety

While delivering all activities, it is important to follow the safety guidelines set out below to ensure a safe and effective learning environment.

- Ensure the playing area is always safe and free of any hazards such as sharp objects, before use.
- Ensure pupils are wearing the appropriate attire and that any shoes with laces are sufficiently tightened.
- Check that equipment is not damaged or torn before each lesson.
- Inform and reinforce to pupils the importance of finding space and not bumping into others during warm-ups and other activities.
- Lay the equipment out before the start of the lesson, where possible, to ensure easy access to resources and a smoother transition between activities.
- Inform and remind pupils of the rules and expectations at the beginning of each lesson.
- When delivering line games or activities in which small queues exist, ensure pupils stand side by side so that you can always see them and they can see what is going on in front of them.
- Use verbal as well as visual signals to regain pupil focus and attention.

Rules

No touching other pupils unless advised to do so as part of the game. Do not play with equipment without an adult supervising the activity.

Lesson 1 Jumping and landing safely

Lesson objective: To introduce safe jumping and landing techniques as well as to learn to travel safely across apparatus whilst forming a *beginning, middle and end*.

Key terms: "squashy landing"; "rotate"; "agility"; "smooth"; "start, middle and ending"

Warm-up: Animal walks and Explode (10 minutes)
Phase 1 – Animals walks: Ask the pupils to travel in the form of various animals, e.g. frog leaps, kangaroo jumps, tall as a giraffe, slither like a snake, bear, panda, bird (flapping the arms), etc. (see Chapter 5).

Phase 2 – Explode: Pupils travel around without touching any mats or equipment. When the teacher calls 'EXPLODE' or 'MATS', pupils must do a running jump on the mats with a squashy landing (knees bent).

Progression
1. Only three pupils are allowed per mat.
2. Only two pupils are allowed per mat.
3. One boy and one girl per mat only per mat.
4. Pupils to think of any different progressions or variations.

Variation
Do the Classic warm-up instead: pupils jog around listening for the teacher's instructions, e.g. 'up' = jump; 'down' = crouch down; 'change' = change direction; 'jog backwards'; 'skip'; 'skip sideways' (call and response).

Key teaching points
- Pupils must show good listening skills.
- Jog on the balls of the feet (tiptoes).
- Look out for other pupils.
- Dodge and weave to find space.
- Use the arms as well as the feet when travelling to develop good practice and co-ordination.
- (This warm up should be used to encourage pupils to think and apply skills learnt from previous lessons about space awareness and teamwork.)

Main lesson: Jumping and landing (20 minutes)
Set out apparatus to include a range of available equipment, e.g.
- tripod stands
- benches for bounding (knees and ankles 'tied' together jumping from side to side by using the arms to elevate themselves)
- vaults
- springboards
- balance beam benches.

(Use as much of the equipment and resources available as possible.)

Set up six stations with five pupils per station. Each station is labelled 1–6. Pupils travel across their station safely and sensibly, display a soft jump landing, with bent knees and arms out in front to finish.

The key is to have a soft, 'squashy' landing.

On the instruction, 'Rotate', pupils travel in a straight and sequenced line to their next station.

Competition
Introduce competition as a means of achieving a higher-quality performance outcome. Introduce a points system for the best performing groups, e.g. award ten points for the best performed groups and five points for the runners-up.

Progression
1. Ask pupils in each team to travel in a sequenced manner, where they are all travelling in the same way, e.g. walking in a straight line, jogging in a straight line, hopping in a straight line, completing star jumps whilst travelling in a straight line, sidestepping in a straight line, travelling on all fours (feet and hands).
2. Encourage independent learning: ask the pupils to think of other creative and safe ways in which they can travel from one station to another.

Health and safety
Only use equipment that is appropriate for the age group – KS1 pupils should always start with the lowest level apparatus, so as to avoid injuries and ensure that lessons are safe.

Key teaching points
- Good breathing patterns when travelling across apparatus – pupils to follow a smooth breathing pattern whilst travelling.
- Ensure pupils demonstrate a *good 'start position', 'smooth middle and clear ending'*.
- Balance and control – pupils to keep their arms out for balance on apparatus.
- Safe jumps – knees and ankles together; hands in a 'swinging' motion by the side to improve velocity momentum and agility.
- Soft and 'squashy' landing with bent knees.
- Arms placed out in front of the body for a complete and *smooth ending to the performance*.

Cool-down: Jump about 1, 2, 3 (10 minutes)
Pupils jump around the playing area following various instructions from the teacher. The teacher explains and demonstrates a sequence of two small to medium height jumps, followed by their biggest jump possible.

Pupils perform the above sequence on the move, using some of the jumping techniques listed below:
- straight jump
- straight jump with a quarter turn left
- straight jump with a quarter turn right
- tuck jump
- star jump with arms fully extended.

Practise good, smooth breathing patterns and high jumps in tuck position – knees and ankles together.

Variation
Play 'Letters': on the teacher's command, pupils control their bodies to form a given letter or shape, e.g. X, Y, h, C, d etc. The aims here are to develop good body posture, develop balance, improve flexibility and *controlled movements*.

Note: Listen carefully and prompt pupils for key terms, including 'squashy landing', 'bent knees', 'travelling safely', 'posture', 'balance', 'three sections – beginning, middle and end'.

Key teaching points
• Pupils must show good listening skills.
• Jog on the balls of the feet (tiptoes).
• Look out for other pupils.
• Dodge and weave to find space.
• Use the arms as well as the feet when travelling to develop good practice in co-ordination and agility.

Plenary
• What types of jumps did we practise today?
• What do we need to remember to do when we land from a jump?

Lesson 2 Jumping and landing using different techniques

Lesson objective: To improve the quality of jumping and landing techniques whilst introducing basic sequencing ideas.

Key terms: "squashy landing"; "agility"; "balance"; "sequence"

Warm-up: Explode (10 minutes)
Phase 1: Pupils jog around the playing space, following various commands from the teacher, e.g. 'jump', 'land', 'high knees', 'skip', 'hop', etc. without touching any mats or equipment.

Phase 2: When the teacher calls 'Explode!' or 'Mats', pupils must do a running jump on the mats with a squashy landing and bent knees.

Phase 3: Ask pupils to jump and land in different ways:
• jump off two legs and land on two legs with legs positioned shoulder width apart
• jump off two legs and land on one leg – attempting to hold the balance steady for one second
• *jump off one leg and land on two legs*

- *jump and do a quarter turn* (90 degrees)
- jump and land on two feet then perform an *arabesque balance* (one leg straight behind the body, parallel to the floor with the opposite arm outstretched in the front of the body – also known as the superman/superwoman pose).

Progression

1. Once pupils have a basic understanding of the game, allow only three pupils or two pupils per mat.
2. Once pupils have displayed a good level of performing the tuck jump, ask pupils to only perform straddle jumps on the mat (in the shape of a star or an X).

Key teaching points

- This dynamic game is for warming up the muscles.
- Increasing awareness of space – pupils to look for the nearest mat.
- Fundamentals development – agility, balance, co-ordination, speed ABCs.
- Pupils to consider why these skills may be important for gymnastics.
- Pupils to reflect on whether they were able to 'hold' their balances.

Main lesson: Jumping off apparatus (20 minutes)

Set out apparatus to include a range of available equipment, e.g.
- tripod stands
- benches for bounding (knees and ankles 'tied' together jumping from side to side by using the arms to elevate themselves)
- vaults
- springboards
- balance beam benches (or other similar available resources).

Phase 1: Tuck jumps only – for advanced groups (and WB pupils) who have achieved the positive outcomes from the previous lesson, teachers may wish to later introduce the *straddle jump (legs apart and coming back together on landing), spin jumps, straight jumps, side jumps, backwards jumps, etc*.

Phase 2: Set up six stations with five pupils per station – each station is labelled 1–6. Pupils travel across their station safely and sensibly, then perform a safe jump landing, with bent knees and arms out in front to finish.

Phase 3: Pupils produce a 'squashy' landing and a forward roll.

Phase 4: On the instruction to 'Rotate', pupils travel in a straight and sequenced line to their next station. Each group could have a different mode of travel, e.g.
- team 1 crawls between stations in a straight line
- team 2 jumps between stations in a straight line
- team 3 skips between stations in a straight line
- team 4 slides between stations in a straight line
- team 5 jogs between stations in a straight line.

Teachers will find it beneficial to use a points system, e.g. award ten points to the team that travels in the straightest line from one station to the next and performs the best sequence. Teachers should look for examples of good *co-ordination and teamwork, positive linking, smooth travelling, fluency of movement* and good overall performances. Those pupils should perform to the rest of the class towards the end of the lesson.

Tips
For all phases, the teacher can add/change various conditions to produce varied outcomes, e.g. stipulate that each team must use only one bench; each team may use only a vault; each team must produce a minimum of three forward rolls and three links of partners; each team must use a hoop to travel through the centre in some way.

Differentiation
WT pupils repeat learning from the previous lesson.
WB pupils progress to learning and practising the backwards roll.

Progression
1. Introduce rhythmic gymnastics equipment such as hoops, balls (tennis balls or sponge balls), skipping ropes, rhythmic bands.
2. Ask pupils to perform various gymnastics skills which develop agility, balance and co-ordination, with use of the equipment provided, e.g. on landing off a vault one pupil who is standing beside the mat, hands a ball to the pupil who has just jumped, who then completes a forward roll with the ball in their hand.
3. To encourage independent learning, it is important to condition the exercise whilst also allowing the children to take three–four minutes to elaborate on their own ideas for their performances, which they will show the rest of the class.

Key teaching points
- Good breathing patterns when travelling across apparatus.
- Balance and control.
- Quality jumps and co-ordination – knees and ankles together; hands in a 'swinging' motion by the side.
- Squashy landing with bent knees – pupils to land on one spot without wobbling.
- Quality tuck jumps combined with a forward roll to finish – see how high pupils can jump whilst maintaining good control of their body.
- Improving techniques of jumping and landing with apparatus – pupils to keep *control of their bodies* both with and without the apparatus whilst jumping, landing and travelling.
- Improving creative development through introducing basic equipment – *pupils to travel in sequence with their team*.
- Pupils to remember some of the shapes and balances learnt in the previous lesson that can be put into their performances at a later stage, e.g. straddle shape/tuck shape.

Cool-down: Group up – letters, numbers and shapes (10 minutes)
Phase 1: Children travel around the playing area, listening carefully for the teachers' instructions. Start by jogging slowly and then slowing down to a walk.

Phase 2: When the teacher calls a number followed by another number, letter or shape, pupils respond by getting into a group of the first number and creating the relevant number, letter, shape or balance as specified by the teacher, e.g.

- 'form the shape of a number 2'
- 'form shape of the letter X'
- 'form a circle/square/triangle/diamond
- balance on one leg/two legs and one hand/one leg and one hand/two knees/*back with legs up and touching each other*.

Key teaching points
- Can you demonstrate good posture by holding your stomach in and keeping your back straight?
- Demonstrate good balance and avoid wobbling by keeping your eyes fixed in a single position.
- Can you link (make contact) with your partner(s) safely and smoothly?

Plenary
- Who can remember the different types of jumps we have practised today?
- Which jumps did you find most challenging and why?
- Which jumps did you find the least challenging and why?

Cross-curricular links

Mathematics: When playing the 'group up' game and other games that involve numbers, challenge pupils' mental arithmetic skills and numeracy skills.

Science: Explain and remind pupils that gravity will be pulling them down when they are completing jumping and landing activities.

Lesson 3 Practising the long jump

Lesson objective: Improve movement skills and jumping distances.

Key terms: "posture", "co-ordination", "long jump"

Warm-up: In the park (10 minutes)
Ask pupils to imagine they are in a park. Tell them to practise various skills, including: jump over the puddles, climb the imaginary ladder, kick the football, swing on the monkey bars, jump and catch the imaginary ball, throw the Frisbee™ for the dog and run after it. Ask your pupils if they can think of any other things they might do in the park?

Variation
Do the Classic warm-up. Pupils jog around the playing area following the teacher's instructions, e.g. jogging, jumping off two feet, hopping on one leg, then alternating, jumping from two legs to one leg, jumping from one leg to two legs, jogging backwards, skipping, jogging whilst rotating the arms, sidestepping.

Progression
Ask pupils to avoid bumping into others by showing a good awareness of space. When the teacher calls a number, such as 2, 3 or 4, pupils must show *fast reactions* to get into a group of that number as quickly as possible and balance on one leg. Include various types of balances.

Key teaching points
- *Good posture* – body upright and head up.
- Constantly in ready position – 'on toes' after each movement is completed.
- Look for spaces and try to be as far away from any other pupils as possible.
- Use dodging skills and change direction (*link to prior learning in invasion games*).
- Focus on the core skills of developing ABCs – agility, balance, co-ordination, speed.
- Remind pupils via questioning of the meaning of 'posture' and how this links to previous topics.

Main lesson: Long jump (20 minutes)
Set out ten stations with up to three pupils per station.

Pupils sit behind a green cone, which is the start of each station. Two red cones are placed approximately 10–12 yards ahead of each team and the two red cones are spaced approximately 1–2 yards apart. On the second red cone is a stack of four cones; pupils will need to use these cones later to place the cone at a further distance based on how far they jump.

One at a time, pupils run up to the first red cone and jump from one leg to two legs, attempting to reach past the second cone.

Pupils practise this skill for a few minutes before progressing to the next type of jump: jumping two legs to two legs, attempting to reach past the second cone.

After pupils have reached the target of jumping beyond the second cone three times, they then lay out another red cone, which they place another foot (or appropriate distance away), and attempt the running jump.

Once pupils can jump beyond the third red cone three times within their team, they then add another cone to the task to ensure constant progress is being made.

Competition
The first team to complete the task of jumping over the fourth and final cone three times within their team, sits down with crossed arms, to show that they have successfully completed the tasks.

Differentiation
Decrease/increase the starting jumping distances for WT and WB pupils respectively.

Group WT pupils together and WB pupils in another group. Challenge pupils according to their ability, and set appropriate jumping distances.

Key teaching points
- SAQ development – SAQs develop the mental-neuro system which trigger the brain to act quickly and respond.
- Developing *co-ordination when moving at speed*.
- Developing teamwork – developing team skills of working together.

Cool-down: Jump relays (10 minutes)
Pupils jog around the space. Tell pupils to imagine they are in the park again, but this time a monkey has left lots of banana skins, which are represented by cones. Tell pupils to jump over as many banana skins as possible while travelling. First they use a two-footed jump. Then a single leg jump.

Progression
Develop leadership opportunities by asking pupils to take over as mini leaders and run exercises themselves in smaller groups to encourage independent learning and practice.

Variation
Remaining in their teams of three, pupils take turns to run to the first red cone and perform four bunny hops between each of the red cones before then turning and running back to his/her team and handing a baton or soft ball to the next person in the line. The next person in the line repeats the activity.

Key teaching points
- Use body parts correctly – soft knees, not falling over, holding ball correctly for exchange.
- Quick feet, using eyes for awareness of surroundings.
- *Good co-ordination and agility*.
- Ask pupils about good techniques that they can use to evade an opponent. Ask pupils if these skills are linked to other games in PE or sports.

Plenary
- What do we mean when we say ABCs?
- What types of jumps did we practise today?
- What jumps did you find the most challenging?

Cross-curricular links

Science: Learning about the body (biology).

Lesson 4 Preparation for sprinting

Lesson objective: To improve co-ordination and body balance for sprinting whilst encouraging teamwork, health and fitness.

Key terms: "bent knees"; "balls of the feet"; "agility"

Warm-up: Domes and dishes (10 minutes)
Divide the class into two teams and provide bibs for each team. Some cones are scattered around the playing area, some are facing upside down (dishes), and others are facing the usual way (domes). One team turns the domes into dishes, and the other turns the dishes into domes. Each team cancels out the efforts of the other team to encourage prolonged running and bending of the knees, to turn the cones over. Pupils must work together as a team to turn the domes/dishes over as quickly as they can.

Variation
The blue team goes first and turns as many cones over as they can within a set amount of time (e.g. ten seconds). The red team are jogging on the spot or doing star jumps whilst waiting. Once the time is over, the red team and the blue team swap places, and the red team reverse the turning of the cones as quickly as they can, to see if they can get the cones all turned back the right way up within ten seconds.

Health and safety
Advise and remind pupils that they are not allowed to touch a cone whilst another pupil is touching it.

Key teaching points
- Bend knees before collecting a cone.
- Quickly identify where the cones are that need to be turned over.
- Run on the balls of the feet (tiptoes).
- Change direction quickly.
- Work together as a team.

Main lesson: Star relay (20 minutes)
Phase 1: Set up ten teams with up to three pupils per team. Each team will have their own hoop that contains beanbags. The first team to collect all of their beanbags and sit down with their hands on their heads is the winning team.

Phase 2: Once pupils have collected their beanbags, they run backwards to their team.

Phase 3: Introduce two appropriately-sized small hurdles between the beanbag and each team. Each pupil must jump over the two hurdles before collecting their beanbag.

Phase 4 – endurance run: Only collecting one beanbag at a time, each pupil must collect all of their beanbags from their hoop.

Variation

Play Robin Hood: divide the class into six teams, each with a different colour. Sit each team at the same distance from the centre. Place 30 beanbags in the centre of the playing area (five of each colour). One member of each team sprints into the middle, picks up a beanbag and sprints back to their team, before giving a high five to the next child in their team. Each team member repeats the process. The team with the most beanbags at the end of the game is the winning team.

Competition

Once all the bean bags have been returned to their team, the pupils sits down with their arms folded to show that they have successfully completed the task.

Tips

Identify the correct start position for sprinting. Pupils must start each relay from the 'sprint position'.

Try to match pupils appropriately according to their speed.

Differentiation

This activity generally works best when pupils are working in groups of mixed abilities, as pupils are able to challenge themselves whilst also supporting their team. However, the teacher may wish to group WB pupils together and progress the WB pupils to phase 3 before the rest of the class.

Key teaching points

- Start in the correct sprint position (see rules).
- Push off and land on the forefoot (balls of the feet).
- *Shoulders low and relaxed*.
- Fast arms – *drive elbows back*.
- *Drive from a low position* to minimise wind resistance (WB pupils).

Cool-down: Sharks in the water (10 minutes)

Explain to the pupils that now they are standing on a magic island by standing in one of the hoops. Outside of the hoops is water, where there may be sharks and other dangerous animals.

Without touching others, pupils must attempt to travel around the island, however, they can only travel by making strides into each hoop. Explain to the pupils that between the hoops is water, with sharks, so they must be in a hoop at all times.

Tips

It is important to ensure that your playing area is not too big or small for this activity, so as to ensure that pupils are able to travel from one to another safely and with a small degree of challenge.

Differentiation

Introduce more hoops/place the hoops closer together for WT pupils.
Place the hoops further apart, whilst ensuring a safe distance for WB pupils.

Variation

Classic cool-down: pupils jog around the playing area, following the teacher's instructions, e.g. 'walk', 'jog', 'hop', 'skip', 'jump', 'high knees', 'sidestep', 'jog backwards', etc.

Health and safety

Remind pupils not to go into congested areas.

Key teaching points

* Improve agility, co-ordination and balance.
* Prepare for jumping skills in previous lessons and lessons that will follow.
* Allow pupils the opportunity to explore space, using skills learnt from previous lessons of identifying space.

Plenary

* What part of the foot should we travel on when sprinting?

Cross-curricular links

Science: Ask pupils about ways in which they can streamline their bodies in order to travel faster. Ask pupils about how wind pressure may affect their speed?

Lesson 5 Sprinting

Lesson objective: To develop knowledge and understanding of the sprinting technique over a 40 yard distance.

Key terms: "speed"; "streamlined"
* Introduce the lesson by asking pupils if they know about any fast sprinters. Ask pupils to discuss with a partner how they use their bodies to run faster.

Warm-up: Traffic lights jogging on the spot and Scarecrow tag (10 minutes)
Phase 1 – Traffic lights: Introduce a gentle pulse-raising activity – jogging on the spot, responding to traffic lights:

- green – jog fast
- amber – jog slow
- red – stand still and make a star shape before commencing phase 2 as shown below.

Phase 2 – Scarecrow tag: five pupils are nominated as taggers, each with a soft ball or bib, to tag others with. The taggers attempt to tag as many pupils as possible. Once tagged, children must stand still in a star shape, as a 'scarecrow'. The scarecrows may be freed when any other pupil runs under both of their arms (or one arm if the space is compact). The game ends after a set time or as commanded by the teacher.

Health and safety
Remind pupils not to scream or shout when moving. If they bite their tongue this could be quite painful.

Variation
This variation activity encourages more independent learning. Pair pupils up with someone of similar speed and endurance to play a 'Tom and Jerry' style game where one person attempts to tag the other using a soft ball or bib. Once tagged, the player takes the bib/soft ball and gives their partner three seconds to get away, before trying to tag them back. The aim of the game is to be the tagger for the least amount of time possible.

Key teaching points
- Pupils to try to evade an opponent by:
  ○ identifying space within the playing area
  ○ changing direction *quickly*
  ○ *changing speed*
  ○ *having good footwork*, *balance and evasion*.

Main lesson: 40 metre sprints (20 minutes)
Phase 1: Create ten teams with three pupils in each team. One by one, pupils practise sprinting from their starting cone to a red cone, which is only 10 metres away; they work on the start of their sprint.

Phase 2: Introduce a yellow cone, which is placed a further 10 metres away, thereby increasing the distance from start to end cone, to 20 metres. Pupils now take turns to practise sprinting form their starting cone and continuing their sprint through to the yellow cone.

Phase 3: Introduce a third cone – a green cone – a further 10 metres away, increasing the sprint distance to 30 metres. Pupils practise running 30 metres whilst maintaining good form.

Phase 4: A final cone marks 40 metres. Pupils now practise the 40 metre sprint, maintaining good form and posture throughout.

Tips
Set all coloured cones out before the lesson to ensure a smooth pace to the lesson. Use the space available effectively, e.g. if you have lots of space, and pupils are relatively fit, the teacher may extend the distances. If it's raining and/or you are in a small hall, practise short

sprinting techniques over shorter distances within your given space or revert to delivering a different main lesson from this section.

Competition
Introduce a competition element where 10 pupils at a time race against each other over a 40 metre distance. Ask pupils to focus on implementing the key tips and teaching points they were practicing in earlier phases of the lesson.

Differentiation
When racing, position pupils so that they run against other pupils of a similar speed. You might also increase the distance for WB pupils and decrease the distance for WT pupils.

Key teaching points
- The core aim is for pupils to run in a straight line and with good posture.
- Start in the correct sprint position.
- Drive low – adopt a streamlined body shape and stay low as long as comfortably possible.
- Once the pupils move past the first 10 metres, they should begin to raise the upper body, with a straight back, ensuring a smooth transition between the cones.

Cool-down: Duck duck goose (10 minutes)
Pupils remain in their teams, and each team sits in a circle. One pupil from each team is nominated as the person to start the game. They jog around the circle, touching each child's shoulder as they go past and saying the word, 'duck', 'duck', 'duck'. . . When they choose to touch a child and call 'goose', that child (the goose) gets up and tries to chase the duck around the circle, back to the space where they found the 'goose.' The 'goose' then repeats the process.

Variation
Classic cool-down: pupils jog around the playing area, following the teacher's instructions, e.g. 'walk', 'jog', 'hop', 'skip', 'jump', 'high knees', 'sidestep', 'jog backwards', etc.

Key teaching points
- Place your hands firmly on the floor so you are ready to spring up, if required.
- Stay as close to the circle as possible when running.

Plenary
Divide the class into pairs. Ask pupils to check their pulse by placing fingers on their wrist or neck. Pupils discuss their heart rate with their partner and *why it increases when they run fast*.
- Why is it important to warm up and cool down at the start and end of each lesson?
- Do we need to be in a low or high position when we start sprinting?
- Why do we need to be in a low position – how does this help us travel faster?

Lesson 6 Preparation for throwing

Lesson objective: To throw a beanbag in a rainbow shape (to prepare pupils for more challenging throwing activities in the next lesson).

Key terms: "cage"; "rainbow shape"; "bent knees"

Warm-up: Bean bag throw (10 minutes)
Phase 1: Ask pupils to move around the space, following the teacher's commands, e.g. 'walking', 'jogging', 'skipping', 'jogging whilst rotating the arms forwards', 'jogging whilst rotating the arms backwards'. Ask pupils if they can rotate their arms in opposite directions.

Phase 2: In pairs, pupils throw and catch the beanbag back and forth to each other whilst on the move. Explore these different ways of throwing and catching:
* throw high
* throw low
* throw with two hands
* catch with *one hand*
* *change direction* after catching the beanbag
* throw the beanbag up whilst jogging, *when you catch the beanbag, you must balance on one leg for three seconds*
* catch the beanbag *above the head/next to the ear, slightly above the shoulder*.

Differentiation
If WT pupils find the activity challenging, ask them to stand still and complete the tasks.

Layered differentiation: Ask pupils to perform the following skills – once they've caught the beanbag three times, they can progress to the next level:
* level 1: stand still and catch the beanbag (WT pupils)
* level 2: jog and catch the beanbag
* level 3: run and catch the beanbag (WB pupils).

Key teaching points
Also remind pupils of what they learnt in previous lessons (sending and receiving – Invasion games).
* Keep your eye on the beanbag: 'eyes on the prize'.
* Throw the beanbag from low to high (in the shape of a rainbow).
* Make a cage with the hands to catch the beanbag (these skills will also be required for cricket lessons and tennis lessons).
* As confidence increases catching the beanbag, pupils should increase their speed.

Main lesson: Hoop targets (20 minutes)
Create up to ten teams with up to three pupils per team. Each team has three hoops in front of them. One at a time, pupils attempt to throw a beanbag into one of the hoops.

If the beanbag lands in the first hoop this is rewarded by 10 points; the second hoop is worth 20 points, and the furthest hoop away is worth 30 points. To start with, pupils should attempt to throw the beanbag slowly. Then, ask pupils to explore different types of throwing and to try it for each hoop, e.g.

- slow/fast
- high/low
- with the left hand/right hand
- underarm/overarm
- with a short follow-through/long follow-through.

Competition
Introduce a friendly competition between the teams to see which team were able to gain the most points in a set time.

Differentiation
For WT pupils, decrease the distance of the hoops; for WB pupils, increase the distance of the hoops.

Key teaching points
- Start with the beanbag by your side.
- Slightly bend your knees before you throw.
- Throw by moving your arm in a forward direction towards the target.
- Point your index finger towards the target once you have released the beanbag from your hand.
- Discuss the different styles of throwing with pupils: which style were they most comfortable with? Which style gave the most success?

Cool-down: Beanbag relay game (10 minutes)
Each pupil has a beanbag and travels around the playing area in the manner specified by the teacher. Pupils throw and catch the beanbag on their own as they travel. Encourage pupils to challenge themselves by throwing the beanbag slightly above their head and by travelling at a steady pace.

Variation
Play 'Travelling cars': ask pupils to travel as if they are driving a car (but without making car noises if indoors). Pupils jog around the playing area, changing their speed according to the number given by the teacher: gear 1 – really slow gear (walking); gear 2 – jogging; gear 3 – running. This may be done on the spot or with pupils travelling around the space.

Note: Always end the game by decelerating, in order to slowly reduce the heart rate; reduce from gear 2 down to gear 1.

Health and safety
Remind pupils of how to throw the beanbag safely so as not to comprise the safety of other pupils. Pupils must throw the beanbag sensibly and not in the direction of others.

Remind pupils of the key rules – no touching, no talking.

Key teaching points

- Throw the beanbag in an upwards direction.
- Make a cage with the hands to catch the beanbag.
- Awareness of space: check left and right to ensure you are in space and avoid bumping into others.

Plenary

- How do we throw the beanbag to make sure it goes towards the hoop?
- What can we do with our index finger to help ensure the beanbag travels towards the hoop?

Cross-curricular links

Mathematics: Ask one pupil from each team to count their scores.

Science: Remind pupils of why it is important to use their arms as well as their legs when jumping.

Science: Briefly explain the science behind why and how the following running techniques affect pupils performance: *Drive the elbows back (push against the wind)*/Drive off the forefoot & land on the forefoot/*Shoulders low and relaxed*/Keep the elbows tucked into the body and by the waist/high hips – lift the knees high.

Unit 3: Net/wall and striking/ fielding games

By the end of this unit, pupils should be able to:

a) Play net and wall and striking/fielding games safely on their own and *with others*.
b) Catch and throw the ball underarm on their own and with a partner *with control and accuracy*.
c) Strike the ball *in a forwards direction*.
d) Understand.

Key: Step 1 | *Step 2*

Equipment required:

- 30 KS1 530 tennis racquets
- bucket containing at least 50 tennis balls
- rack of cones
- set of 30 spots (desirable)
- 15 cricket bats for KS1 pupils (approximately 51 cm in length)
- 15 cricket stumps.

7 Tennis

What do I need to know?

Net and wall games are part of the National Curriculum for PE and include sports that involve a net such as tennis and badminton.

The National Curriculum for net and wall, and striking and fielding games, requires that pupils in KS1 are taught the basic skills of:
* *catching and throwing*
* *striking the ball.*

Safety

While delivering all activities, it is important to follow the safety guidelines as set out below to ensure a safe and effective learning environment:

* Ensure the playing area is safe and free of any hazards such as sharp objects before use.
* Ensure pupils are wearing the appropriate attire and that any shoes with laces and sufficiently tightened.
* Check that equipment is not damaged or torn before each lesson.
* Inform and reinforce to pupils the importance of finding space and not bumping into others during warm-ups and other activities.
* Lay the equipment out before the start of the lesson, where possible, to ensure easy access to resources and a smoother transition between activities.
* Inform and remind pupils of the rules and expectations at the beginning of each lesson.
* When delivering line games or activities where small queues exist, ensure pupils stand side by side so that you can always see them and they can see what is going on in front of them.
* Use verbal as well as visual signals to regain pupil focus and attention.
* When using racquets, always ensure pupils are a safe distance away from each other.
* Use soft balls or mini tennis balls during lessons.

Rules

* No talking while the teacher is explaining something to the group or demonstrating a task.
* No talking whilst others are explaining something to the group or demonstrating a task.
* No touching other people or equipment without the teachers' permission.

The two key rules you will need to know for teaching primary school tennis are:

* The ball may only bounce once in order for play to continue – except when the teacher has conditioned the game to make it easier in practice and allows two bounces.
* The ball must travel over the net and remain in court for a point to be scored. If the ball is not returned over the net and into court, a point is awarded to the person who originally sent the ball.

Lesson 1 Hand-eye co-ordination tennis

Lesson objective: To improve balance and hand-eye co-ordination with the racquet and ball; pupils should be able to trap the ball and send it back in a straight line.

Key terms: "agility"; "balance"; "co-ordination"; "racquet control"; "fitness"

Warm-up: Tennis circuit (10 minutes)
Set up several small circuit stations, which involve several jumps, bounds and tennis-related quick feet manoeuvres, e.g.
• Set out 6 cones – children start by being sideways on and quickly placing one foot at a time in-between each space.
• Six small mini cones for pupils to jump over
• A throw-down line, cone or *mini hurdle* to act as a river for pupils to jump over, landing on two feet
• Ladder for pupils to run with quick feet through, landing one foot in each hoop
• Cones set out for side shuffle from one cone to another
• Diagonal cones set out for pupils to move sideways between.

Children work together in small teams of up to five pupils per station. All pupils may be working on the same agility skill, e.g. hurdles. Alternatively, if time and resources are available, the teacher may wish to have different activities at different stations so that pupils can practise at different stations throughout the warm-up.

Tip
ABCs explanations:
• Agility: short quick movements
• Balance: remaining steady
• Co-ordination: different body parts working together.

Key teaching points
• Explain the meaning of ABCs in a simple way (see Tip above). Later in the lesson, ask pupils to discuss these with a partner and remind you what these terms mean.
• Prepare for tennis-related movements: good balance and foot control.
• Fitness and endurance.

Main lesson: Carry on tennis and floor tennis (20 minutes)
Phase 1 – Carry on tennis: Pupils practise balancing the ball on the racquet and holding it still for five seconds. Then, ask pupils to walk whilst balancing the ball on the racquet. When this is secure, ask pupils to jog slowly with the ball on the racquet, keeping the ball steady. Suggest pupils imagine the ball is an egg, and they cannot drop it, or it will crack. After some time, introduce the rule that if the ball falls to the floor at any time during the activity, pupils must put down their racquet and ball and complete three star jumps before continuing.

Phase 2 – Floor tennis: One pupil has the tennis racquet in their hand and the other pupil has the ball. Pupils start by standing either side of their 'gate' facing each other (ask pupils if they remember what a 'gate' is from previous lessons and invasion games).

Pupils take three paces back. The pupil with the ball rolls it at a steady speed along the floor to their partner. The pupil with the racquet traps the ball with the racquet head and gently steers the ball back to their partner. The aim is to get the ball straight through the gate along the floor.

Competition
If time allows, move the pupils to ten teams with three pupils in each team for these races.
- Rolling race: One at a time, pupils roll the ball with the racquet to the red cone, stop the ball and push it through the green gate (two green cones spaced approximately 2 yards apart, which is placed approximately 3 yards ahead of the red cone). The next person goes once the person ahead has reached the green cones.
- Relay race: One at a time, pupils carry the ball on the racquet to the designated line and return to their team.

Differentiation
Progress WB pupils onto the progression activities below quicker, whilst WT pupils can work on the stationary tasks, before progressing to the next phase/s.

Progression
Phase 1:
1. Tap the ball up whilst travelling with the ball on the racquet.
2. Tap the ball down on the floor whilst travelling.
3. *Group up: when the teacher calls a number, e.g. 'two' or 'three', pupils respond by forming a group of that number and touching their racquets together by holding their racquets out in front of their bodies or to the side of their bodies, whilst also keeping the ball on their racquets. For each pupil in a group that achieves the task successfully, they get one point.*

Phase 2:
1. Pupils place their racquet on the floor in front of them; hold the tennis ball at shoulder height, drop the ball onto the racquet and catch it.
2. For pupils who can perform this activity well, ask them to drop the ball on the racquet springs before catching the ball.

Key teaching points
- Try to keep the ball at the centre of the racquet.
- Try to keep your hand in a steady position with a bent elbow.
- Work on hand-eye co-ordination: *pupils to make contact with the ball and the centre of the racquet*.
- Pupils should always be on the balls of the feet ready to move their body in line with the ball.
- Roll the ball in a *straight line* and at a *steady speed*.
- Trap the ball safely and push it back in a straight line to a partner.
- Follow through towards the target using the index finger to point to the direction they wish for the ball to travel.

Cool-down: Relay races (10 minutes)

Play the numbers game (see Introduction, pxii) to get pupils forming groups of two. Then ask pupils to sit down sensibly before demonstrating the next exercise below.

In small teams, pupils complete footwork relay races across short distances (8 yards, 10 yards and 15 yards). The racquet can be used as a baton to increase focus of the group and allow pupils to become used to sprinting with the racquet in their hand.

Pupils should concentrate on staying low to the floor and 'pushing off' the back leg when turning as opposed to running around in a circular motion.

Key teaching points
- Get low when starting to run.
- Turn and change direction quickly.
- Discuss why it is important to exercise, warm up and cool down.
- Discuss what pupils have learnt in the lesson; look for *key terms* such as 'balance,' 'bent knees', 'trapping the ball', 'pushing the ball'.

Plenary
- Who can tell me what we mean by: agility; balance; co-ordination?
- What part of the racquet should we use to make contact with the ball?

Lesson 2 Floor tennis

Lesson objective: To send and receive the ball with a tennis racquet (hand-eye co-ordination).

Key terms: "rally"; "agility"; "balance"; "co-ordination"

Warm-up: High and low fives (10 minutes)
Begin in the style of the Classic warm-up whereby pupils are travelling around the playing area in different ways as instructed by the teacher, e.g. jogging, hopping, skipping, sidestepping, bounding, jogging backwards, travelling with 'quick feet'. When the teacher says, 'High five', pupils react quickly by giving a high five to the nearest person to them whilst continuing to travel.

Extend the activity by introducing 'low five' and 'middle five':
- high five – above the head
- low five – below the knees
- middle five – at waist height.

Once pupils are confident following the teacher's instructions, they should continue to travel in various directions around the playing area, giving high, low and middle fives to other pupils as they pass.

Key teaching points

- Make positive eye contact before making contact.
- Signal to the nearest person high, middle or low.
- Keep alert and on the balls of your feet.

Main lesson: Floor tennis – two racquets (20 minutes)

Ask one pupil to collect two cones of the same colour and make a gate two yards wide before selecting a partner.

Demonstrate the game, floor tennis, learnt in the previous lesson. (If pupils did not progress to this phase in the previous lesson, begin with only one pupil using the racquet and their partner rolling the ball to them.) Working in pairs, the first pupil strikes the ball along the floor to their partner at a steady speed and in a straight line. The ball should travel through the 'gate' (pair of cones). The second pupil traps the ball with the racquet before gliding it back along the floor. Repeat this process before ensuring pupils swap roles safely.

Competition

Once pupils have developed the required skills, make this game into a small competition. Pupils count their rallies 1–10. When pupils reach ten successful rallies through the gates, they must place their racquets on the floor and complete ten star jumps before sitting down and placing their hands on their heads to demonstrate that they have completed the task.

Tip

Explain to pupils that a 'rally' means that the ball is travelling through the cones and being sent back.

Differentiation

Increase or decrease the size of the gate for WT and WB pupils respectively.

Progression

Progress to both pupils using racquets and striking the ball back and forth to each other.

Key teaching points

- Keep your eyes on the ball – 'eyes on the prize'.
- Try to get your body in line with the ball before trapping it.
- Place the racquet behind and slightly on top of the ball to trap it.
- Glide the ball along the floor, *following through towards the target*.

Cool-down: Listen and respond – side steps (10 minutes)
Ask pupils to sidestep around the playing area, whilst travelling on the balls of their feet. When the teacher says 'Down', pupils quickly bend low and touch the top of their shoes. When the teacher says 'Catch', pupils make the shape of catching with their hands. When the teacher says 'Rally', pupils make a pretend rally shot with their hands.

Key teaching points
- Alertness – React quickly to the teachers instructions.
- 'Rally' – perform a 'C' shape with the racquet to emulate a forehand shot.

Plenary
- If the ball is travelling to either side of my body, where do I need to position my body before I collect the ball?
- Do I trap the ball by placing the racquet face down or do I place the racquet at an angle?

Lesson 3 Catching and throwing the tennis ball

Lesson objective: To improve rolling, catching and throwing skills in pairs.

Key terms: "low, middle high"; "communication"; "balls of the feet"; "cupped hands"

Warm-up: Spin, swap, jump
Phase 1: Red and blue cones are spread around the perimeter of the playing area. Pupils begin by walking around the playing area, looking for spaces. When the teacher says 'Cone', pupils quickly run to a cone and stand still next to it.

Repeat this two or three times, then instruct two pupils to go to each cone so that they are in pairs ready for phase 2.

Phase 2: In pairs and standing either side of a cone, pupils face their partner and follow the teachers' movement instructions, including, but not limited to:
- jog on the spot
- hop on the spot
- star jumps on the spot
- criss-cross their feet repeatedly on the spot
- forwards and backwards movement with the feet repeatedly on the spot
- spin (360 degrees turn)
- swap (swap positions with their partner)
- jump.

When the teacher calls 'Cone', the first pupil out of each pair to pick up their cone, gains one point.

Progression
Rotate pupils' positions by asking them to move to a new space and play with a different partner.

Variation
Use a soft tennis ball instead of or placed on top of a cone.

Key teaching points
- Listen carefully for instructions.
- Always stay on the balls of your feet – on tiptoes.
- Always have knees a little bit bent ready to bend down quickly.
- To react quickly to the instruction.
- Do not attempt to snatch/grab the cone whilst another person has made contact with it, as this can be dangerous.

Main lesson: Low, middle, high (20 minutes)
In pairs, pupils stand facing each other 3 yards apart with one tennis ball between them.

Pairs pass and catch the ball in different ways with their partner, starting by rolling the ball (low along the floor) before progressing to middle and high passes once they have achieved the desired outcomes/skills:
- low pass – roll the ball along the floor
- middle pass – bounce the ball between you and your partner (underarm throw)
- high pass – throw the ball direct to your partner without the ball bouncing.

Differentiation
Pair WB pupils together and extend their practices where necessary, e.g. travelling faster and/or increasing the distance of their throwing.

Pair WT pupils together and give them more time to practise the low roll and medium throw before progressing to high throws.

Progression

Ask pupils to perform the skills whilst moving around the playing area calling the words 'low', 'middle' or 'high' as they throw the ball.

Key teaching points

- Develop catching skills – pupils to keep their eyes on the ball.
- Watch the flight of the ball – pupils to *get their body behind the ball*.
- Bend the knees when catching the ball.
- Pupils to *cup their hands*, ensuring little fingers are touching and thumbs are facing up, with fingers spread out when catching the ball. (Revisit and remind pupils of the key teaching points from previous lessons in basketball, p12.)
- Sideways movement and quick footwork.
- Communication between pairs – pupils to tell their partner, 'low', 'middle', or 'high', when they are about to throw the ball.

Cool-down: Tunnel express (10 minutes)

Pupils begin by standing at one end of the hall or playing area behind a set of red cones. The teacher stands at one side with a bucket of soft tennis balls. When the teacher calls 'Go', pupils attempt to get to the other side and beyond the red cones without being hit by a travelling ball, which the teacher gently rolls across the hall. Pupils who are hit by a ball on the feet or legs join the teacher by kneeling down at the side and attempting to roll the balls.

Health and safety

Remind pupils to be sensible and to look out for others when travelling.

Variation

1. For each round the teacher asks a question. If the answer is 'yes', only then do pupils travel across the hall, e.g. 'Do you have long hair?' 'Are you a girl?' 'Are you a boy?' 'Do you have a white t-shirt on?' 'Do you like salad?' Be mindful to ask questions which relate to healthy eating/ lifestyles.
2. Classic cool-down: Pupils travel around the space responding to various instructions from the teacher (see p33).

Key teaching points

- Peripheral vision – look out for where the balls are travelling from.
- Use variations in speed to get across the tunnel and avoid being hit.

Plenary

- What skills did we practise today?
- Why are these skills important for tennis?
- Does anybody know any types of shots in tennis? Which are high, medium or low?

Lesson 4 Flight of the ball

Lesson objective: To develop skills bouncing the ball and judging the flight of the tennis ball and reacting accordingly through throwing and catching.

Key terms: "underarm throws"; "catching"; "bounding"

Before the lesson, set out cones on the perimeter of the playing area with a tennis ball on top of each cone.

Warm-up: Shadow shots and Bounce about (10 minutes)
Phase 1 – Shadow shots: Pupils walk around the playing area, listening to the teacher's instructions. The teacher calls out tennis-related movements from the lesson 2 cool-down, including: 'forehand', 'rally' (make a pretend rally shot with their hands), or 'down' (touch the foot). Progress to pupils jogging around the playing area, touching the shoes of other pupils instead of their own on the command, 'Down' (stretching the leg and arm muscles).

Phase 2 – Bounce about: Pupils are selected one at a time to take a ball from the cones which are situated on the cones on the outside of the grid. Pupils begin bouncing and catching the ball whilst travelling. After a short practice on their own, pupils are asked to follow and repeat the process, 'walk, bounce catch'. Progress to 'jog, bounce catch'.

Differentiation
Be aware that some WB pupils will be able to jog confidently with the ball, bouncing and catching, whilst WT pupils will feel more comfortable walking with the ball. Allow pupils to start at their own level and make individual progress as they grow in confidence.

Some pupils will be confident catching the ball in one hand. Encourage them to extend their skills further if they are able.

Variation
Select two or three pupils to be taggers who hold the tennis ball in one hand. When the teacher says, 'Tag', pupils attempt to stay clear of the taggers, using dodging and weaving skills, learnt from previous lessons. If tagged, pupils must stand still with their arms out until another player runs under their arms to set them free.

Health and safety
Explain to pupils that they can only tag others gently on the shoulder. They must not push or pull any other children.

Key teaching points
- Raise the heart rate.
- Stretch the muscles.
- Get mentally prepared for activity.

Main lesson: Catch tennis (20 minutes)

Play the numbers game (see Introduction, pxii) to organise pupils into pairs for the next activity.

If nets are available, place tennis nets (or suitable alternative such as benches or cones) across the playing area. Pupils face their partner. One pupil has the ball and their partner has a down-turned cone, ready for catching the ball in. The first pupil throws the ball underarm, over the net, allowing the ball to bounce once, before their partner catches the ball in the cone. Their partner then throws the ball to return it using an underarm action. Ask pupils to reverse rolls after approximately two minutes.

Competition

Once pupils have achieved the desired objectives, continue the game above instructing pupils to reach ten catches as quickly as they can. After ten successful catches in the downturned cone, pupils sit down with their legs and arms crossed to show that they have completed the task.

Differentiation

Progress WB pupils using the progressions listed below. WT pupils may use beanbags as opposed to tennis balls, or work closer to their partner, or work with their partner but not using the net.

Progression

1. Increase the number of catches required for task completion.
2. Remove the use of the downturned cone. Pupils catch the ball in their hands.

Health and safety

Inform pupils not to touch the nets or any other large objects. Tell pupils that if their ball goes astray (e.g. under a table or in bushes) not to go and get the ball, but to inform the teacher and ask for a new ball/collect one from the bucket.

Key teaching points

- Pupils to keep their eyes on the ball.
- Throw the ball from the 'knees to trees' (low to high) or 'in the shape of a rainbow'.
- Pupils to get their body behind the ball, with bent knees for catching.
- Pupils to strike the ball *over the net/bench and in a straight line*.

Cool-down: Bounding (10 minutes)

Give each pupil a throw down line/flat marker (or a cone) and ask them to place it in an open space. Pupils place their feet on either side of the cone and perform small jumps on the spot over the throw down line or cone. Next, ask pupils to perform 'quick feet' (small quick steps on the spot).

Progression

Ask pupils to jump from side to side of their throw down line. Repeat the jumps for ten seconds.

Pupils may compete with their partner who will record their scores.

Key teaching points

Can you keep your feet and ankles together whilst jumping?

Can you use your arms to help you swing through the jump and keep a smooth rhythm?

Plenary
- What do we need to keep our eyes on as the ball is travelling towards us – the racquet or the ball?
- What do we do if the ball is travelling too far away from our bodies?

Inform pupils that next lesson they will be using the racquets and practising bounce rallies, so to practise if or when they can before the next lesson.

Lesson 5 Mini tennis

Lesson objective: Develop catching skills and the ready position for tennis, potentially progressing to striking and catching the ball with a tennis racquet, in pairs.

Key terms: "mini tennis"

Warm-up: Classic warm-up and warm-up relays (10 minutes)

Phase 1 – Classic warm-up: pupils travel around the space warming up their bodies. At the end of the activity, play the numbers game to ask the pupils to quickly get into groups of 3 and to sit sensibly in their teams, before demonstrating the next game.

Phase 2 – Warm-up relays: Pupils sit in teams of three behind a red cone. One at a time, pupils skip to a blue cone 5 yards in front of them before skipping back and giving a high five to the next pupil in their team. (While waiting, other pupils should be completing star jumps, jogging on the spot, completing tuck jumps or twisting their feet in a standing shuffle.)

Extend the activity by asking pupils to:
- jog to an end line of white cones and complete five star jumps, before returning to their team
- jog to the white cones and bounce a tennis ball on the spot twice, before running back to their team
- sidestep to the white cones and sprint back to their team.

Ask pupils if they can think of any other ways to travel for their warm-up relay.

Progression
Develop pupils' leadership skills – select well-behaved pupils to set out the red and white cones at the beginning of the lesson and instruct them where to place each cone and ball.

Health and safety
Remind pupils to give their teammate a gentle high five and not hit others on the hand or any other part of the body.

Key teaching points
- Explain to pupils that it is not a race and that each task must be performed with skills they have learnt in previous lessons.

Main lesson: Mini tennis (20 minutes)
In pairs, pupils stand facing each other on either end of a small 1x1 yard grid of cones. Pupil A holds the tennis ball at shoulder height and drops it into the square, whilst pupil B watches the ball bounce once before gently striking the ball upwards, so that it lands back in the grid. After one bounce, pupil A catches the ball and repeats the activity.

The first pupil to reach five or six successful catches sits down to demonstrate that they have successfully completed the task. *Progress to ten catches.*

Differentiation
Allow pupils to progress at their own pace, e.g. WT pupils don't use racquets; WB pupils use racquets. Vary the number of successful catches required for pupils of varying abilities.

Key teaching points
- Keep moving on the balls of your feet.
- Bend your knees and position the racquet underneath the ball.
- Contact the ball with the centre of the racquet.

Cool-down: Hear the bounce – ready position (10 minutes)
Pupils travel around the playing area quietly, listening to the sound of when the teacher bounces the ball (or if in a noisy area, when the teacher claps his/her hands). When pupils hear the ball bounce, pupils respond by jumping into the 'ready position'. Ask pupils to travel by walking, jogging, sidestepping and hopping.

Key teaching points
- Inform pupils that the 'ready position' is similar to the 'jump stop' position that they learnt in invasion games – basketball: knees bent, shoulder width apart, hands out in front of the body, with eyes focused ahead.

Plenary
- How do we stand in the ready position?
- Why is it important to get into the ready position?

Lesson 6 Striking the tennis ball

Lesson objective: To introduce pupils to striking the ball with the tennis racquet (large surface area) in preparation for striking the ball with a cricket bat (smaller surface area) in future lessons.

Key terms: "strike"; "red arrows"

Warm-up: High five and low (10 minutes)
Pupils travel around the playing area, listening to various teacher commands including: walking, jogging, skipping, hopping, changing direction, jumping or bounding and sidestepping.

When the teacher says, 'High five', pupils continue moving in the given fashion and give a high five to their classmates as they pass them. Repeat with a low five, and then repeat with a medium level five (in the shape of a racquet swing).

Health and safety

Ensure the space is large enough to minimise the risk of pupils bumping into each other.

Inform pupils that there will be some waiting required in this lesson, so that they all can play the full game of the tennis and rounders variation game safely. Remind pupils that they must be sensible whilst waiting.

Key teaching points

- Pupils to ensure they connect smoothly with their partner's hands, keeping their eyes focused until a clear connection is made.
- Inform pupils that these skills will be needed for the main lesson when using the racquets.

Main lesson: Tennis and rounders variation game (20 minutes)

Create at least six teams with three different playing areas. Each playing area has a fielding team and a striking team. The first pupil from the striking team stands in one hoop, with the bowler from the fielding team standing in another hoop approximately 5 yards away.

The aim of the game is for the striker with the tennis racquet to hit the ball as far as they can and then run through the red cones (situated at a 45 degree angle from the strikers hoop and approximately 12–15 yards away) before re-joining the back of their line. The next person in their team then steps forwards into the striker's hoop. As soon as the striker has run and the bowler has received the ball back from the other fielders, the bowler attempts to bowl the ball so it lands in the striker's hoop ready for the next person to strike the ball. The striking team gain one point for each successful run through the red cones, whilst the fielding team gains one point for each time they bowl the ball into the hoop.

After a set amount of time (7–10 minutes, depending on the length of the lesson), pupils swap roles.

Differentiation

Enable WT pupils to work in the same playing area together, whilst WB pupils work together in a different playing area. You can then differentiate the speed at which the game is played and the distance between the bowler and the striker, dependent upon the skill level of the pupils. For example, WT pupils will bowl from a shorter distance than that of WB pupils.

If WT pupils find it difficult to hit the ball, then the teacher may assist by holding the end of the racquet and assisting the connection with the ball. Alternatively, these pupils may have the ball rolled to them along the floor.

If some pupils find it difficult to bowl the ball accurately, the pupil rolls the ball along the floor.

Health and safety

Use a soft sponge ball. Ensure you have a 'waiting area' for each team at least 5 yards behind the striking hoop.

Key teaching points

- Strike the ball as far as you can and run through the red cones (known as 'red arrows').

- The next person from the striking team must be ready to run into the hoop and strike the ball straight away, so as to not lose a point.
- Keep your eyes on the ball with slightly bent knees.
- Make contact with the ball at the *centre of the racquet*.
- *Follow through in the direction you want the ball to travel*.
- Give pupils two or three opportunities to strike the ball before applying the differentiation of moving the bowler closer to the person who is striking the ball.

Cool-down: Creep up on the teacher (10 minutes)

The teacher stands at one end of the playing area and the pupils line up at the opposite end. The teacher faces away from the children. All pupils creep forwards until the teacher turns to face them, at which point they must stand still. If pupils are caught moving by the teacher, they are asked to restart from the starting line or take five paces back (whichever is most appropriate).

Progression

Select one sensible pupil to play the role of the teacher.

Variation

Select a different cool-down game from other lessons in this book, e.g. the classic cool-down (p33).

Key teaching points

- Pupils are learning to develop *balance and control* of their bodies.
- When the teacher turns and faces the pupils, explain to pupils that they must adopt the 'ready position' (link to prior learning of tennis, which is also needed for cricket fielding).

Plenary

- What did you learn and practise in today's lesson?
- What can we do to improve and refine our skills in future lessons?

8 Cricket

What do I need to know?

Cricket is a striking and fielding game in which pupils develop the fundamental skills of catching, throwing and striking the ball at distance, whilst working in a team. 'Kwik cricket' is a fast-paced children's version of the game, implemented to ensure pupils are more actively involved and engaged in each cricket lesson. In order to develop key skills, it is advised that pupils play versions of cricket in smaller teams of three pupils and work on a rotary basis to practise these skills.

Safety

While delivering all activities, it is important to follow the safety guidelines set out below to ensure a safe and effective learning environment.

- Ensure the playing area is always safe and free of any hazards such as sharp objects, before use.
- Ensure pupils are wearing the appropriate attire and that any shoes with laces are sufficiently tightened.
- Check that equipment is not damaged or torn before each lesson.
- Inform and reinforce to pupils the importance of finding space and not bumping into others during warm-ups and other activities.
- Lay the equipment out before the start of the lesson, where possible, to ensure easy access to resources and a smoother transition between activities.
- Inform and remind pupils of the rules and expectations at the beginning of each lesson.
- When delivering line games or activities in which small queues exist, ensure pupils stand side by side so that you can always see them and they can see what is going on in front of them.
- Use verbal as well as visual signals to regain pupil focus and attention.
- Keep safe distances between the pupil with the bat and fielders and/or other pupils.
- Use soft balls as opposed to hard tennis balls.

Lesson 1 Striking the ball with a cricket bat

Lesson objective: To improve striking and fielding skills with a cricket bat from the floor.

Key terms: "batting"; "fielding"; "bowling"

Warm-up: Light up (10 minutes)
The teacher spaces out lots of cones of different colours (e.g. red, white, blue, green, yellow) in the playing area. Alternatively, for more independent learning, give pupils one cone (of various colours) each and ask them to place the cone in an open space, within the given area.

Pupils travel around the playing area following the teacher's instructions (jogging, hopping, skipping, jogging backwards, sidestepping, jumping/bounding, etc.). When the teacher calls a colour, pupils must run to a cone of that colour as soon as possible and make a star shape.

Progression
Pupils must make contact with the cone once they get near it. Ask pupils to be creative in how they make contact with the cone, without lifting it from the floor, e.g. touch it with their hand, foot, elbow, knee, heel, etc.

Variation
When pupils get to the cone, they perform a skill, e.g. jump over it, jog around it, complete three star jumps.

Key teaching points
- Find the space whilst travelling.
- Listen to instructions carefully.
- Stay clear of other pupils, and travel in their own space.
- Pupils to make a *mental note* of when they travel past a cone, as they may need to turn quickly to get to that cone.

Main lesson: Roll and go (10 minutes)
In groups of three, pupils begin by holding hands in a triangle shape, then taking six steps back. Pupil A rolls the ball to pupil B who catches the ball and rolls it on to pupil C. Throughout the activity, pupils keep moving into a new space within the playing area.

Differentiation
WT pupils work together and the teacher or TA provides the necessary support (if a TA is present).

WB pupils work together and are provided with appropriate challenges, e.g. to bowl the ball underarm as opposed to rolling it along the floor.

Progression

Ask pupils to bounce the ball to each other as opposed to rolling it along the floor.

Key teaching points
- When rolling the ball: hold the ball by your ankle from a lunge position, bending the knees when rolling the ball.
- Roll the ball forwards ensuring your hand points towards the person you are rolling the ball to.

Match play (10 minutes)

Create teams of three pupils per team and allocate the members of each team a number, 1, 2 or 3:
- player 1 is the batsperson (stands in front of the wicket)
- player 2 is the bowler
- player 3 is the fielder.

The bowler rolls the ball along the floor to the batsperson, who hits the ball in any forwards direction; the fielder collects the ball quickly and returns it to the bowler.

After a few minutes of practice, ask pupils to rotate positions.

Invite one group to demonstrate good practice.

Tips

Ensure pupils are taught the basic rules for the game, e.g. where and when to run.

Key teaching points
- Hold the ball next to the ankle to bowl.
- Bend the knees when rolling the ball.
- Bowlers to ensure their hand *follows through in a straight line* towards the target pupil (remind pupils of prior learning).
- Remind bowlers to always be ready and to adopt the 'ready position', learnt in previous lessons.
- Front foot batting – the batter stands sideways to the wicket (sideways on).
- Pupils to hold the bat correctly – teach pupils the correct hold position for holding the bat *(writing hand lower than non-writing hand forming two Vs facing downwards)*.
- Fielders to catch the ball *quickly* and get it back to the bowler – pupils to remember the 'cage' technique from previous lessons.

Cool-down: In-goal fielding (10 minutes)

In groups of three, pupils stand in a line, keeping a 6 yard distance from each other: the pupil in the middle has two cones on either side of them, which are approximately 3 yards apart; the pupils on the outside both have soft balls or tennis balls.

One of the pupils on the outside bowls the ball towards the cones. The pupil in the middle must sprint towards the ball, gather the ball and roll it back to the player, stretching for it if necessary (if indoors and it is safe to do so), ensuring the ball does not go past the cone.

Once the ball has been returned, the other outside pupil does the same; the pupil in the centre turns to face them.

After a set number of seconds, the teacher should ask pupils to rotate positions so that a different pupil goes into the middle.

Health and safety
Ensure any diving for balls that takes place is in a safe area. Teach pupils how to dive by leading with their lower bodies first. If it is not a safe area for diving/stretching, ask pupils to move their feet quickly to get their body behind the ball.

Variation
Pupils walk, skip or jog around the space throwing and catching the ball on their own. As pupils gain confidence, they progress to jogging at a faster pace and/or throwing the ball higher above their head, keeping their eyes on the ball and making a cage with their hands to ensure they catch the ball successfully.

Key teaching points
- Pupils should keep their eyes on the ball.
- Pupils should keep on their toes and be ready to move.
- The two pupils on the outside should roll the ball *at a 'steady speed'*; not too fast nor too slow.

Plenary
- Where do we hold the ball when we are bowling – near our shoulder or near our ankle?
- When we are batting the ball, do we stand straight or sideways on?

Lesson 2 Throwing towards a target

Lesson objective: To improve accuracy of throwing towards a target and striking towards a target (striking and fielding – cricket).

Key terms: "hold position"; "target"

Warm-up: Roll it on team (10 minutes)
Phase 1: Pupils travel around the playing area responding to the teacher's instructions, including sidestepping, skipping, jogging backwards, hopping, bounding. Ask the pupils to call out key words during the activity, including 'up' (jump), 'down' (almost touch the floor) and 'change' (change direction).

Phase 2: Play the numbers game using the numbers two–five. When the teacher calls a number, pupils respond by getting into groups of that number.

Phase 3: Introduce a tennis ball/soft cricket ball into the activity to help develop independent learning. The teacher calls for a group of a certain number, e.g. 'three'; pupils find their groups and roll the ball to different players in their group, while keeping on the move. Pupils must ensure good practice and work well together to ensure that all of their team members share the ball appropriately. How many passes can they make within their team while moving around the playing area?

Differentiation
If WT pupils find this exercise challenging, they may complete the task in pairs, or revisit some of the skills from prior lessons, e.g. static rolling in pairs.

Key teaching points
- Transferring the cricket ball – pupils to roll it *quickly and accurately* by following through towards the target person.
- Developing catching skills – pupils to make a cage, as learnt in previous lessons.
- Warming up the muscles and preparing the mind for the more advanced elements of the lesson.
- Pupils without the ball to find *good space before calling for the pass*, e.g. not standing behind somebody else but moving to where the pupils with the ball can clearly see them and get the ball to them easily.

Main lesson: Target! (10 minutes)
In groups of three, pupils practise throwing a beanbag into a target zone or hoop, one by one before sprinting to collect their beanbag and returning to their group. (The hoop is placed approximately 3–4 yards away.)

Competition
Pupils gain one point each time the beanbag lands inside the hoop or target zone. The first team to reach five points wins the round. Repeat this activity three or four times.

Progression
Pupils throw a ball instead of a beanbag into the target zone or hoop.

Variation
Lay out two hoops for each team. One hoop is 3 yards away and the other is 5–6 yards away from their cone. Pupils gain 10 points if their beanbag lands in the first hoop, and 20 points if it lands in the second hoop.

Key teaching points
- Before throwing bend your knees slightly, holding the beanbag by your side.
- Throw the beanbag in a shape of a rainbow.
- Point your index finger towards the target once you have released the beanbag.

Match play (10 minutes)
This is a continuation from the previous lesson.

Divide the class into groups of three and allocate each pupil in the group a role: pupil 1 – batsperson; pupil 2 – bowler; pupil 3 – fielder.

The bowler either rolls the ball along the floor or bowls it underarm to the batsperson, who hits the ball in any direction, the fielder collects the ball quickly and returns it to the bowler.

Differentiation
If some WB pupils have achieved the target aims for the previous lessons, then use the 'target zone' (two cones placed at a 45 degree angle from the batting spot) for these pupils only, as an *extension activity*. The bowler shall gain one point for each time the ball travels through the target zone.

Key teaching points
- Ensure pupils are using the correct 'hold' position for the ball – ask pupils to show you their thumb and its two nearest fingers ('snake' fingers) and ask pupils to practise using only these three fingers to 'hold' the ball.
- Ensure that pupils use their bat or racquet to follow through towards their target (remind pupils of prior learning from invasion games).
- Pupils to be 'sideways on' when batting.

Cool-down: Footwork ladder drills (10 minutes)
Ladders are laid out in the middle of the playing area and in between two cones (one starting cone for each team). Three pupils begin on one side of each ladder behind the red cone, and two pupils begin on the other side of the ladder, behind the blue cone. Each cone should be five yards away from the ladder.

The teacher selects the style in which pupils travel through the ladder for each round, e.g. sideways footsteps, hops, two-footed jumps, two feet in each space, one foot in each space, etc.

On exiting the ladder, each pupil must roll the ball underarm to their teammate opposite and joins and the back of the queue on the opposite end.

Tips
If ladders are not available, use small cones or throw down lines for the pupils to travel through.

Differentiation
WT pupils might prefer to complete the footwork activity without using a ball.

Key teaching points
- Keep eyes ahead to be able to see where to place feet.
- Don't travel too fast – be careful not to fall on the ladder/cones.

Plenary
- Why are the skills we have learned relevant to cricket?
- What are some of the key terms we have learned?
- How do we hold the ball when we are bowling it?
- What do we follow through towards when we are bowling the ball?

Lesson 3 Striking from an underarm bowl

Lesson objective: Develop skills of striking the ball from an underarm bowl; learn the basic rules of the game and implement them safely.

Key terms: "underarm bowl"; "batting"

Warm-up: Bowl out (10 minutes)
Ask two or three pupils to be bowlers; the rest of the class are the runners. Using sponge or soft tennis balls, the bowlers must bowl the ball low on the floor and attempt to hit the legs of the runners.

A pupil who is hit (below the knees only) takes possession of the ball and assumes the role of the bowler, taking the ball that he or she was hit with and attempting to 'bowl out' at another pupil. The pupil who was originally the bowler moves away from the ball and attempts to avoid being hit by any of the bowlers.

Tip
Pupils must keep moving at all times.

Variation
A pupil who is hit by the ball assumes the scarecrow position (legs and arms apart). Scarecrows can only be freed by another pupil running under their arms and calling out, 'Freed!'.

Key teaching points
- Awareness – pupils to try to stay away from the bowlers.
- ABCs – pupils to dodge, show lots of changes of direction, and jump, so as not to get hit by the ball.
- Timing – pupils to try to jump over the rolling ball to avoid getting hit.
- Pupils to understand that a warm-up raises the heart rate, in preparation for further activity.
- Pupils to roll the ball flat and straight.
- Revisit why it is important to warm up.

Main lesson: Underarm bowling and batting (20 minutes)
This activity provides a good assessment opportunity.

Divide the class into teams of three–six pupils, each team with one bowler, one batter and one–three fielders. The bowler bowls the ball underarm to the batter, who hits the ball into an open space and then runs around the wicket (to the left of the batsperson). The fielders collect the ball as quickly as they can and return it to the bowler. After two or three minutes, ask pupils to swap roles.

Differentiation

Provide support for WT pupils, e.g. rolling the ball along the floor, which will make it easier for them to hit the ball.

Progression

If time allows and pupils have reached the desired objectives, progress the activity. Each batter starts with 20 runs, and one run is deducted from their score for each time they are bowled out or caught out.

Key teaching points

- Revisit why it is important to hold the bat correctly – discuss with pupils why it is important to aim their shot.
- Ensure pupils are reminded of the rules of the game.
- When bowling, hold the ball next to the knee.
- Bend the knees when rolling the ball.
- Ensure the hand follows through in *a straight line towards the target pupil*.
- Reiterate the correct 'hold' position for the bat – non-writing hand on top of the bat, with the writing hand lower down; the thumbs and fingers should form a V shape facing downwards towards the floor when the pupil is holding the bat correctly.

Cool-down: relay bowl (10 minutes)

Divide the class into teams of five. Each team lines up with three children at one end and the remaining two children facing them 10 yards away.

The first pupil in each line bowls the ball to their teammate at the opposite end, then sprints to the back of the opposite line. The receiver of the ball repeats the same skill. After the first round, alter the type of movement to sidestepping, then to jogging backwards.

The first team to have all players returned to their original position, sitting down with their hands on their laps, gains a point.

Key teaching points

- Remind pupils of key teaching points as above for rolling the ball flat and in a straight line.

Plenary

- What do we mean when we say the word agility?
- Were we practising overarm or underarm bowling today?
- How do we hold the ball when delivering an underarm bowl?

Lesson 4 Doubles cricket

Lesson objective: To understand the basic rules of doubles cricket while developing the core skills of striking, throwing and catching in cricket.

Key terms: "bowling"; "fielding"; "striking"; "teamwork"; "doubles cricket"

Warm-up: Classic warm-up and Beanbag relay (10 minutes)
Phase 1 – Classic warm-up: Pupils travel around the playing area responding to various teacher instructions, e.g. 'Up', 'Down', 'Change direction' (see p15). Provide leadership opportunities by asking one pupil at a time to select the next movement action or to call the commands.

Phase 2 – Beanbag relay: Divide the class into teams of three or four. Pupils sit sensibly behind their team cone. Each team cone has a red cone approximately 10 yards ahead of it, then ahead of the red cone is a hoop. One at a time, a pupil from each team runs towards their red cone and aims to thrown the beanbag into their hoop. The target should be 3–6 yards away from the red cone that they throw from. Whether they score or miss, pupils jog back to their team, and the next person in the line repeats the process.

Differentiation
Ensure pupils are challenged but also have a suitable chance of scoring and achieving the objectives.

WB pupils could throw tennis balls at two or three static large cones; they would gain one point for each accurate throw.

The teacher may split the teams into groups that are of similar abilities. They could also alter the distance of the targets for pupils of different abilities.

Health and safety
Remind pupils that only one pupil from each team may go at any one time, to avoid collisions or the risk of being hit by a beanbag.

Key teaching points
- Revisit skills learnt in previous lessons for bowling underarm, including 'throw it in a rainbow shape' or 'from low to high' with 'bent knees' and keeping the 'eye on the target'.

Main lesson: Doubles cricket (20 minutes)
This activity provides a good assessment opportunity.

Divide the class into four teams (or six teams if space allows). Set up playing spaces for pairs of teams to play each other. Create a safe middle section of boundary cones which divides the playing areas from each other.

Explain the rules of doubles cricket.

- Two batters start – the first batter is positioned at the bowler's stumps and the second batter at the fielders' stumps.
- The bowler bowls the ball underarm to the first batter.
- When the first batter hits the ball, both batters run to the opposite stump with their bat.
- Each team starts with 10 runs. Each batter has three hits. Batters gain one run for each successful run, but lose one run for each successful catch or bowl out at the stumps.
- After the first two batters have had their three bats of the ball, the teacher instructs the batters to safely place their bats on the floor, and two new batters to step forward.

Tips

Explain to pupils that at some points of the lesson they will need to wait patiently to bat. Alternatively, pupils can practise balance and control games, e.g. balancing the ball on the racquet, tap ups or floor tennis games.

Ask pupils to observe the performances of their classmates, so that they can improve their own performance. You could ask pupils to write down key points on mini whiteboards, e.g. can they make a clean connection with the ball? Remind pupils not to swing the bat but to guide it safely.

Remind pupils not to scuffle over loose balls, but to work together to get the ball back to the bowler, hitting the stump as soon as possible.

Differentiation

Repeat a main lesson activity from previous lessons to develop the skills of catching, bowling and striking further, if required.

Health and safety

Ensure sufficient space is available for these games. If sufficient space is not available, then play the game with two teams or play a different game with similar learning outcomes.

Create a 'safe zone' for the batters who are waiting, so they can wait and watch safely without causing interruption to the flow of the game. This can be a rectangle of cones or a bench where pupils sit.

Progression

If time allows, repeat this game with different teams playing each other.

Key teaching points

- Accurate bowling towards the target – remember from previous lesson to throw it in the shape of a rainbow.
- Letting the ball bounce before it reaches the bat.
- Fielders are to be in the ready position at all times (as learnt in previous lessons).
- Fielders are to throw the ball as *quickly* as they can to the stumps or back to the bowler – discourage fielders from running with the ball.

Cool-down: Body parts (10 minutes)

Pupils walk around the playing area. When the teacher says the name of a body part, pupils must balance on that part of the body, e.g. 'knees', 'two feet and two hands', 'one foot and two hands', 'back', 'bottom'. Ensure body parts called are appropriate for the space being used.

Variation

Pupils stand in a circle with their team. Pupils practise throwing the ball gently (underarm) to their teammates without dropping the ball.

Progression

If pupils cover all the supplied cricket lessons within the space of one academic year, repeat one of the lessons where time was cut short or which the pupils particularly enjoyed and learnt a lot from, e.g. match play games or hold mini tournaments.

Key teaching points

- Hold your stomach in tight.
- Use your arms for balance.

Plenary

- What did you learn and practise in today's lesson?
- What can we do to improve and refine our skills in future lessons?

Cross-curricular links

Science: Explain the relationships between the amount of force used to strike the ball and the distance the ball travels.

Part 2:
Key Stage 2

Purpose of study

A high-quality physical education curriculum inspires all pupils to succeed and excel in competitive sport and other physically demanding activities. It should provide opportunities for pupils to become physically confident in a way that supports their health and fitness. The opportunity to compete in sport and other activities builds character, and helps to embed values such as fairness and respect.

Aims

The National Curriculum for physical education aims to ensure that all pupils:

- develop competence to excel in a broad range of physical activities
- are physically active for sustained periods of time
- engage in competitive sports and activities
- lead healthy, active lives.

Attainment targets: by the end of each key stage, pupils are expected to know, apply and understand the matters, skills and processes specified in the relevant programme of study. Schools are not required by law to teach the example content in [square brackets].

Subject content

Key Stage 2:

Pupils should continue to apply and develop a broader range of skills, learning how to use them in different ways and to link them to make actions and sequences of movement. They should enjoy communicating, collaborating and competing with each other.

They should develop an understanding of how to improve in different physical activities and sports and learn how to evaluate and recognise their own success. Pupils should be taught to:

- use running, jumping, throwing and catching in isolation and in combination
- play competitive games, modified where appropriate [for example, badminton, basketball, cricket, football, hockey, netball, rounders and tennis], and apply basic principles suitable for attacking and defending
- develop flexibility, strength, technique, control and balance [for example, through athletics and gymnastics]
- perform dances using a range of movement patterns
- take part in outdoor and adventurous activity challenges both individually and within a team, compare their performances with previous ones and demonstrate improvement to achieve their personal best.

DFE Physical Education requirements KS2

Teaching should ensure that when evaluating and improving performance, connections are made between developing, selecting and applying skills, tactics and compositional ideas, and fitness and health.

During KS2, pupils enjoy being active and using their creativity and imagination in physical activity. They learn new skills, find out how to use them in different ways, and link them to make actions, phrases and sequences of movement. They enjoy communicating, collaborating and competing with each other. They develop an understanding of how to succeed in different activities and learn how to evaluate and recognise their own success.

Knowledge, skills and understanding

Through the delivery of high quality PE, children should develop knowledge, skills and understanding of a breadth of sports within the National Curriculum framework for PE.

Pupils should be active for the majority of the PE lesson – approximately 80% of the time – and should be supported by effective modelling, peer and self-evaluation, putting the learned skills into practice through conditioned or unconditioned games, match-play scenarios and/or full games.

Effective modelling

Through effective modelling, pupils should have a clear understanding and be able to explain what 'good' PE looks like, and how they can make progress.

Peer- and self-evaluation

By outlining the learning objectives, questions, intentions and key words on the board/via PowerPoint presentations, and regularly referring to them throughout the lesson, you can encourage pupils to constantly assess where they are in terms of their skill level, where they have progressed from and what they can do to increase the challenge and/or make further progress. To support this, it's good practice to outline three representations of the success criteria on the board using a colour-coding system such as Gold, Silver and Bronze:

- Bronze – I can pass the ball to my partner
- Silver – I can pass the ball to my partner with accuracy and control (through the cones)
- Gold – I can pass the ball to my partner with accuracy and control whilst on the move

Though not referenced within the lesson plans in this book, teachers can use the success criteria as a method of assessment for each lesson to provide clarity for learners and encourage continuous progress.

Putting learned skills into practice

In KS2, teachers should look for examples of where they can implement layered differentiation, and enable pupils to progress at their own pace with a high threshold. For example, when delivering a game where pupils have to dribble the ball to point X and strike/throw the ball at a target, set out cones at three different distances from the target. Pupils must dribble to the cone nearest the target, and hit the target a set number of times (e.g. three) before progressing to striking/throwing the ball from the second furthest cone. This enables pupils to challenge themselves independently and without teacher intervention whilst working in a group setting.

The four A's as set out below outline key elements that provide a basis for each lesson or phase of learning offered in this book.

Activate

Pupils should enjoy being active throughout their PE lessons, and following necessary introductions such as health and safety, discussions about learning objectives, questions and intentions. Pupils should actively engage in an inclusive warm-up activity that prepares them for the learning to come.

Acquire

Pupils should be allowed time to observe good practice, usually through effective modelling, before practicing their own skills and self-assessing/peer assessing their performance against the set model so that they can make continual progress.

Apply

Pupils should be given time to put the skills into practice, both independently and in pairs or small teams, before discussing key ideas about the learning and how to make progress.

Assess

Pupils should understand how to evaluate their performance against the learning objective, intention or question, and have a clear understanding of how they can improve.

Unit 1: Invasion games

9 Basketball

What do I need to know?

Basketball is a high-tempo, high-scoring end to end invasion game. As there are a maximum of just five players per team on the court at any one time, tactile ball control and individual skill is very important. As such, pupils should be encouraged to practise their dribbling and ball handling skills whilst also learning how to work effectively in a team.

Key teaching points may include:

- defending
- basketball stance
- team spacing on attack
- safe side passing – passing the ball on the opposite side of the defender
- pass and move
- person ahead principle – encourage pupils to get the ball forward early
- creating space near the basket
- scoring – lay-up shots and set shots
- control of the ball
- rules of the game.

Note: This unit would typically be delivered in autumn term 1.

By the end of this unit, pupils should be able to:

a. Dribble the ball in various directions *with accuracy and control* | **whilst under pressure from opponents**.
b. Pass the ball using various techniques including the bounce pass and chest pass, *with accuracy and control* | **whilst under pressure from opponents**.
c. Understand and be able to discuss the basic rules of the game including travelling, double dribble and *various tactics* | **and use this knowledge to positively influence the game**.
d. Use the correct stance to defend against an opponent.

Key: Step 3 | *Step 4* | **Step 5**

Equipment required:

- 30 size 5 basketballs
- stack of cones
- class set of bibs including six colours with at least five bibs of each colour.

Safety

While delivering all activities, it is important to follow the safety guidelines as set out below to ensure a safe and effective learning environment:

- Ensure the playing area is safe and free of any hazards such as sharp objects before use.
- Ensure pupils are wearing the appropriate attire and that any shoes with laces and sufficiently tightened.
- Check that equipment is not damaged or torn before each lesson.
- Inform and reinforce to pupils the importance of finding space and not bumping into others during warm-ups and other activities.
- Lay the equipment out before the start of the lesson, where possible, to ensure easy access to resources and a smoother transition between activities.
- Inform and remind pupils of the rules and expectations at the beginning of each lesson.
- When delivering line games or activities where small queues exist, ensure pupils stand side by side so that you can always see them and they can see what is going on in front of them.
- Use verbal as well as visual signals to regain pupil focus and attention.

Rules

- No talking while the teacher is explaining something to the group or demonstrating a task.
- No talking whilst others are explaining something to the group or demonstrating a task.
- No touching other people or equipment without the teacher's permission.

The two key rules that teachers will need to know and understand in basketball are:

- **Travelling:** Pupils are not allowed to travel with the ball more than one complete step (not including the landing foot), unless the ball is bouncing in a continuous bouncing motion.
- **Double dribble:** A double dribble is a violation in which a player dribbles the ball, clearly holds it with a combination of either one or two hands (while either moving or stationary), and then proceeds to dribble again without first either attempting a field goal or passing off to a teammate. Double dribbling can also occur if a pupil tries to dribble using both hands at the same time.

Lesson 1 Dribbling the ball

Lesson objective: To improve confidence in dribbling the ball with both hands and in various directions, whilst identifying space and progressing to playing a one vs one invasion game.

Key terms: "jump stop"; "stride stop"; "crossover"; "V shape"

Warm-up: Jump stop traffic lights (10 minutes)
Phase 1: Pupils start by travelling around the playing area by following the teachers instructions which will include, walking, jogging, hopping, bounding, jogging backwards, side-stepping and so on. Pupils should respond to the traffic light cones when they are shown by the teacher: red cone – stop (progress to introducing the 'jump stop'); orange cone – jog on the spot; green cone – go (or increase speed).

Phase 2: All pupils start travelling with a basketball in their hand, while bouncing the ball in a repetitive motion. When the teacher raises the red cone and calls, 'Red', all pupils must stop and stand still. Progress to the pupils performing a 'jump stop'. On 'Green' the pupils then continue travelling around the playing area with the ball. Explore different ways of travelling with the ball:
- dribble with the right hand only
- dribble with the left hand only
- front crossover – *from right hand to left hand or vice versa* (the ball should travel across the front of the body in a V shape)
- low dribble (below the knees).

Tip
A jump stop position is when a player lands on two feet, usually shoulder width apart. This is also known as the triple threat position as players have three options from this position: pass, shoot or dribble – the 'triple'.

Progression
1. Teacher introduces new instructions, such as yellow cone – change direction with the ball; 'switch' – exchange balls with another pupil by leaving their ball and *quickly* finding another; 'increase speed' (for 5 seconds or 3 paces).
2. Introduce the green cone to indicate an increase of speed from each pupil.
3. Introduce *new ball familiarisation skills* as players' skill level improves, e.g.
   - a diagonal crossover (between the legs)
   - push up position on the ball – with arms extended on top of the ball and back straight
   - V dribble – dribble the ball back and forth with the right hand, bouncing the ball on the outside of the right foot. Pupils to 'claw' the ball pushing the ball forwards then backwards.

Key teaching points

- Legs shoulder width apart.
- Knees bent.
- Hold the ball firmly in both hands at the centre of the body.

Main lesson: Pick me up (20 minutes)

Divide the class into ten teams with three pupils in each team. Each team lines up beside a cone or spot. There is a hoop 8 yards ahead of them containing a number of cones.

One at a time, pupils from each team dribble the ball to their hoop and collect a cone, then dribble back to their team with the cone in their other hand, place the cone on the floor, then join the back of their line. Then the next person in the line has a turn. Note that the next person cannot travel until their teammate has placed their cone on the floor.

Competition

The first team to return all of their cones to their area is the winning team. All cones in the middle must be picked up before each round comes to an end.

Differentiation

WT pupils should cuddle the ball in one hand before picking up the cone from the floor.

As WO and WB pupils improve in upper KS2, encourage them to continue bouncing the ball, whilst picking up the cone with their other hand.

Progression

When the pupil is five paces away from their team, they pass the ball to the next in line before placing their cone on the floor.

Key teaching points

- Dribble the ball at a steady speed.
- Keep your eyes looking ahead to avoid bumping into other people.
- Keep good *balance and control*.
- Place the cone on the floor before the next person in the line can go.
- Using *peripheral vision and planning ahead* – pupils to see where the cones are and select early the cone they will collect.

Match play (20 minutes)

Set up: Set out a red end zone on one end of the playing area and a green end zone on the opposite end. The space between end zones should be approximately 10–20 yards. Pupil A starts in the red end zone and passes to pupil B (who starts 5 yards away from pupil A. Pupil B then turns and dribbles the ball towards the end zone. Pupil A attempts to chase pupil B as a 'passive defender' | *Semi passive defender* | **Active defender**.

Key teaching points

- Use your arm to 'shield' the defender away.
- Keep good dribbling technique including keeping the ball on the outside of the foot, with fingers spread and looking ahead.

Cool-down: Crabs (10 minutes)

One pupil is selected as the crab. The crab can only travel in the 'squat' position. All the other pupils are dribblers who attempt to dribble across the beach without the crab touching their ball. If unsuccessful, the dribbler must place the ball in the bag and become a crab. The game ends when there are too many crabs, which renders the area unsafe. For most school halls, this would end with ten crabs and the remaining pupils as dribblers.

Differentiation

Play this game without the basketball until pupils are more confident dribbling the ball under pressure.

Depending on ability of the group, crabs can also travel on their bottoms only (easier for dribblers) or their knees only.

Variation

Classic cool-down: Pupils travel around the playing area pretending they are dribbling a basketball. Practise various dynamic stretches including jumps, twists and turns. Give pupils bonus points for finding and creating their own space within the playing area.

Key teaching points
- Keep on the balls of the feet.
- Keep looking for spaces, staying as far away from others and objects as possible.

Plenary
- What part of the hand do we use to dribble the ball?
- Where should we be looking when we dribble the ball – at the ball or around us? Why is this important?

Cross-curricular links

Mathematics: Encourage pupils to count how many cones their team has collected. For older pupils, the teacher may wish to ask various mental arithmetic questions to keep the pupils thinking, e.g. 'How many cones did you collect? = 9! Good – now hands up if you can tell me 9 threes?'

Lesson 2 Travelling with the ball

Lesson objective: To improve skills of passing the ball and dribbling whilst under pressure and to understand the basic rules of travelling.

Key terms: "jump stop"; "stride stop"

Warm-up: Pass and move (10 minutes)
Phase 1: Introduce a basic warm-up for a few minutes to increase heart rate, such as the Classic warm-up (see p15) and/or dribbling with a ball in an open space, as an extension of lesson 1.

Phase 2: In pairs, pupils practise passing the ball to each other and moving looking for a new space. Ask pupils to use only the 'bounce pass' to transfer the ball to their partner first, then only the 'chest pass'. After completing the pass, pupils must sprint in a new direction and call for the next pass whilst on the move. Pupils must dribble the ball whilst their partner is moving to a new space.

Key teaching points
1. Dribbling – pupils to keep the *ball below the waist*.
2. Bounce pass – by *flicking the wrist* and pointing the thumbs down.
3. Chest pass – by flicking the wrist and pointing the thumbs down.
4. After the pass, pupils should *quickly* look for a new space.
5. Communication with their partner – the pupil without the ball must say and signal where they wish to receive the pass and when (the teacher may wish to inform pupils that this links to the hockey lessons and other invasion games).

Main lesson: Stride stop and freeze tag (20 minutes)
Explain the rules of travelling and double dribble before commencing these activities.

Phase 1 – Stride stop: Pupils run freely around the playing area but stop when instructed to do so by the teacher using either a stride stop or a jump stop, according to the teacher's command:
- **'Stride stop':** The pupil lands on one foot, which then becomes the pivot foot. The trailing foot strides forwards and secures balance on landing. This is a natural running action involving a one-two rhythm with knees bent, weight evenly spread and head up.
- **'Jump stop':** The pupil lands on two feet simultaneously. The knees should be bent on landing with feet shoulder-width apart, slightly ahead of the body. The chin should be up so that the pupil can scan for spaces or teammates. Either foot may then be selected as the pivot foot.

After making a clear stop, the pupils move off again.

Rules: A pupil is allowed one pace when holding the ball in their hands. This means contact with the floor with the landing foot, followed by contact with the floor with the following foot.

Phase 2 – Freeze tag: The teacher nominates 2–4 pupils as taggers. The taggers hold a bean-bag in their hands and attempt to 'tag' other pupils with the beanbag. Once tagged by a tagger, pupils must stand still with their hands out to the side, until a teammate runs under their arms to set them free.

Progress to giving each pupil a basketball. *Pupils dribble the basketball whilst playing the game*. The taggers attempt to 'tag' as many pupils with the basketball as possible within a set number of seconds, e.g. 10 seconds. Once tagged, pupils must stand with their ball above their head and legs apart. Other pupils may set their classmates free by bouncing the ball under their arms (*legs*) and collecting the ball on the other side.

Progression
In phase 1, the teacher calls a number to indicate which type of stop the pupils should use: 'one' for a jump stop, and 'two' for a stride stop. Pupils respond by calling the name of the stop: 'jump stop' or 'stride stop'.

For WB pupils, the teacher may then wish to swap the numbers around to increase the mental challenge.

Variation
If a person is tagged, they must stand on the spot and bounce the ball five times before being allowed to move around with the ball again.

Key teaching points
- Balance – pupils to bend knees once 'frozen' to be ready to move off again once freed (remind pupils of the 'jump stop' position from previous learning).
- Balance and co-ordination – pupils to come to a complete stop without wobbling; once tagged, pupils run into the *stride stop position*.
- **Dribbling the ball under pressure** – pupils to keep away from the taggers.
- Dribbling speed – pupils to think about and identify **when to dribble slow and when to dribble fast**.
- The stride stop – practicing quality footwork.
- Peripheral vision – pupils to keep an eye out for the taggers.

Match play (20 minutes)
One vs one | *two vs two* | **three vs three**

Layer the process: start with one vs one. Once pupils have demonstrated that they can per-form to the desired objectives competently, progress to two vs two, then three vs three, where appropriate.

Set up mini playing areas for each match. Pupils score by dribbling the ball to the end zone safely. **Pupils score only by catching the ball in the end zone**.

Progression
Introduce the five second rule: pupils can only stand in the end zone for a maximum of five seconds.

Key teaching points

Look for common misconceptions and where pupils can improve which may include things like:

- Dribbling into the space.
- Accuracy of passing.
- Communication with teammates (if more than one vs one).

Cool-down: Creep up on the teacher (10 minutes)

Play this at first without **and then with** a basketball. Pupils run towards the teacher who is standing at the opposite end of the playing area facing the other way. When the teacher turns to face the pupils, they must stop straight away by landing in the stride stop position. If a pupil is caught off-balance or still moving, they are sent back to the start line. The winner is the first pupil (or pupils) to reach the end line.

Variation

If basketball hoops are available, practise the lay-up shot instead.

The basic action is to take two steps towards the hoop, jump off one foot and hit the ball off the backboard to score. If right-handed, pupils should jump up towards the basket off the left foot using the right hand.

Develop the technique in stages:

- Pupils perform the shot from a standing position under the basket.
- Pupils take one step towards the basket before jumping off the left leg; ensuring the shooting hand is behind the ball (for right-handed shooters).
- Pupils take two steps in towards the basket to produce a full lay-up shot.

Key teaching points

- Hold the ball firmly in both hands on approach to the basket.
- Jump off one leg upwards.
- Extend the arm towards the basket.
- Push the ball towards the inner square of the backboard (the black box on the rim of the basketball hoop).

Plenary

- Why do we pass and move – why do we not just dribble the ball all the time?
- Can you explain the jump stop?
- Can you explain the stride stop?
- When in a game would we use the jump stop or stride stop?

Lesson 3 Passing the ball

Lesson objective: To develop tactical ideas and skills for *quick passing on the move*, and to develop awareness skills through dribbling and passing games, and further to introduce the 'fast break'. This is when a team gains possession and quickly attacks towards the opposition's basket.

Key terms: "pass selection"; *"disguise the pass"*; *"fast break*"

Warm-up: Swap (10 minutes)
Phase 1: Pupils travel around the playing area, following various teacher instructions, e.g. walk, jog, hop, skip, change direction, jump, down (pupils bend their knees and pretend to touch the floor).

Phase 2: All pupils are dribbling a basketball around the playing area. When the teacher calls, 'Swap', pupils place their ball on the floor and begin to walk around. When the teacher calls, 'Collect', pupils all quickly pick up the nearest ball to them.

Health and safety
Ensure that pupils are told that if someone has their hand on the ball first, not to challenge for the ball, but to react quickly and look for another ball.

Progression
1. Pupils swap balls by leaving their own ball and quickly collecting another whilst it is still bouncing.
2. The teacher gradually takes some of the balls out of the game; this means that the pupils who start without the ball must anticipate early which ball they will collect and dribblers must react very quickly to find a new ball.

Key teaching points
- Dribble the ball confidently with the ball being bounced on the outside and slightly in front of the foot (at 'two o'clock' on a clock face).
- Spread your fingers to increase grip and ball control whilst dribbling.
- Peripheral vision: look around whilst dribbling; avoid looking at the ball.

Main lesson: Pass and move (20 minutes)
Divide the playing area into three lanes. Each lane will have ten pupils. Pupils work in pairs so there will be 5 pairs in each of the three lanes. Large cones should be placed in the centre of each lane and be spaced approximately 5 yards apart.

In pairs, pupils use chest passes to pass a basketball between each other, moving in a forwards direction until they reach the opposite end of the court or playing area. They then sprint back down the sides of their lane as fast as they can back to the start. The next pair of pupils in the lane has their turn.

Progression
WB pupils **sidestep down the channels back to the start delivering overhead passes to each other, over the heads of the oncoming passers of the ball**. This requires accuracy of passing and good footwork.

Key teaching points

- Tactics – pupils to *pass ahead of the receiver and* show their receiving hand as the furthest hand away from the ball.
- Communication – pupils to call for the pass.
- Improve passing technique – start with the ball held with the thumbs behind, fingers alongside, wrist slightly cocked back.
- Pass with *sharp extension of arms,* wrist and fingers, keeping elbows close to the body.
- Developing the chest pass on the move.
- Developing speed up the court.
- Improving basic balance, agility and co-ordination.

Match play (20 minutes)

By this point, pupils should have developed passing and moving skills to enable them to play the games with increasing success and tempo. Choose the number of opponents according to the ability of your pupils: one vs one | *two vs two*| **three vs three**.

In small teams, pupils play a one vs one, two vs two or three vs three basketball game. As opposed to using hoops to score a point, pupils score a point by catching the basketball behind the end line or behind the end line and inside one of two hoops which are laid out at the end of each teams playing area.

During the game, focus on:
- footwork faults – the teacher calls the fault and asks pupils to explain why there was a fault.
- developing the 'fast break' – once possession is won, pupils should be encouraged to pass the ball forward quickly and get up the court.

Differentiation

For more advanced groups, or WB pupils, the teacher may reduce this time to 1–2 seconds; pupils must catch the ball in the hoop only on landing (stride stop or jump stop landing).

Progression

1. Pupils can only score by passing the ball to a teammate who is standing in the hoop.
2. *Pupils are not allowed to stand in the hoops for more than three seconds.*

Key teaching points

Refer to the key teaching points taught throughout the lesson and previous lessons including:
- Passing and moving quickly.
- Passing accurately.
- Communicating about where you would like to receive the ball.
- Moving when you don't have possession of the ball.

Cool-down: Bull in the ring (10 minutes)

Divide the class into groups of ten and ask each group to form a circle. One child in each group is nominated as the 'bull', and their task is to stand in the centre of the circle and attempt to intercept the ball as it is passed between the other members of the group. If the ball is lost outside the circle or intercepted, the pupil responsible for giving away the ball becomes the bull.

Health and safety
No physical contact between players is allowed.

Key teaching points
- Pass the ball quickly – teachers can help increase the speed of passing by insisting that each pupil has a maximum of three seconds to pass the ball.
- *Select whether to use the bounce pass or chest pass* by looking at the position of the bull.
- Pupils to trick the bull by *disguising the pass* using their eyes or a 'fake' pass (pretend to pass to one person, before passing the ball to another person) and passing **with speed and accuracy**.

Plenary
- What should we do when we wish to receive a pass from a teammate?
- How do we hold the ball and send it to our teammate to ensure a quick and accurate pass?

More lesson ideas and activities for basketball

Slalom sprints/slalom dribble
Divide the class into ten teams with three pupils per team. Basketballs or cones are placed diagonally down the court or playing area for each team.

Pupils sprint diagonally down the court (without a ball), pushing off the back leg to go around the balls or cones before returning to their group.

Progress this activity by introducing the basketball. Ensure that the pupils dribble the ball on their 'safe side' – when dribbling to the right, pupils should use the right hand; when dribbling to the left, the left hand should be used.

As the pupil approaches the ball or cone that they need to go round, they should ensure a crisp front crossover from one hand to the other, e.g. if approaching a ball or cone on the left, the pupil will need to change from the left hand to the right hand.

Competition
To add an element of competition, ask pupils to set off as soon as the person before them has reached the first ball. They then **chase the person ahead** of them and attempt a gentle tag on the back. However, pupils should imagine a wall between each ball or cone. Pupils cannot tag others 'through the wall'. They must go fully around the ball or cone, pushing off the back leg to catch up with the player ahead.

Progression
If hoops are available, the teacher may instruct pupils to finish by **completing a lay-up shot** before collecting their ball and restarting the activity.

Health and safety

Advise and remind pupils not to cross their feet over.

Knockouts basketball

All pupils are in the playing area, dribbling the ball and practising various dribbling and ball-handling skills. When the teacher calls, 'Knockouts', or, if you prefer, 'Play', pupils attempt to steal other players' basketballs and knock them safely out of the grid.

Once a pupil's ball is knocked out of the grid, they must collect their ball and dribble to the end of the court or playing area before re-joining the game. If only a small space is available, ask pupils to dribble around the outside of the playing area before re-joining the game.

Each game lasts only 20–30 seconds. After this time, the teacher blows the whistle; all pupils who are in the playing area when the whistle blows are winners.

Tips

It is important that pupils can keep control of their ball without 'travelling' or a 'double dribble' offence. Ensure pupils are able to dribble competently before attempting this game.

Progression

If a pupil's ball is knocked out of the playing area, they have to dribble the ball using only their non-writing hand.

Crossover passing in pairs

Pupils practise passing the basketball up the court in pairs running diagonally across each other in a pass, follow and catch, dribble sequence.

The two pupils start about 5 paces apart. Use cones at the start to mark out this distance. The first pupil passes the ball to the other, then both pupils run forwards diagonally. The pupil with the ball dribbles the ball diagonally behind the other pupil as they cross. Once they are level with the cones, the pupil with the ball passes it to the other pupil and they swap roles. They repeat the process until they reach the end line.

Passing in fours

Divide the class into groups of four. Each pupil stands by a cone set out in the shape of a square. Pupils pass the ball, using a specific pass indicated by the teacher, around the square, with the aim of delivering effective passes and not dropping the ball. Next, introduce dummy passing and 'fake' passing (pretending to pass to one person before passing to another).

Competition

Add a competition element by setting a number of successful passes for the groups to achieve. Once a group has completed the set number of successful passes, they sit down with their hands on their heads. The group that makes the set number of successful passes in the shortest time is the winning team.

Progression

Progress this activity by playing the game on the move with pupils moving around the perimeter of the square. Pupils must be standing by a cone when they receive the pass. This game requires good movement, timing and passing skills.

Drill 101

Drill 101 incorporates speed of catching, passing and moving.

Set the cones out before the lesson, so pupils will know where to stand. A line of 15 blue cones facing a line of 15 red cones opposite, or where space is limited, set out a line of 8 blue cones facing 8 red cones and repeat the same set up twice. Divide the class into pairs. Each pair lines up facing their partner in a circle or rectangle formation, standing approximately 6–8 yards apart.

All pupils on the outer side of the circle/rectangle or on the blue cones start with basketballs in their hand. They pass the ball to their partner and then move one space to their right. The pupils on the inside of the circle/rectangle (standing by a red cone) receive the ball and pass it back to their new partner.

Pupils continue passing the ball until the outside pupils are back in their original positions.

Competition
Time how quickly every pupil can return to their start position.

Ball familiarisation skills
All pupils stand still with a basketball in their hands. Alternatively the teacher can ask pupils to complete the same exercises sitting down or on their knees.
- **Finger-tip ball squeezes:** Pupils tap the ball between their fingertips. Progress to doing this activity quickly.
- **Around the body**: Pupils circle the ball around the waist, transferring the ball from hand to hand. It's important that pupils spread their fingers to maintain grip. Progress to circling around the neck or making a figure of eight in between the legs. Advise pupils to try not to look at the ball, keep their head straight and tap the ball repeatedly between the fingertips.

Seated position ball
From a seated position, pupils tense their stomachs and raise one leg at a time before passing the ball under the raised leg from one hand to the other.

Competition
Add a competition element by seeing who can be the first to 20 successful passes. Alternatively, the teacher can organise two teams: one pupil at a time from each team comes to the middle and the other pupils count the number of passes they achieve in a set number of seconds e.g. 10.

This is a good game for team-building, improving co-ordination and technical skill.

Shooting
Pupils practise the BEEF/BELIEF technique by shooting the ball and attempting to make the ball land on a cone, or inside a hoop ahead of them. Always use as many baskets as possible for shooting practice.

Teach the BEEF or BELIEF netball shooting techniques:

Lower KS2 (Years 3 and 4):
- **B**alance
- **E**ye
- **E**xtend
- **F**ollow through.

Upper KS2 (Years 5 and 6):

- **B**alance (knees shoulder-width apart and slightly bent)
- **E**ye (on the target)
- **L**ine (elbow in line with the knee)
- **I**ndex (finger centre of the ball)
- **E**xtend (the arm upwards)
- **F**ollow through (towards the target).

Arrangements

Divide the class into three teams. Each team lines up, with the front pupil from each team standing at a different station along an arc in front of the net.

The front pupil from each team either shoots simultaneously or one at a time, then joins the back of their line.

Once their team has scored at set number of points, e.g. five baskets (depending on the number of pupils involved), they move to the next station.

The first team to score five baskets at each station wins.

This is a positive way to end a lesson with a light shooting practice.

10 Football

What do I need to know?

Football is the UK's most popular sport, so many pupils will have had prior practice and experience playing football. With this in mind, it is important to reinforce the need for control before speed. As pupils' control develops, pupils should be encouraged to increase the speed of their activities whilst maintaining and continuously improving their control of the ball.

Note: *This unit would typically be delivered in autumn term 2.*

By the end of this unit, pupils should be able to:

a. Dribble the ball, using changes of direction and control whilst under pressure.
b. Send and receive the ball to and from a partner whilst on the move and under pressure.
c. Strike the ball accurately towards a target with control and accuracy whilst under pressure.
d. Understand why exercise is important for health, the benefits of warming up and cooling down and can explain the short-term and long-term effects of exercise.

Key: Step 3 | *Step 4* | **Step 5**

Equipment required:

- 30 size 3 footballs (Years 3 and 4)
- 30 Size 4 footballs (Years 5 and 6)
- class set of cones
- class set of bibs of at least 6 different colours.

Safety

While delivering all activities, it is important to follow the safety guidelines set out below to ensure a safe and effective learning environment.

- Ensure the playing area is always safe and free of any hazards such as sharp objects, before use.
- Ensure pupils are wearing the appropriate attire and that any shoes with laces are sufficiently tightened.
- Check that equipment is not damaged or torn before each lesson.
- Inform and reinforce to pupils the importance of finding space and not bumping into others during warm-ups and other activities.

- Lay the equipment out before the start of the lesson, where possible, to ensure easy access to resources and a smoother transition between activities.
- Inform and remind pupils of the rules and expectations at the beginning of each lesson.
- When delivering line games or activities in which small queues exist, ensure pupils stand side by side so that you can always see them and they can see what is going on in front of them.
- Use verbal as well as visual signals to regain pupil focus and attention.

Rules

- No talking while the teacher is explaining something to the group or demonstrating a task.
- No talking whilst others are explaining something to the group or demonstrating a task.
- No touching other people or equipment without the teacher's permission.

The key rules that teachers will need to know and understand whilst teaching football lessons are as follows:

- If the ball travels outside of the playing area, this results in a 'throw in' for the opposing team. Rules for five-a-side may vary depending on who is hosting the competition as some rules will state that pupils should pass the ball in with their feet, whilst others will stipulate that the ball should be rolled into play underarm.
- The offside rule is generally not applied in school football until pupils reach KS3 (Year 7).

Lesson 1 Dribbling the football

Lesson objective: To introduce dribbling skills, so that pupils develop confidence travelling with the ball at their feet both on their own and with a partner.

Key terms: "close ball control"; "foot-ons"; "peripheral vision"

Warm-up: Traffic lights football (10 minutes)
Phase 1: Pupils begin by travelling around the playing area in various ways (walking, jogging, skipping, hopping, changing direction, high knees, quick feet). Stand in a space where pupils can see you. Introduce the traffic light signals one at a time:
- red cone – stop (pupils stand still and say, 'Control')
- yellow cone – get ready (pupils jog on the spot)
- green cone – increase speed for three seconds.

Begin by calling the colour as well as raising the cone, then you can progress to just raising the cone to improve awareness.

Practise each colour cone for a few turns before introducing the next one. Demonstrate each skill and remind pupils to look around them and avoid bumping into others.

Phase 2 – Traffic lights football: All pupils start with a football at their feet. They dribble the ball around the playing area, responding to the teacher's traffic lights signal. Introduce each colour cone one by one, allowing pupils time to become skilled at one activity, before progressing onto further skills through showing other cones:
- red cone – all pupils must stop and put their foot on top of the ball, demonstrating *good ball control*
- yellow cone – pupils respond by placing alternate feet on top of the ball one after the other three times, *five times* | **eight times** (foot-ons)
- green cone – pupils respond by taking three quicker touches with the football and increasing their speed *with precise control* before stopping the ball and slowing down again.

Differentiation
Change the yellow cone signal to mean a change of direction as opposed to foot-ons.
Teachers can also be creative and use various ball familiarisation techniques, such as stop turn, *drag turn,* or **Cruyff turn**. Teachers can also introduce new cones for pupils of various skill levels: toe taps (tapping the ball between the toes), knee touches (touching the ball with alternative knees *quickly*).

Progression
Increase the number of foot-ons and the number of touches for dribbling at speed, e.g. *five* or **eight–ten** foot-ons, and *five* or **eight ** touches dribbling at speed.

Key teaching points
- Awareness of space – pupils to look round them so they don't bump into anybody or anything.

- Close ball control – pupils to keep the ball *close to their body* (ask pupils to stretch their arms out and draw a circle around themselves; they must try to keep the ball within that distance of their bodies, within their 'magic circle').
- Peripheral vision – the teacher must encourage pupils to keep their eyes ahead and looking around for the new cone as well as for spaces to travel into.

Main lesson: Take a stand (40 minutes)

Demonstrate the next activity with two pupils, before requesting that the other pairs stand by their cones. It's a good idea to have a line of blue cones and a line of red cones on opposite ends of the playing area, so that you can signal where pupils should go.

Children are placed in pairs, facing their partner at opposite sides of the playing area. Each pair has one ball.

The first pupil in each pair dribbles the ball towards their partner, stopping the ball approximately 8–12 yards away. Their partner comes forward and takes controls of the ball and completes foot-ons whilst the first pupil runs behind their back and returns to their start position. The partner repeats the activity.

Competition

Once each pair has completed 4, 8 or 12 complete runs, they sit down with their hands on their heads.

Differentiation

Extend the distance, where possible, for WB pupils, and reduce it for WT pupils.

Key teaching points

- Improving close ball control within pairs.
- Co-ordination between two pupils – *if pupils trap the ball using the right foot, they should move left to avoid a collision with the oncoming player*.
- Communication – pupils call 'Stand' when they place their foot on the ball.
- Timing – pupils to move towards the ball as their partner is travelling towards them.

Cool-down: Ball familiarisation (10 minutes)

Each pupil should have a ball each or a ball between two.

Phase 1: Pupils walk with or dribble the ball practising various skills and movements with the ball, as designated by the teacher.

Phase 2: After every three touches of the ball, pupils must perform a skill designated by the teacher, e.g.
- stop the ball and change direction
- put your right foot over the top of the ball then trap it with the sole of the foot
- pupils to perform three foot-ons (alternately placing the feet on top of the ball) or three toe taps (tapping the ball in between the toes).

Key teaching points
- Keep the ball close to your feet.
- Dribble the ball with knees slightly bent for control.
- Use various parts of the foot to dribble and control the ball.
- Peripheral vision – always be looking around for spaces.

Plenary
- Why is it important to keep the ball close to our feet?
- Do we look at the floor or ahead when we are dribbling? Why is this important?

Cross-curricular links

Languages: Call the numbers in a language your pupils are studying, e.g. in French.
Mathematics: During demonstrations or short breaks in activity, ask pupils mathematical questions that relate to the activity, e.g. 'Can you show me three foot-ons? Now can you tell me three times three.' 'Can you perform three foot-ons whilst counting up in threes?'

Lesson 2 Passing the football

Lesson objective: To build upon ball familiarisation skills from the previous lesson, and to improve passing skills in pairs.

Key terms: "sole of the foot"; "inside of the foot"; "weight of the pass"

Warm-up: Classic warm-up and Switch (10 minutes)
Lay 30 footballs spaced out around the playing area or on either ends of the playing area. Refrain from keeping the balls in a bag as this will negatively affect the pace of your lesson.

Phase 1 – Classic warm-up: Pupils travel around the given space in various ways as expressed by the teacher, e.g. walking, jogging, hopping, bounding (jumping off two feet), sidesteps, jogging backwards, sprinting, etc. When the teacher calls various instructions, pupils respond by repeating the instruction or extending upon it, e.g.
- Teacher: 'Change' – pupils respond: 'Change' or 'Direction'
- Teacher: 'Up' – pupils respond: 'Up'.
- Teacher: 'Down' – pupils respond: 'Down' and almost touch the floor.
- Teacher: 'Groups of two' – pupils respond: 'Two', and quickly find a partner.

Phase 2 – Switch: Pupils dribble the ball within the coned area. To dribble, they should use only the insides of the toes, and take three short, quick touches with the right foot, before stopping the ball and then repeating with the left foot.

When the teacher calls, 'Switch', the pupils must stop their football immediately and find another football that has been left by another person.

Tips
If doing phase 1 outdoors, advise children to 'almost' touch the ground but do not actually touch it so as to avoid grazes.

In phase 2, it is important that the teacher explains that pupils are not to tackle – once some-one else has their foot on the ball, pupils must quickly scan the area for a different ball which is spare.

Differentiation
Pupils should have learnt the skills of 'switch' in previous lessons. However, for younger or WT pupils for whom further help is needed, the teacher should introduce the 'stop' and 'change' skills as two separate instructions. When the teacher calls, 'Stop the ball', pupils follow the command before walking around the playing area. The teacher then calls, 'Change' or 'Collect a ball' and pupils then place their foot on top of a nearby ball. Once the teacher is satisfied that all pupils have a football, the pupils can be instructed to continue dribbling.

Key teaching points
- Find lots of space whilst dribbling the ball – develops an awareness of space.
- Dribble the ball *using the tops and insides of the feet*.
- Think quickly – pupils to try to find a different ball as soon as possible.
- Awareness of space – pupils to find the nearest ball.
- Dribbling *with eyes ahead and chin up* and close ball control (as lesson 1) **with speed and control**.

Main lesson: Gold star passing (20 minutes)
Phase 1: In pairs, pupils stand facing each other in between two cones with one ball per pair. Pupils then each take three steps back.

Pupils begin by passing the ball to their partner. The receiving pupil controls the ball before passing it back using the inside of the foot.

Phase 2: Pupils continue passing the ball in their pairs, but now pupils must control the ball with their left foot, before passing with their right foot. After a short practice, ask pupils to change to controlling with the right foot, then passing with the left.

Competition
Once pupils have become familiar with the basic skill of trapping and passing, introduce a competition element, e.g. when each pair has completed ten successful passes, they sit down with their hands on their heads to signify that they have completed the task. The first pair to have sat down sensibly are the winners. Progress this to pupils completing *15* or **20–30** successful passes.

Differentiation

Decrease or increase the number of passes required for WT and WB pupils, or increase or decrease the distance between the pupils.

For WB pupils (Years 5 and 6), when the ball travels between the cones, the receiver must push the ball at a 45 degree angle away from the cone before passing to their partner – using alternate feet.

Key teaching points

- Always be on your toes (balls of the feet) ready to receive the ball.
- Trap the ball using the sole of the foot – heel down, toe up – so that the ball does not slide under the foot.
- Communicate in pairs – pupils to call for the pass.
- Pass with the inside of the foot.
- *Weight of the pass* – not too fast, nor too slow.
- Footwork speed – pupils to adjust their foot position quickly to get the *body behind the ball*.
- First touch – pupils to demonstrate good ball control on the floor, *pushing the ball gently into the direction they intend to travel* and **with control and precision**.

Match play (20 minutes)

One vs one, *two vs two* or **three vs three**

Create several small teams (ideally six or eight teams using three or four playing areas) with each team facing towards the pitch, so they can observe their peers. One at a time, individual pupils from two different teams play one vs one; one pupil attempts to dribble the ball past the other pupil to reach the end zone or score in the goal.

Other pupils watch and observe their teammates and give them support when necessary. Each game ends either when the ball goes out of play, or the teacher signals that time is up. Games will typically last for 10–30 seconds, dependent on the ability level of the pupils.

Where the game is two vs two or more. . .
1. Pupils should be encouraged to make quality forward passes within their team.
2. Pupils should be encouraged to make space and not to crowd the ball.

Differentiation

The teacher may find it helpful to group pupils according to their ability so that all pupils can make progress at their own pace.

Progression

If pupils have demonstrated the required skills for the tasks above, progress to *two vs two* or **or three vs three**.

Key teaching points

- Always be looking for spaces in the playing area when you are/your team is in possession.
- Dribble with confidence and attack the spaces *using skills learnt in the lesson and/or changes of pace*.

- Look for quick passes and pass forward where possible.
- Move to a new space once you have completed the pass.

Cool-down: Quick feet (10 minutes)
Divide the class in half: pupils in each half stand side by side facing the opposite half. Place a ladder (or cones spaced one foot apart) between the two halves.

Pupils complete fast feet drills on the ladders before tagging the next player:
- one foot in between each space on the ladder.
- two feet in between each space on the ladder – right foot leading then left foot leading.
- bunny hops between each space – keeping bent knees with feet and ankles together.
- Repeat bunny hops as above but this time facing left – jumping with two feet in each space followed by facing right – two feet in each space.

Differentiation
For WB pupils, **introduce a ball between these drills**. Pupils go through the ladder with the ball in the hands before throwing the ball to the next pupil, or gently passing the ball down the side of the ladder and collecting it on the other side.

Key teaching points
- Maintain good balance and control throughout with slightly bent knees.
- Use your arms to help you travel as quickly as you can.

Plenary
- What part of the foot did we use to trap the ball?
- What part of the foot did we use to pass the ball?
- Why do you think this is the most common part of the foot used to make a short pass?

Lesson 3 Passing the football on the move

Lesson objective: To improve skills passing in pairs on the move, whilst also improving dribbling skills and running with the ball.

Key terms: "foot-ons"; "toe taps"; "stop turn"; "drag turn"

Warm-up: Classic warm-up and ball skills (10 minutes)
Phase 1 – Classic warm-up: Begin with a classic warm-up (see lesson 2) and gentle pulse-raising activity without equipment before progressing to the ball skills warm-up below.

Phase 2 – Ball skills: Pupils practise dribbling the ball and completing various footwork exercises, e.g.
- when the teacher says, 'Change', pupils change direction with the ball

- foot-ons – pupils place alternate feet on top of the ball 6–10 times (depending on the ability of the class)
- toe taps – pupils tap the ball between the toes 6–10 or *15* times (depending on the ability of the class)
- dribble with the left foot only
- dribble with the right foot only
- roll the ball with the sole of the foot
- dribble the ball with the outside of the foot.

Tips
Introduce the 'drag turn' or various other ways of changing direction with the football. This is where a pupil places their foot on top of the ball before dragging it, using the sole of their foot, across their body in order to change direction (usually 180 degrees).

Variation
Introduce any basic dribbling skill that can be used to go past an opponent by breaking it down into two or three simple steps. Depending on the ability of your class and environment, pupils can practice on the spot, before progressing to completing the skills on the move, e.g. step over – Phase 1 – step over the ball (demonstrate and allow pupils to rehears on the teachers' command. Phase 2 – push the ball in a new direction (demonstrate and allow pupils to rehearse). Phase 3 – Accelerate into the space.

Key teaching points
- Start by completing the skill slowly and then steadily increase your pace as pupils develop in confidence.
- Exaggerate the step over, feint or dummy in an attempt to move the imaginary defender off balance.
- Accelerate into space once the space has been created.

Main lesson: Through the gates (20 minutes)
Paired colour cones are laid out all over the playing area 2 yards apart; these are known as 'gates'. Ask pupils to quickly get into pairs before demonstrating the activity below.

In pairs and whilst jogging on the spot, pupils pass the ball back and forth to their partner through a gate.

Progression
Once pupils are confident passing the ball to each other through one gate, after each successful pass, pupils dribble the ball to a new space, listen and look for their partner's signal that they are ready to receive the ball, and pass through a new gate. Pupils must only pass the ball through the coloured gates which are laid out on the floor.

Competition
Pupils complete a set number of successful passes through a series of gates *with control and accuracy*, **and speed**, before picking the ball up and sitting down in their pairs. The first pair to complete the set number of successful passes through the gates and sit down, is the winning team.

Differentiation

Make the gates larger (easier) or *smaller* (harder) in accordance with the ability levels of the pupils. WT pupils can walk with the ball at their feet, whilst WB pupils should be encouraged to dribble at a much quicker pace. WB pupils can also be challenged further by asking them to perform various skills, e.g. turns or changes of direction after travelling through each gate.

Key teaching points

- Passing in pairs – focus on *the quality of pass* i.e. the weight of the pass (not too hard or too soft) and *accuracy of the pass* (is the ball travelling to where my partner wants to receive it?).
- Awareness of space – pupils to find a gate which is free *quickly*.
- Communication in pairs – pupils to communicate where to pass (between which colour cones) and **when to pass, e.g. as the player is arriving on the other side of the cones; not when another person is in the way**.

Match play (20 minutes)

Create several small teams (ideally six or eight teams using three or four playing areas) with each team facing towards the pitch, so they can observe their peers. One at a time, individual pupils from two different teams play one vs one; one pupil attempts to dribble the ball past the other pupil to reach the end zone or score in the goal.

Other pupils watch and observe their teammate and give them support when necessary. Each game ends either when the ball goes out of play, or the teacher signals that time is up. Games will typically last for 10–30 seconds, depending on the ability level of the pupils.

Progress from one vs one to two vs two then three vs three.

Progression

Progress to four vs four.

Key teaching points

- Exaggerate the teaching points of the main lesson activity.
- Encourage accurate passes and immediate movement after the pass.
- Encourage good communication skills.
- Pupils should develop a basic understanding of where to dribble the ball and understand the key purpose for the dribble.
- Pupils to observe each other and analyse the performances for self-improvement and improvement of others, e.g. they have whiteboards out to write down:
  ○ what went well and what could be improved (team analysis)
  ○ what went well and what could be improved (Individual pupil/player analysis).

Cool-down: Dribble and strike (10 minutes)

This game is about achieving success through scoring goals in a simple manner. The pupils simply dribble, shoot, pick up their ball and return to the end of their line. The teacher should use positive encouragement words such as: 'success', 'excellent goal', 'good control', 'outstanding effort', etc. This will send the pupils back to class with a smile on their faces, knowing that they have achieved something positive.

Divide the class into several small groups or a maximum of three groups of ten.

Each pupil in a group has six seconds to dribble the ball to the opposite end of the playing space and pass the ball or *strike* the ball into an empty goal. The next person in the group can only begin their dribble once their teammate ahead has released their shot *with control and accuracy*. Pupils can count down from 'six' to encourage the dribbling player in their team to score. The team that scores the most goals within 60 seconds wins.

Alternatively, the teacher may wish to complete this game as a whole class activity with each pupil having one shot on goal before then putting their ball away ready to reflect on the lesson.

Key teaching points
- Running with the ball.
- Shooting on the move.
- Improving confidence of dribbling and striking the ball.

Plenary
- What part of the foot did we use to pass the ball?
- What do we look for after we've passed the ball?
- What is the difference between dribbling the ball and running with the ball?

Cross-curricular links

Science (forces): The more force placed behind the ball, the quicker it will travel. Teach pupils that the amount of friction on the floor will also be a determining factor as to how fast or slow the ball travels.

More lesson ideas and activities for football

Head for goal (Match play conditioned games)
In groups of two or three, pupils pass the ball by throwing and move with their partner towards the goal. When they are close enough, one player calls 'Header' and the other attempts to head the ball into the empty net.

Progression
Progress to a *two vs two* or **three vs three** game whereby the above rules apply.

Alamo
Set up several small pitches and allocate each pitch two teams. The red team starts in one corner and the blue team in the opposite corner. Each team has a 'receiver' – someone who stands in the middle and receives the pass.

The first person in each team passes the ball to the receiver and then runs in a curved line (marked out by cones) towards the goal where they receive a pass from the receiver and passes the ball or *strikes the ball*, aiming for the 'far corner' for the goal. Once a pupil shoots for goal, they collect their ball and run behind the goal before transferring to the opposite queue.

Competition

Cones may be placed by the 'far corner', and pupils gain one point for hitting the target and three points if they hit the corner.

Progression

Introduce a goalkeeper. Pupils gain three points per goal scored and one point if the shot is saved but on target.

12 gates

Pupils have 12 gates to dribble through. All pupils dribble at the same time. They have 30 seconds to dribble through as many gates (pairs of cones) as possible. Pupils count the number of gates they successfully travel through as they go along.

Encourage pupils to plan ahead and think about which gates they are going to travel through whilst also avoiding collisions.

Body parts

Pupils dribble the ball around the playing area. When the teacher calls a body part, pupils respond by placing that part of the body onto the ball, e.g. 'hand', 'foot', 'chest' 'knee' 'elbow' 'back' etc.

Progression

The teacher may be more specific with relation to the body parts that they call out, e.g. 'quadriceps', 'hamstrings', 'gluteus maximus' and 'hip flexors' to help develop pupils' understanding of their body parts (link with Science).

Dutch vision (Futsal)

Dutch vision is a Dutch method of playing football which encourages pupils to complete lots of passes on the floor. Teachers should also encourage pupils to practise this game at lunchtimes, during after-school clubs and outside of school.

This is a small-sided game: two vs two, three vs three or four vs four. The basic rules are:
- The ball is not allowed in the air/above waist high.
- Throw-ins are replaced by 'pass-ins' and there are no corners.
- Goals are only one yard apart to increase pupil accuracy and encourage positive passing.

Progression

Two successive passes must be made before a goal can be scored.

11 Hockey

What do I need to know?

There are quite a few core skills for pupils to learn for playing hockey.

Stick handling

Pupils in Year 3 and above should learn and understand the different parts of the stick and what they are used for.

- The long part of the stick, known as the 'shaft' is used for trapping the ball, scooping the ball, interceptions and blocking.
- The bottom of the stick, known as the 'toe end' of the stick is commonly used for push passing, dribbling and shooting.

Start by teaching the pupils stick rotation using their non-writing hand. Pupils place their non-writing hand near the top of the stick and flick their wrist to the opposite side as if they are opening a bottle of water. Pupils should practise moving the stick from the 'open side' (outside of the 'writing hands' foot) to the 'reverse side' (outside of the non-writing hands leg). Good teaching technique is to get the pupils rotating the stick from a stationary position using the 'group calling' technique: the teacher calls instructions and the pupils respond with the stick movement, e.g. 'Open side', 'Reverse side', 'Open side', 'Reverse side,' and so on. Teachers can also use a visual aid, e.g. showing one finger for open side; two fingers for reverse side. Remember this is using the left hand only for rotating the stick in accordance with best practice. Once the pupils understand the stick, gain good wrist action and keep their eyes up, the teacher can then introduce the ball. Obvious progressions involve using a ball and then doing the skill in a *stationary position, and then *while walking*, and then **while running**.

Hockey stance

Once you have taught pupils that the non-writing hand is the operational hand for stick rotation, it is then important to teach them where to place the writing hand and why.

The writing hand should be about halfway down the stick; knees should be bent and level with the hips, or no lower than a right angle with the floor. Ensure pupils keep their backs straight, heels firm into the ground and stick outside the writing hands' foot – at about two o'clock.

Pupils should be encouraged to keep the ball ahead of the writing hands' foot (at two o'clock) whilst dribbling.

The push pass

The push pass is a fundamental skill. The ball should start at about two o'clock. The pupil should use the non-writing hand to then push the ball towards their teammate, using the writing hand as support only. The ball should stay in contact with the stick for as long as possible, keeping the non-writing elbow high on release of the ball. There is no draw back on this type of pass. It is the quickest type of pass, used often for short, quick passes.

The reverse stick

This is an advanced skill for WB pupils. It is most commonly used when dribbling on the left flank or cutting in from the right; disguised passing and shots from the left side.

The ball should be positioned at ten o'clock with the non-writing elbow up in the opposite direction you wish to travel.

Note: This unit is typically delivered in spring term 1.

By the end of this unit, pupils should be able to:

a. Dribble the ball, using various techniques, *with control and accuracy* | **whilst under pressure from opponents**.
b. Send and receive the ball *with control and accuracy* | **whilst under pressure from opponents**.
c. Strike the ball accurately into a target area *with control and accuracy* | **whilst under pressure from opponents**.
d. Understand the basic rules *and tactics of the game* and **use this knowledge to influence team games**.

Key: Step 3 | *Step 4* | **Step 5**

Equipment required:

* 30 plastic hockey sticks
* 30 sturdy hockey sticks
* class set of cones and or spots
* class set of bibs of at least six different colours.

Safety

While delivering all activities, it is important to follow the safety guidelines set out below to ensure a safe and effective learning environment.

* Ensure the playing area is always safe and free of any hazards such as sharp objects, before use.
* Ensure pupils are wearing the appropriate attire and that any shoes with laces are sufficiently tightened.

- Check that equipment is not damaged or torn before each lesson.
- Inform and reinforce to pupils the importance of finding space and not bumping into others during warm-ups and other activities.
- Lay the equipment out before the start of the lesson, where possible, to ensure easy access to resources and a smoother transition between activities.
- Inform and remind pupils of the rules and expectations at the beginning of each lesson.
- When delivering line games or activities in which small queues exist, ensure pupils stand side by side so that you can always see them and they can see what is going on in front of them.
- Use verbal as well as visual signals to regain pupil focus and attention.

In KS2 hockey lessons, some teachers use plastic sticks, whilst others opt to use stronger sticks. Plastic sticks are a safer option, whilst stronger sticks give pupils a more realistic experience in preparation for KS3 and enable pupils to develop more tactile ball control.

With this in mind, I recommend that teachers use plastic sticks for game-based activities and stronger sticks for individual technical activities where the activity does not require or encourage pupils to make contact with others.

Rules

- No talking while the teacher is explaining something to the group or demonstrating a task.
- No talking whilst others are explaining something to the group or demonstrating a task.
- No touching other people or equipment without the teacher's permission.

The key rules that teachers will need to know and understand whilst teaching hockey lessons are as follows:

- The stick should never come up above the knee (also known as the 'safety line').
- Sticks are not allowed to collide – on defence or attack – this is a foul against the defending opponent.
- Only the flat side of the stick should be used; use of the outer stick will result in a free pass being awarded to the other team.
- Pupils should keep their eyes ahead at all times and scan the space for others on their team and opponents.
- Pupils are not allowed to tackle from behind; this will result in an automatic foul and possession will be awarded to the opposing team, even if the ball is won successfully.
- Any aggressive play shall result in a time out.
- When the teacher signals to stop play or says, 'Freeze', pupils should gently bend their knees and place their hockey stick on the floor. When using sticks for the first time or at the start of a new unit, it is good practice for teachers to test pupils' response time to help ensure that pupils will respond appropriately when the teacher needs to refocus pupils' attention.

Lesson 1 Dribbling the ball

Lesson objective: To improve control whilst dribbling the ball, including looking ahead and holding the stick correctly, and to improve balance and control, whilst travelling.

Key terms: "two o'clock"; "shaft"; "push pass"; "speed"

Warm-up: Traffic lights hockey (10 minutes)
Ask pupils to find a space within the playing area. Explain that they can only begin to travel when they see the green cone displayed.

Ask what the red cone might mean. Give the answer: pupils are to stop, look at the teacher and point to their ears and say, 'Listen'.

Introduce varied movement styles using the red and green cones to indicate when to stop and go including some or all of the following examples: walking, jogging, bounding, hopping, skipping, skipping and rotating the arms, sidestepping, jogging backwards.

Introduce the yellow cone, and explain that this will signify a change of direction.

Tip
At the beginning of this activity, when you display the cone say the name of the colour as well so that pupils receive a visual and verbal cue. As pupils reaction skills improve, tell the pupils that cone will be shown but verbal cues will not be given.

Progression
1. Give each pupil a stick and repeat the traffic lights game above. Teach the correct position for holding the hockey stick (non-writing hand near the top and writing hand lower down).
2. Give each pupil a ball and repeat the traffic lights game.

Key teaching points
- Responding to teacher instructions.
- Teach pupils the correct way to hold the stick (non-writing hand on top, with writing hand lower down and bent knees).
- Awareness of space – praise pupils moving in the most space.
- Close ball control – pupils to keep the ball close to their body and at an angle (two o'clock on a clock face).
- Changing direction (with the ball).
- Developing *speed* (with the ball).
- Peripheral vision – pupils to keep their eyes ahead and look around (scan) for space as well as to look for the colour of the next cone being raised by the teacher.

Main lesson: Gold star passing and duos (20 minutes)
Pupils stand in pairs 5 yards apart, at opposite ends of the playing area, one pupil behind a red cone and one behind a blue cone.

Pupils pass the ball using a push pass to their partner who will trap the ball before passing it back. Repeat this process.

Tips
Look out for pupils with a good passing technique.

Competition
The first pair to complete ten successful passes calls 'Gold star' and sits down with their hands on their heads. As pupils improve their performance, *increase to 20 passes*.

Differentiation
Decrease the distance between the pupils for WT pupils and increase the distance for WB pupils. *Introduce ball skills* between passes for WB pupils. WB pupils should push the ball slightly away from the body into the two o'clock position, ready for the pass.

Progression
Duos: after trapping a pass, the pupil completes 2, *4* or **6** (depending on the pupil's ability) stick shifts, shifting the ball from right to left using the 'open' and 'reverse' stick. While they do this, their partner runs around their back and returns to their starting position before calling for the pass.

Key teaching points
- Lay the long part of the stick along the floor, keeping two hands on the stick, and call 'Shaft' when trapping the ball.
- Push passing – keep the ball in contact with the stick for as long as possible by pushing the toe end (bottom) of the stick through the ball.
- Ensure that the *weight is transferred from the back foot to the front foot* on release of the ball, keeping the non-writing hand elbow high.
- Co-ordination – pupils to try to pass the ball at the *same speed* to each other.
- Communication between partners – pupils to call for the pass, by calling 'Pass'.

Match play (20 minutes)
If time and space allows for match play, create several small teams (ideally six or eight teams with three or four playing areas) to play one vs one.

Place two balls on a spot or cone in the centre of each playing area (one for each team). One at a time, pupils sprint to their own ball and dribble it to the end line before picking it up and placing it back on the spot or cone. Repeat the task with the next pupil in each team. Each pupil who completes the task gains a point for their team.

Key teaching points
- Travel as quickly as you can towards the ball.
- Keep the ball close to the stick while dribbling, remembering the key techniques learnt in the lesson and in previous lessons.

Cool-down: Creep up on the teacher (10 minutes)
Pupils start at one end of the playing area and attempt to jog towards the end line where the teacher is standing with their back to their them.

When the teacher turns and looks at the pupils, they must freeze, demonstrating *good balance and control*. If a child is moving when the teacher turns, they are asked to go back to the beginning or to take three large paces backwards. The first pupil to reach the end line is the winner.

Progress to playing the game with the *stick and ball*, further **emphasising balance and control with the stick and ball**.

Key teaching points
- Focus on good balance and control.
- Use short quick steps as opposed to large steps.

Plenary
- What part of the stick do we use to trap the ball?
- Why would we use that part as opposed to the toe end of the stick?
- When might we use the toe end of the stick?
- How long do we keep the stick in contact with the ball when delivering a push pass?

Cross-curricular links

Science: Transfer of weight (forces) and friction between the ball and the stick.
Foreign languages: Call the numbers in French or Spanish (depending on which language they are learning in school).

Lesson 2 Dribbling the ball in tight spaces

Lesson objective: To improve dribbling skills, co-ordination and peripheral vision, which will be required for future learning.

Key terms: "peripheral vision"; "control"; "accuracy"; "speed"

Warm-up: Gateway dribble (10 minutes)
Phase 1: Pupils travel through the gates that have been laid out around the playing area following various instructions from the teacher, including: walking, jogging, skipping, bouncing, jogging with high knees, rotating the arms and giving high fives and low fives to other pupils.

Phase 2 – Gateway dribble: Set out the playing area with a number of gates (marked by two cones of the same colour). Pupils dribble the ball freely around the playing space, keeping their non writing hand elbow high and their writing hand near the centre of the stick. They attempt to dribble through as many gates as possible, avoiding other players within the playing area.

Differentiation

Pupils travel at their own speed – the speed at which they can comfortably dribble the ball, e.g. walking, jogging or running (according to ability).

Layered differentiation: Pupils walk through the first three gates with the stick and ball. Once they have completed that skill successfully without losing control or bumping into anybody, they progress to jogging through the next three gates. If they feel really confident and have not lost control of the ball or bumped into anybody, they try running with the ball through the next three gates.

Progression

Encourage pupils to plan ahead; *to think one gate ahead and plan which gate they will go through next before making their move* and to carry the task out **with speed, accuracy and control**.

Request pupils have their hockey stick and ball touching each other to emphasise good ball control.

Key teaching points
- Pupils to find space.
- Pupils to improve their confidence dribbling *at speed*.
- Pupils to improve their confidence of changing direction with the ball.
- Peripheral vision – pupils are encouraged to keep their eyes ahead scanning for new gates to travel through. Remind pupils of skills learnt in the Traffic lights game in the previous lesson and not to bump into others.

Main lesson: Slalom dribble (20 minutes)
Ask pupils to set out the playing area by demonstrating how each pupil should place three cones of the same colour down in a space, leaving one complete foot space in between each cone. Advise pupils not to place their three cones too close to another persons' cones.

Phase 1: Pupils dribble a ball through their set of cones to the opposite end; they pick the ball up in their hands and jog back to their start point before repeating the activity.

Phase 2: Ask pupils to get into pairs then quickly sit down behind an end cone. Pupils complete the activity one at a time using only one ball. When they have dribbled through the slalom, pupils turn and pass the ball gently to their partner. The pupil then runs back to the starting point as their partner repeats the process.

Key teaching points:
Advise and remind pupils to:
- Dribble around the cones using the toe end of the stick then pass the ball to their teammate at the other end.
- Not use the curved end of the stick.
- Trap the ball using the shaft when receiving the ball and then set off to repeat the process.

Competition
The first team to have all of their team complete the dribble and return back to their original position, sitting down with their hands on their heads is the winning team.

Differentiation
Complete the task with more or less cones, according to the ability levels of the pupils.

Progression
After the pass, WB pupils sprint around a cone 20 yards away before sprinting to the end of the playing area to await their next turn.

Key teaching points
- Pupils should be on the balls of their feet, ready to receive the pass.
- Keep your eye on the ball as it travels.
- Trap the ball using the shaft.
- Dribbling using the toe end, open and reverse stick (emphasise slow control).
- Pupils to sprint to the end of the playing area after the pass is released.
- WB pupils should try to pass the ball at the *same speed as their teammates* (focusing on the co-ordination between the three players in their team) and **pass with speed, control and accuracy**.
- Communication – pupils communicate with their teammates using the words 'pass' and 'trap'.

Match play (20 minutes)
Create six or eight small teams of approximately three–four pupils per team (and in three or four playing areas). Place two balls on a spot or cone in the centre of each playing area (one for each team). The first pupils from each team sprints to their own ball and attempts

to score in their goal. They then collect the ball and race to return it to their cone. Repeat the task with the next pupil in each team. Each pupil who scores a goal gains a point for their team. A bonus point is awarded to the pupil who is the first to return their ball onto the cone.

Progression
Progress from one vs one (with other members of the team observing and analysing the performance and reflecting on how they could enhance their own performance), to **two vs two**. Build upon dribbling skills from the previous lesson.

Key teaching points
- Travel as quickly as you can.
- Strike the ball as early as you feel comfortable when attempting to score.
- Push pass technique – keep the ball in contact with the stick as much as possible and follow through with the hockey stick towards the goal. **If more advanced pupils use the 'clip hit' technique which involves a short backlift of the stick and striking the ball towards goal, this should not be discouraged.**
- Return the ball to the middle as quickly as possible.

Cool-down: Ladders SAQs (10 minutes)
Use the same layout as the main lesson with the cones approximately one foot space (one foot) apart. Travelling without the ball, pupils place one foot in-between each cone before tagging the next person on the opposite end. After a couple of turns each, introduce a different footwork exercise, e.g.
- two feet placed quickly in between each space.
- two feet placed quickly in between each space (facing left/facing right).
- bunny hops, keeping the knees and ankles together, swinging the arms for leverage.
- keeping the right leg on the side of the ladder or cones, raise the left leg quickly, planting the toe of the foot quickly into each space; then repeat this with the right foot.
- **while travelling backwards**, perform bunny hops through the ladders or cones.
- single leg hops through each space in the ladder.

Progression
Provide leadership opportunities: ask the pupils if they can think of any other ways to travel through the ladders or cones to improve co-ordination, balance and speed.

Key teaching points
- Travel on the balls of the feet (commonly referred to as the 'tippy toes').
- Use the arms in a running motion to coordinate with the legs.
- Keep the stomach muscles tight.

Plenary
- What are the key things we need to focus on when dribbling the ball?
- What are the key things we need to focus on when passing the ball?

Lesson 3 Striking the ball

Lesson objective: To develop basic team-play skills, dribbling and striking skills.

Key terms: "trap"; "45 degree angle"; "peripheral vision"; "reverse stick"

Warm-up: Bandit (10 minutes)
Stage 1: Play the game 'Bandit' with no sticks and using soft balls only.

Create five teams, each with six pupils (for a class of 30 pupils). Each team has a hoop as a home base with two or three soft hockey balls in. On a signal to start, each pupil collects a ball from another team's hoop and brings it back to their home base. The game ends after a set amount of time, e.g. 20 seconds. The team with the most balls in their hoop at the end of the game wins a point.

The rules are:
- pupils are allowed to collect balls from any other teams' hoop
- pupils are not allowed to touch anyone else or block other pupils
- pupils are <u>not allowed</u> to defend their hoops or to tackle others.

Stage 2: Play the game Bandit using hockey sticks.

Create three teams, each comprising ten children, and divide each team into five pairs. Each pair has a hoop as a home base, containing two or three soft hockey type balls or tennis balls, as above. This time pupils dribble the ball back to their own base once they have collected it from another team's base. They must use only their own stick to play the ball and may only attempt to dribble one ball at a time.

Tips
During the game, encourage pupils to make good decisions and dribble the ball safely, thinking about the skills they learnt in the previous lesson.

Remind pupils to focus on *control and speed* and **quality decision-making**.

Differentiation
Use beanbags instead of balls which will get pupils familiar with the concept of how to play the game fairly.

Variation
The game Bandits is fast-paced and is recommended for pupils who are safe and well-mannered and have demonstrated positive behaviour in previous lessons.

As an alternative, teachers can deliver a different game, such as dribbling and looking for spaces whilst encouraging spatial awareness, good decision-making and control.

Key teaching points
- Keep two hands on the stick at all times.
- Dribble at a steady speed, keeping good *control of the ball*.

- Develop the skill of changing direction with the ball.
- How to compete in a fair and friendly manner – ensure pupils follow the rules fairly and that pupils are made aware of consequences for ignoring the rules.
- **Peripheral vision and planning ahead – encourage pupils to scan ahead and at all angles to see where most of the balls have been deposited, in order to gain a numerical advantage**.

Main lesson: Dribble and strike (20 minutes)

Phase 1: Split the class into small teams (of up to three). Set out the playing area with a set of cones for each team to dribble around and a goal at the end (which can be represented by two cones spaced approximately two yards apart).

Pupils take it in turns to dribble the ball towards the cones, dribble in and out of the cones and then striking the ball towards the goal.

Phase 2: Two pupils from each team set off together. Pupil A dribbles the ball towards the cones then passes the ball to Pupil B, who receives the ball on the left. Pupil A performs a footwork drill to travel through the three cones (as designated by the teacher); Pupil B *quickly* traps the ball and rolls the ball gently in front of the cones and towards goal at a 45 degree angle. Pupil A reaches the ball and strikes the ball into the goal. The next pupils in each team then repeat the exercise.

Tips

Pupils must be confident doing the slalom dribble (see lesson 2), before progressing onto this more advanced exercise. Teachers may find that they need to repeat the slalom dribble activity instead. Ensure that at least eighty percent of the class are confident in that activity before progressing to dribble and strike.

Differentiation

Decrease the number of slalom cones for WT pupils and increase the number for WB pupils.

Increase the size of the goal for WT pupils and decrease the size for WB pupils.

Ask advanced pupils to:
- trap the ball **using the reverse stick** and push the ball onto the open stick for the shot.
- trap the ball using the reverse stick before producing a **snap shot using the reverse stick**.

Competition

The first team to score five goals wins the round.

For more advanced pupils, increase the amount of goals needed to complete the game.

Key teaching points
- Keep control of the ball.
- Pass the ball *accurately and at a steady speed* (weight of the pass).
- Demonstrate *quick footwork and good posture* to race through the cones.
- Strike the ball accurately using the push pass technique **or using the clip hit technique for more advanced learners**.

Match play (20 minutes)

Create six or eight small teams consisting of three or four pupils per team and three or four playing areas to play a match as described in lesson 2.

Practise basic one vs one | *two vs two* | **three vs three** games, thus building upon skills learnt in previous lessons.

Key teaching points
• Emphasise the key teaching points from the main lesson as above.

Cool-down: Cross the sea (10 minutes)

Pupils stand behind a designated line. On the teacher's command, 'Sea', pupils must jump ahead of the line, and on the command, 'Shore', they must jump behind the line. Pupils' feet must not touch the line and they must be encouraged to react quickly.

Progression

The teacher walks along the line, *throwing a tennis ball underarm to various pupils*, who catch the ball and return it to the teacher.

If the teacher calls, 'The waves are coming', pupils respond by ducking down with their hands covering their heads.

If the teacher calls, 'The sharks are coming', pupils respond by sprinting to the opposite end of the designated playing area.

Health and safety

If there is a wall, net or fence present, teachers must ensure that they tell pupils not to touch these things as touching the walls, nets or fences can scrape their hands. With this in mind, it's always best to tell them to sprint to a line marking on the floor, as opposed to a wall or any other potentially dangerous area.

Variation

Complete ladder and footwork exercises, as described in lesson 2.

Key teaching points
• Improving balance and steadiness.
• Stretching different parts of the legs and developing an awareness of different muscles working:
  ○ calf muscles (used in the spring upwards)
  ○ abdominal muscles (tighten for increasing balance and steadiness)
  ○ quadriceps (used for power and elevation).

Plenary
• At what angle should we push the ball when we receive it? Why?
• How do we ensure the ball reaches its target when striking the ball to a target?

Cross-curricular links

Science: Ensure pupils develop an awareness and knowledge of names of various parts of the body, including calves, abdominal muscles and quadriceps.

Science: Ask pupils to focus on the weight of the pass and link this concept to 'forces' in science.

Mathematics: Ask the pupils how they will decide where to take the next ball from? Pupils must use good mathematical skills to make intelligent decisions, based on distance of the ball or beanbag and how important it is to win the ball or beanbag from the other team.

More lesson ideas and activities for hockey

Traffic lights V drag
The V drag is a common technical skill used to beat an opponent in a game of hockey. It is very similar to a drag back in football. Imagine a V shape in front of you now. You have an orange cone (centre), a red cone (top left) and a green cone (top right) in the shape of a V. Approach the orange cone slowly, move the ball diagonally towards the red cone. Check back (move the ball back) to the orange cone, then gear off to the green cone, exploding into space. By this time – ideally – the defender should be off balance.

End to End
Pupils stand facing their partner, approximately 20 yards apart (vary pitch length according to the age group and ability levels of the pupils). One pupil dribbles the ball to the end, where the partner is; their partner then takes control of the ball, dribbles back down to the other end and back up. Pupils then swap over again.

Encourage pupils to have their knees bent, with the ball at two o'clock, non-writing hand elbow high and eyes ahead.

Variation
This game has many variations and, as is often the case, it can be used with various sports. Variations include: duos, dribble halfway and leave the ball for your partner who then takes the ball from the halfway point.

As the pupil dribbles, the pupil about to receive the ball should put up a number of fingers. The dribbler must *call out the number of fingers being held up*. Alternatively, the passer asks the receiver the hold the stick either up or down. The *passer must call 'Up' or 'Down'* just before making the pass.

Progression
Once pupils develop their dribbling skills to a competent level, the teacher should facilitate pupil progress by specifying particular skills at various parts of the activity, e.g. only use the push pass; dribble on the reverse side; hit pass (little drawback); V drag then pass, etc.

Player in the middle
One pupil is the defender. Five pupils stand in a circle or pass and move about the given space, whilst trying to keep the ball away from the defender. Pupils roll the ball with their hand or *pass the ball with the stick* to their teammates. The pupil who loses possession of the ball to the defender trades places with the defender.

Shadow me
This game often acts as a good cool-down game and builds positive rapport between pupils and the teacher.

The teacher has a stick and ball, as do all of the pupils who are facing the teacher in a line, standing shoulder by shoulder. Whichever way the teacher travels, the pupils must shadow them, e.g. if the teacher travels forwards, pupils travel backwards the same distance.

Triangles and rectangles

This is a game for WB pupils.

Set up a rectangle approximately 12 yards by 6 yards marked out using four cones: two blue and two red (red cones are diagonally opposite each other and blue cones are diagonally opposite each other). Use a green cone to make a triangle at the top of either end of the rectangle.

One pupil stands at each of the blue and red cones; two pupils stand at the green cone to start. Pupils move clockwise, they dribble along the sides of the rectangle and pass round the triangle. Pupils follow their passes.

The first pupil sets off from the green cone. They pass the ball to the player at the next cone and follow the pass. The next player dribbles the ball to the next player, etc.

• Blue cone to red cone: dribble.
• Red cone to green cone: pass.
• Green cone to red cone: pass.
• Red cone to blue cone: dribble.

12 Netball

What do I need to know?

Netball is an invasion game that can be incorporated into the National Curriculum as an invasion game. Most primary schools adopt high five netball rules to support adaptability to various positions and ensure a high level of inclusion.

Note: Netball is an optional section of the yearly planning and may not always be taught in an academic year cycle as it engages a similar concept to basketball.

By the end of this unit, pupils should be able to:

a. Send and receive the ball to and from a teammate on the move, *with accuracy and control*, **while under pressure from opponents**.
b. Understand the rules *and tactics* in netball and **use this knowledge to influence the game**.
c. Use the right technique for shooting into a hoop *consistently* and **while under pressure from an opponent**.

Key: Step 3 | *Step 4* | **Step 5**

Equipment required:

- 30 netballs
- 30 hoops
- stack of cones and (spots)
- set of bibs (5 × 5 different colours)
- netball hoops (desirable).

Safety

While delivering all activities, it is important to follow the safety guidelines set out below to ensure a safe and effective learning environment.

- Ensure the playing area is always safe and free of any hazards such as sharp objects, before use.
- Ensure pupils are wearing the appropriate attire and that any shoes with laces are sufficiently tightened.
- Check that equipment is not damaged or torn before each lesson.

- Inform and reinforce to pupils the importance of finding space and not bumping into others during warm-ups and other activities.
- Lay the equipment out before the start of the lesson, where possible, to ensure easy access to resources and a smoother transition between activities.
- Inform and remind pupils of the rules and expectations at the beginning of each lesson.
- When delivering line games or activities in which small queues exist, ensure pupils stand side by side so that you can always see them and they can see what is going on in front of them.
- Use verbal as well as visual signals to regain pupil focus and attention.

Rules

- No talking while the teacher is explaining something to the group or demonstrating a task.
- No talking whilst others are explaining something to the group or demonstrating a task.
- No touching other people or equipment without the teacher's permission.

Some of the high five netball rules that teachers should know and understand include:

- Pupils must pass or shoot within four seconds.
- Five pupils per team on court with seven–nine pupils per team in total.
- Pupils must rotate positions each quarter.

Lesson 1 Passing and moving

Lesson objective: To develop passing and moving skills for invasion games (which will be required for two vs one games in future lessons).

Key terms: "shadow"; "change of speed"; "chest pass"; "bounce pass"; "lob pass"; "shoulder pass"

Warm-up: Scarecrow tag (10 minutes)
Phase 1: The teacher will need to introduce a light, pulse-raising activity such as the Classic warm-up (see p15) before progressing onto phase 2 of the warm-up, as shown below.

Phase 2 – Scarecrow tag: The teacher selects a number of pupils to be the taggers; they each have a soft ball in their hand. All the other pupils are spread out around the playing area.

On the teacher's command, the taggers attempt to 'tag' as many players as possible within 30 seconds (or the given time). A 'tag' is a gentle tap on the body with the soft ball. No pushing or pulling is allowed.

Once a pupil is tagged, they must stand with their legs apart and arms spread. Pupils can free their teammates by running under both of their arms and calling the word, 'Free'.

After the set time, the teacher blows the whistle or calls, 'Time', and identifies how many pupils are still frozen.

Differentiation
Tag other pupils without a ball in the hand.

Key teaching points
- Movement and staying free – pupils to change direction frequently *to successfully evade opponents*.
- Speed – pupils to change speed frequently *and with good timing to successfully evade opponents*.
- Teamwork and supporting other players – pupils free their teammates if they have been caught.

Main lesson: Shadow my moves (20 minutes)
Phase 1: In pairs, one pupil is the leader who gives commands and instructions; the other pupil responds to the commands and follows instructions accordingly. The leader gives movement instructions such as: jog to the left, sidestep right, hop on one leg, jump up, jump to the left, etc. Progress to including a ball in the activity.

Phase 2: In pairs or small groups, pupils line up across the court or playing area before proceeding to make several forward passes with the ball back and forth to their partner, travelling gradually towards the end line. They should be taught one passing technique at a time. The first pair or group to reach the end line and place the ball on top of their head to show good control is the winning pair.

Differentiation
The teacher should select the amount of children in each group based on the ability levels of the pupils and the space available.

Key teaching points
- Communication – pupils tell their partner what to do and then copy them.
- Use a range of passing styles – teach each pass, one technique at a time. Once pupils have demonstrated confidence delivering the given passing technique, move on to the next: chest pass, bounce pass, lob pass or shoulder pass.
- Passing and moving, using a variety of techniques.
- Footwork and co-ordination – pupils to move their feet *quickly* to get into a *good 'receiving position'*.
- Developing basic passing skills – pupils to demonstrate effectively the chest pass, shoulder pass and bounce pass.

Match play (20 minutes)
Set up several mini-courts or playing areas (ideally set up between five and ten mini courts, depending on the space available) and create several two vs one games.

The two attacking pupils should be encouraged to pass and move to get from one end of the court to the other. A goal is scored when a pupil receives the ball in the 'scoring zone' or behind the end line. If the defender wins the ball, they give the ball back to the attackers, to give them another opportunity to score.

Tips
A generic approach to footwork should be looked at closely. Encourage pupils to practise good footwork (not running with the ball) and good movement. The higher the ability levels of the pupils, the more closely footwork skill should be analysed.

Differentiation
The teacher may wish for WT pupils to work together and WB pupils to work together to ensure sufficient challenge for each pupil and group. WT pupils may practise four vs one or three vs one. **WB pupils may progress to two vs two.**

Key teaching points
Focus on and reinforce the key teaching points from the main lesson.

Cool-down: Shooting for success (10 minutes)
Divide the class into the number of netball hoops there are available to use. Each pupil has one shot at the hoop, then re-joins the back of their line.

Differentiation
Layered differentiation: Set out three cones for each station. Pupils start by attempting to score by shooting from behind the red cone which is nearest the hoop. If and when a pupil has got the ball in the hoop three consecutive times, they must then start to shoot from the cone second furthest away pick up the hoop and move it one pace further away.

Variation
Ask pupils to stand on a spot or behind a line before placing their hoop a few feet away from the designated starting point. Pupils practise shooting the ball upwards in a netball shooting style into the hoop. Pupils gain one point each time they successfully throw the ball at least three metres above their head and in the hoop. After shooting the ball, they retrieve it and repeat the exercise.

Key teaching points
Teach the BEEF or BELIEF netball shooting techniques.

Lower KS2 (Years 3 and 4):
* **B**alance
* **E**ye
* **E**xtend
* **F**ollow through.

Upper KS2 (Years 5 and 6):
* **B**alance (knees shoulder-width apart and slightly bent)
* **E**ye (on the target)
* **L**ine (elbow in line with the knee)
* **I**ndex (finger centre of the ball)
* **E**xtend (the arm upwards)
* **F**ollow through (towards the target).

Lesson 2 Moving into space

Lesson objective: To refine skills for evading an opponent (dodging and weaving), and receiving the ball in open spaces.

Key terms: "45 degree angle"; "pivot"; "I step"; "checking in"; "checking out"; *"half roll"*; *"full roll"*

Warm-up: Light up (10 minutes)
Note: this game should be delivered without a ball first, before netballs are introduced to the activity in phase 2.

Phase 1: Pupils jog around the playing area; when the teacher calls the name of a colour, pupils quickly stand by a cone of that colour. Introduce different ways of travelling and dynamic stretching, including: walking, jogging, skipping, swinging the arms across the chest, twisting, turning, jumping sprinting, etc.

Phase 2: Lay out four cones for each of four different colours around the playing area. Pupils pass the ball and move around the court, performing a variety of passes, including the bounce pass, chest pass, shoulder pass and lob pass.

When the teacher calls out the name of a colour, the receiving player may only receive the ball whilst standing by a cone of that colour.

Progression
Develop *leadership opportunities: ask one pupil to lead the activity and call the next colour of cone that pupils should travel to*.

Key teaching points
- Finding spaces – pupils to ensure they are in good space *at all times*.
- Instant reactions – pupils to react to the instructions *quickly and accurately*.
- WB pupils to be passing using *various techniques and intelligent pass selection*, e.g. a short pass should be a bounce pass or a chest pass; a longer pass may require a lob, overhead or shoulder pass. Pupils should *complete these skills accurately with consistent good choices*.

Main lesson: Get open (20 minutes)
Divide the class into groups of three. Each group stands in an area approximately six square yards. One pupil is the defender, another is the passing player (this pupil stands still), and the third is the receiving player. The aim is for the passing player to pass the ball to the receiving player who uses a variety of movement patterns to get away from the defender and receive the pass.

Teach and demonstrate each movement skill listed below in turn, and allow the pupils to practise and improve that movement skill before moving on to the next:
- sideways movement
- 45 degree angle moving forward (also known as 'checking in')
- 45 degree angle moving backwards (also known as 'checking out')
- *I step – the pupil makes a forward movement before 'peeling' (moving off quickly) left or right*
- *move left then forwards at a 45 degree angle, or move right then forwards at a 45 degree angle*
- *double up – the player moves forwards then backwards to get free*
- zigzag – the player moves diagonally left, then diagonally right.

For each skill, after some time (e.g. 90 seconds), ask pupils in each group to rotate roles.

Competition
Add a competition element: the receiver is awarded one point for every successful catch from the passer. Which pupil has the most points after the pupils have played all three roles.

Tip
Allow time for pupils to discuss key concepts of movement in their small groups to help facilitate pupil progress.

Differentiation
Pupils work with pupils of a similar ability: WT pupils work together; WB pupils work together.

WB pupils practise more complex movements to 'get free' from the defender.

Layered differentiation: Once pupils have succeeded in receiving the ball three times using one type of movement, *progress to attempting a different type of movement*. *Encourage pupils to make progress at their own pace – this encourages independence.*

Progression
Introduce turning rolls:

'Half roll': The receiving pupil rolls their body 180 degrees around the defender's body. They then sprint out to receive the ball on the angle.

'Full Roll': The receiving pupil turns their body 360 degrees around the defender's body to receive the ball on the opposite side of the defender.

Key teaching points
- Independent learning and improving decision-making skills – introduce new movement skills one by one for evasion but then allow pupils to *make their own decision* as to which movement pattern to follow on which occasion.
- *Timing the run and effective changes of speed* – pupils to **time the run successfully and consistently to gain points**.
- Communication – the receiving pupil should signal or call for the pass from the passer.
- Passing – pupils to pass accurately and with appropriate speed to their partner.
- Marking and intercepting the ball – the defender should stay on their toes and stay close to the receiver.

Match play (20 minutes)
Set up several mini-courts or playing areas (ideally set up between five and ten mini courts, depending on the space available) and create several two vs one or *two vs two* games.

The two attacking pupils should be encouraged to pass and move to get from one end of the court to the other. A goal is scored when a pupil receives the ball in the 'scoring zone' or behind the end line. If the defender wins the ball, they give the ball back to the attackers, to give them another opportunity to score.

Tips
A generic approach to footwork should be looked at closely. Encourage pupils to practise good footwork (not running with the ball) and good movement. Other pupils should be analysing the performance of their peers, looking out for good technique and examples of good passes and pass selection.

Key teaching points

Focus on the key teaching points as outlined above in the main lesson.

Cool-down: Slalom (10 minutes)

All pupils are on the court or in the playing area following various movement patterns and dynamic stretches as shown by the teacher, e.g. skipping, bounding, sidestepping, jogging with knees up, quick feet, etc.

When the teacher calls out the name of a colour, pupils must sprint to a cone of that colour as quickly as possible and place their hands on their heads.

Progression

Only three children are allowed to stand by any one cone. Any pupils who do not find a cone of the correct colour must complete three star jumps before re-joining the game.

Key teaching points

- Look around the playing area whilst travelling to identify and explore space.
- React quickly to instructions using short, quick steps

Plenary

- What movement patterns can we use to make space for ourselves or lose a defender?
- What movement patterns did you find most effective and why?
- *What types of passes did we find to be most effective today and why?*

Cross-curricular links

Mathematics (angles): Angles of support.

Lesson 3 Developing game play

Lesson objective: To further develop skills for dodging and weaving and collecting the ball safely in a two vs one situation and with a passive defender (progressing to two vs two).

Key terms: "end zone"; "pivot"; "movement off the ball"

Warm-up: Scarecrow tag and **Double paired invasion** (10 minutes)

Phase 1 – Scarecrow tag: Play the game Scarecrow tag. All the pupils attempt to stay clear of a number of selected taggers. For a class of 30 pupils, starting with three taggers is a good baseline. *The teacher can then progress the game by introducing more taggers if the level of challenge needs to be increased.* Once tagged, children stand still and wait to be freed by a teammate who runs under their arms.

Phase 2 – **Double paired invasion**: Divide the class into three equal teams who each start the game in their own third of the playing area. Each team member is assigned a number. Each team is assigned a 'third' to invade on the teacher's command.

The teacher starts the game by calling out two numbers. The two pupils called from each team invade the opposing team's third. The 'double paired invaders' try and tag as many people as they can within the specified time (e.g. 10–15 seconds). The pupils then return to their third of the court and the game is repeated.

Differentiation
WB pupils may progress to including a ball. Pupils in each team pass the ball amongst themselves. When the 'invaders' enter, they are only attempting to tag a pupil who has possession of the ball. This encourages pupils to pass the ball quickly and effectively, ensuring good pass selection.

Key teaching points
- Movement and fast feet co-ordination – pupils to try to stay away from the taggers.
- Being alert – pupils to listen for their number to be called.
- Increase the heart rate.
- Closing down in pairs – pupils to work as a team of taggers **by closing off angles and making play predictable in order to force an error or interception**.

Main lesson: Netball rugby three vs one (20 minutes)
Create several mini courts or playing areas. Divide the class into an equal number of teams of three to five pupils. Allocate each team an opposing team and position them facing each other in the playing area.

The aim of the game is for the pupils to pass the ball to each other, moving up the court, attempting to score a goal over the try line. For the purposes of this game, pupils are allowed to run two steps with the ball. One pupil starts with the ball and begins the game by rolling the ball through their legs to their teammate behind.

If a pupil is tagged by the opposition whilst holding the ball, the team must restart the game. Alternatively, if a pupil is tagged whilst holding the ball, the game is paused; the tagger moves five steps back and the game restarts (similar to the rules used in tag rugby).

The team with the ball has five attempts to get the ball over the try line. A goal is scored when the ball is placed on the floor over the try line or caught in the end zone.

Ensure time is given for teams to swap roles.

Competition
The competitive element is inherent in the game. This game develops team play and the concept of moving the ball quickly.

Differentiation
Increase the number of attackers in each team for WT pupils and decrease the number for WB pupils and in accordance with pupils' ability levels. *Progress to attacking against two defenders to increase the difficulty level.*

Variation
Pupils are only allowed to travel on their hands and knees and without standing up. This helps pupils to understand that they are not allowed to move (except in pivoting) whilst in possession of the ball.

Key teaching points
- Teamwork – pupils to find space.
- Quick passing – pupils to find a pass *quickly and accurately*.
- Movement 'off' the ball (when not in possession) – pupils to *receive the ball at a good angle*.
- Getting close – defending and **making play predictable**.
- Defending as a team (basic principles) – if playing with more than one defender (see differentiation for WB pupils above), pupils who perform all of the above skills consistently and effectively are working at attainment step 5 for this activity.

Match play (20 minutes)
Create several mini courts or playing areas (ideally create eight small playing areas) for a two vs two match. The two attacking pupils should be encouraged to pass and move to get from one end of the court to the other. A goal is scored when a pupil receives the ball in the 'scoring zone' or behind the end line. If one of the defenders wins the ball, they give the ball back to the attackers, to give them another opportunity to score.

Tips
A generic approach to footwork should be looked at closely. Encourage pupils to practise good footwork (not running with the ball) and good movement. Other pupils should be analysing the performances of their teammates and opponents to assess how they can improve their skills and the skills of others.

Key teaching points
- Reinforce the key teaching points above from the main lesson.

Cool-down: Land and sea (10 minutes)
All players stand on the baseline or any designated line by the teacher. When the teacher calls, 'Sea', pupils must jump forwards across the line using their arms for leverage. When the teacher calls, 'Land', pupils jump backwards behind the given line.

Progression
The teacher then uses trickery to catch players off guard and to ensure good listening and reaction skills. This drill can be done with or without the netball.

Key teaching points
- Maintain good balance and control of your body by keeping your stomach in, knees together and slightly bent.
- Reaction speed – listen carefully and respond quickly to instructions.

Plenary
- Who can remind me of why it is important to warm up?
- What techniques or movement patterns did we use to evade opponents?
- What parts of the game did you find most challenging? Why?

Cross-curricular links

Mathematics (angles): Teach pupils about 'angles of support' for receiving good quality passes. Remind pupils of the differences between acute and obtuse angles.

More lesson ideas and activities for netball

Gold star passing
In pairs, pupils stand facing each other, toe to toe before each taking three, *five* or **eight** steps back. Pupils begin passing the ball back and forth to each other using the passing style directed by the teacher, e.g. chest pass, bounce pass, *shoulder pass*. The first pair to reach a set number of passes, sits down and calls 'gold star'.

Passing through the gates
In pairs, pupils practise passing the ball to each other back and forth whilst on the move. Pupils may only receive a pass which travels through a gate. Pupils will need to demonstrate good awareness to avoid other pupils.

The receiving pupil should progress to calling the colour of the gate and signalling with their hand where they wish to receive the ball in advance. The passing pupil should demonstrate good timing of the pass and awareness, using an appropriate passing technique to ensure the ball reaches their partner quickly and effectively.

Pivot patrol
In pairs, one pupil stands holding the ball in both hands and their partner stands approximately one pace away. The person in possession of the ball uses their pivot foot as well as placing the ball in various positions out of reach to keep the ball away from their partner. The person without the ball attempts to touch the ball as many times as possible and counts each time they make contact with the ball. After a set time, e.g. 10 seconds, *15 seconds or **20 seconds**, pupils swap roles.

Pass and retreat

In pairs, pupils stand facing each other approximately five yards apart. Pupil A passes the ball to their partner and follows their pass in a forwards direction. The receiving partner catches the ball and quickly returns the pass before jogging backwards towards the end line. Pupils continue to pass the ball back and forth to each other whilst moving towards the end line, until Pupil B reaches the end line. Once pupil B reaches the end line, roles are reversed and pupil B begins to travel in a forwards motion, whilst pupil A travels backwards. (The end line will simply be a line of red cones across the given playing area. The distance between the two end lines will be dependant on space available and ability of your pupils. Typically 20–30 yards between each end line would be appropriate.)

Variation

Alter the types of passes: chest pass, bounce pass, shoulder pass or a combination of passing styles.

Explode netball

Create an outer grid of red cones and an inner grid of blue cones In pairs, pupils pass and move within the inner grid. When the teacher calls 'Explode', the pupil who is not in possession of the ball sprints out to a cone on the outer grid and calls for the pass before receiving it. The receiving pupil then returns the *long distance shoulder pass* and returns to the inner grid. Pupils continue to repeat this task.

Getting through the zones

Divide the class into several groups of eight pupils each and allocate each group to a mini court or playing area. Divide each playing area into three small sections.

Six pupils are lined up on the outsides of the court (three on each side; one per section), facing inwards towards the playing area or court. The other two members of the group become an attacker and a defender who start on opposite ends of the mini court or playing area.

The attacking pupil must pass and move, using the teammates on the outside of the court as support. The aim is for the attacker to get to the other end of the court without travelling with the ball (or causing a violation) and *without allowing the defender to intercept the ball*.

The attacking pupil must receive the ball in each section of the court or playing area before progressing to the next section.

Once the ball is lost or the attacking pupil reaches the end, a new attacking person and new defender is selected to repeat the exercise.

13 Tag rugby

What do I need to know?

Tag rugby was developed to introduce the basic skills of rugby to children, whilst reducing the risk of injury and the physical contact side of the traditional game.

Note: Tag rugby lessons are typically delivered in spring term 2, but lesson topics can be moved around in accordance with school competition dates and to suit the needs of your school.

By the end of this unit, pupils should be able to:

a. Demonstrate good ball handling skills.
b. Understand the rules *and tactics* of the game for tag rugby and *use this knowledge to positively influence team games*.
c. Demonstrate the ability to pass and receive the ball confidently on the move, *with accuracy and control*, **while under pressure from opponents**.
d. Demonstrate good co-ordination with their feet and agility skills *to evade an opponent*.

Key: Step 3 | *Step 4* | **Step 5**

Equipment required:

* 30 tag rugby balls
* stack of 100 cones
* set of bibs (in five different colours)
* 30 pairs of tags (five different colours).

Safety

While delivering all activities, it is important to follow the safety guidelines set out below to ensure a safe and effective learning environment.

* Ensure the playing area is always safe and free of any hazards such as sharp objects, before use.
* Ensure pupils are wearing the appropriate attire and that any shoes with laces are sufficiently tightened.
* Check that equipment is not damaged or torn before each lesson.
* Inform and reinforce to pupils the importance of finding space and not bumping into others during warm-ups and other activities.

- Lay the equipment out before the start of the lesson, where possible, to ensure easy access to resources and a smoother transition between activities.
- Inform and remind pupils of the rules and expectations at the beginning of each lesson.
- When delivering line games or activities in which small queues exist, ensure pupils stand side by side so that you can always see them and they can see what is going on in front of them.
- Use verbal as well as visual signals to regain pupil focus and attention.
- The use of tags in tag rugby helps to separate tag rugby from rugby. It is important to place the tags on safely so as to minimise the risk of injury and ensure pupils feel safe.
- Advise and remind pupils to always place the tags on their hips, not on the front or back of their bodies.
- Ensure tag belts are tied safely and are not too tight or too loose.
- Advise and remind pupils not to overlap the tag belts or tie the tags underneath the main central belt. This is both an infringement of the laws of the game and is unsafe to themselves and others.

Rules

- No talking while the teacher is explaining something to the group or demonstrating a task.
- No talking whilst others are explaining something to the group or demonstrating a task.
- No touching other people or equipment without the teacher's permission.

Some of the key rules teachers will need to know and understand in tag rugby include:
1. No hands off – pupils are not allowed to 'defend' their tags by using their hands to guard, fend off or shield other players or pupils.
2. If the tag is taken, the defensive team must retreat (five yards) before the game restarts with the attacking team. If more than a set number of tags (usually between three and seven, depending on the age and ability of the group) are taken from the attacking team within any given round, the ball is automatically transferred to the other team. It is useful to have the cones on the perimeter of the playing area, spaced by five yards. This way, pupils know approximately what line to move back to.
3. For a try to be successful, the player must hold the ball in two hands and place it on the floor in the end zone. If the ball is held in only one hand, in the legalities of the official game, this will not stand as a try.
4. Pupils must call 'Tag' when they have successfully won a tag from an offending player. The referee shall then blow the whistle, the defensive players retreat (a set number of yards back) before play continues.
5. A free pass (tap and pass) is awarded for any infringement. In the official game, this happens in the centre of the pitch where the defensive player passes it to the attacking player for the game to resume.
6. If a player slides into the end zone or falls to the ground, the try is disallowed. It is therefore important to explain to pupils that they must stay on their feet and to hold the ball in two hands at all times.
7. No forward passes are allowed. This is penalised by awarding a free pass to the non-offending team. Passing sideways (also known as a 'square pass') is accepted within the rules.
8. Knock on: this is when a player attempts to catch the ball but fumbles it in a forward motion. Play continues as normal in this situation.
9. There are no scrums and line outs.
10. Ball away – this is when a ball carrier is tagged in the act of passing and the referee has ruled in favour of the attacking team; the tag is not counted as a proper tag. In this situation the referee should call, 'Ball away, play on'.

Lesson 1 Creating space and passing

Lesson objective: To emphasise the need to find and create space within the game of tag rugby and to improve basic footwork skills and the technique for 'pop passing', which will be required for future learning.

Key terms: "space"; "agility"; "balance"; "co-ordination"; "speed"

Warm-up: Find the space (10 minutes)
Give all pupils two tags at the beginning of the lesson and inform them that they will be needed at various points throughout the lesson.

Phase 1: Give each pupil a ball to hold. Pupils start by jogging in any direction in the grid (or playing area) trying to avoid contact with other pupils by running into space. When the teacher calls, 'Freeze', all pupils must be at least one metre from the nearest person. The teacher may insist that pupils place their ball on the floor and stretch their arms out when 'freeze' is called, to help ensure they are not touching anybody and to contextualise the importance of space. The pupils found in the most space are given a point.

Phase 2: When pupils are used to finding space, introduce new instructions for them to follow while travelling at their own pace e.g.
- 'Up' – pupils throw the ball up and catch it, or *clap once (or twice) before catching the ball*, or **clap several times before catching the ball**.
- 'Switch' – pupils must place their ball on the floor and quickly find another ball.
- 'Change' – pupils respond by shaping to travel in one direction before sprinting in another direction.

Differentiation
WB pupils (and gifted and talented) could **complete a full circle spin before catching the ball**.

Layered differentiation: Ask pupils to throw the ball up just to their head height and catch it as they are travelling. Explain that once they have made five consecutive catches without dropping the ball, they can proceed to throwing the ball one metre above their head. After catching the ball five consecutive times again, they progress to throwing it two metres above the head, and so on.

Key teaching points
- Stay on the balls of the feet.
- Look for spaces and try to be as far away from any other person as possible.
- Use dodging skills and change direction *frequently with control and precision*.
- Practise good ball familiarisation skills – two hands on the ball and catch the ball with two hands.
- ABCs – agility, balance, co-ordination, speed.

Main lesson: Pop passing and line games (20 minutes)

Phase 1: Pupils line up in teams of three. The first pupil in the line must sprint with the ball in their hands to a cone placed 15–20 yards ahead. They sprint around the cone and return, handing the ball gently to the next person in line. Progress to a short 'pop pass' to the next player and then to a 'longer pass with speed, control and accuracy'.

Phase 2: Place three small cones in the playing area between the start and end line and instead of sprinting to the cone, pupils develop SAQs (Speed Agility Quickness Suppleness) through a range of speed and co-ordination exercises, e.g.

- sidesteps between the cones
- bunny hops over the cones
- *forwards and backwards lateral movements* through the cones
- diagonal sprints around the cones
- sprint to the first cone, jog to the second cone, walk to the third cone and then sprint to the end line.

In addition to the SAQ exercises in between the start and end cone of each line, pupils are asked to form a variety of ball-handling skills at the end cone before sprinting back towards their team, e.g.

- *throw the ball above the head before catching it*
- *rotate the ball around the waist three times* and **with speed, accuracy and precision**
- *pass the ball between their own legs in a figure of eight*.

Competition

For each round, one team is awarded 10 points for being the quickest team to have applied the relevant skill correctly. The team with the most points after a set period of time wins the game.

Differentiation

The teacher may wish for WT pupils to work together in a team and WB pupils to work together in a team in order to help monitor progress effectively.

Decrease the amount of central cones or ladder size for WT pupils and increase it for WB pupils. Change the footwork techniques for WT and WB pupils in accordance with their skill level, e.g. WB pupils complete the above activity whilst moving their feet *backwards and forwards* and **quickly and accurately**.

Key teaching points

- SAQ development – to develop the mental-neuro system which triggers the brain to act quickly and respond.
- Ball familiarisation – pupils to spread the fingertips for more *tactile ball control*.
- Developing the basic 'pop pass' technique: throw the ball from the hips, with fingers spread and thumbs up; follow the hands towards the direction of the pass, *snapping the wrist for extra ball rotation*.

Match play (20 minutes)

Divide the class into four or six teams on two or three small pitches to play one vs one tag.

Pupils from two opposing teams (e.g. red and blue) line up facing each other five yards apart. The first pupil in the red team passes to the first pupil in the blue team. The pupil from the red team then turns and runs to the top of the playing area; the pupil from the blue team turns and runs to the opposite end of the playing area. The pupil in blue then attempts to use evasive skills to get back to their original end line and make a 'try' before being tagged by his/her opponent.

After being tagged or a try being made, the next pupil in each line goes. Pupils outside the playing area should observe and analyse the game and think about what they can do to improve their performance or the performances of their peers, writing down key points on a mini white board.

Differentiation
Pupils should play against peers of a similar ability so as to increase challenge and accelerate progress.

Key teaching points
- Attack the space – sprint to the end as fast as you can to gain an advantage on your opponent.
- Use evasive skills such as dummies and feints in an attempt to put the defender off balance.
- Explode by running as quickly as you can once the defender is off balance or once you see a clear gap of space to travel into.
- Defenders stay low and watch the attacker's knees to anticipate/decide which way the attacker will go.

Cool-down: Follow the leader (10 minutes)
Organise the pupils in groups of two or three with one ball per group. The leader holds the ball and can run in any direction, and the others must follow like a snake with their hands on the shoulders of the person in front of them.

When the teacher calls, 'Pop pass', the leader must stop and hold the ball out to the side so the next person can take the ball and continue jogging. The original leader then joins the back of the group.

The teacher can introduce new instructions as they go along to increase attention and reaction speed, e.g.
- 'Touch left' – touch the floor with the left hand
- 'Touch right' – touch the floor with the right hand
- 'Side shuffle only'
- 'Hips' (or other part of the body) – pupils must quickly but gently hold on to the person in front of them by the designated part of the body.

Progression
Introduce **larger group sizes**.

Key teaching points
- React quickly to the instructions.
- Work cohesively as a team.
- Hold the ball out to the side at waist height with hands near the bottom of the ball, so that the other pupil can easily take hold of the centre of the ball.

Plenary
- Why is it so important to find space in tag rugby?
- What do we mean by the term SAQ?
- What skills or techniques can we use to beat an opponent in a one vs one situation?

Cross-curricular links

Science: Teach pupils about changing direction quickly by adopting a 'low centre of gravity' and bending their knees.

Lesson 2 Evading opponents and passing in pairs

Lesson objective: To develop fundamental movement skills of changing direction, including maintaining a *low centre of gravity and transferring their body weight*.

Key terms: "tag"; *"peripheral vision"*; "agility"; "balance" ;"co-ordination"; "speed"

Warm-up: Ten tag (10 minutes)
Phase 1: Repeat the warm-up phase 1 and 2 from lesson 1.

When pupils have developed the relevant skills of finding space, progress to phase 2 below.

Phase 2: Divide the playing area into three smaller playing areas and split the class into three groups of ten. Nominate two taggers in each group. The taggers are given a set period of time (e.g. ten seconds) to win as many tags as possible from the other pupils by releasing the tag strips.

The tagging pair who has won the most tags within the given time period is the winning pair. A new pair is then nominated as the taggers for each group.

Progression
Make the game more challenging by asking the pupils wearing the tag belts to run with:
- *both hands behind their back*
- *both hands held high above the head*.

Variation
All pupils play within the same playing area, and a small number of pupils are the nominated taggers, e.g. for a class of 30 pupils have two–five taggers (depending on the age and ability of the group).

Key teaching points
- ABCs – agility, balance, co-ordination, speed.
- Use dodging and awareness skills to find spaces *and evade opponents*.
- Engaging and strengthening the core stability muscles – especially if pupils have their hands held high above their heads.
- Low centre of gravity – pupils to get low to rip the tag; a low centre of gravity allows for *good balance and control*. (Revisit the learning outcomes from previous lessons on bending the knees and getting low, e.g. hockey lessons.)

Main lesson: Gold star passing (20 minutes)
In pairs, pupils practise the skills of passing back and forth to each other (using any type of pass) whilst looking for and travelling into space.

Once pupils have learnt the key skills, the teacher should introduce a rule that the first pair to reach a set number of passes should sit down and say the words 'gold star' to signal that they have successfully completed the task.

Tips
Pupils should be confident with basic catching skills learnt from previous lessons and topics before progressing onto the competition phase.

Competition
Time trial: each team is timed to see how long it takes them to get to the other end and complete the try.

Key teaching points
- Being on the balls of the feet.
- Being ready to receive the ball – having their hands up, fingers spread and thumbs together.
- Throwing the ball from the hips and into the hands of their partner – hands travel from the level of the 'hips to lips'.
- Peripheral vision – pupils to identify and quickly move into the spaces.
- Communication – pupils to call for the pass and inform their partner of where to pass the ball.
- Receiving the ball safely and *prepare your next pass quickly*.
- Passing the ball safely and accurately to their partner.
- Pupils to **complete all of the above skills consistently and effectively to influence team games**.

Match play (20 minutes)
Play a game of one vs one or *two vs two* tag rugby.

Set up several mini pitches or playing areas (up to 15 mini pitches approximately 10x20 yards if time and space allow). Each playing area has a red cone and a blue cone placed five yards apart near the half way point on the perimeter of the playing area, which marks the starting point for each pupil or team. At the corner and on the same side as the starting cones of each playing area is another tall cone which pupils must travel around before facing their opponent for the one vs one / *two vs two* activity.

The first pupil behind the red cone passes to the first pupil behind the blue cone, both of whom turn and run around their end cones. The blue player attempts to make the 'try' before being tagged by the red opponent.

After each round, the roles are reversed.

Key teaching points
- Attack the space and travel as quickly as you can to gain an advantage.
- Hold the ball firmly in two hands.
- Use feints and changes of body movements to get the defender off balance.
- Stay low in order to push off in new directions quickly.

Cool-down: Make the try (20 minutes)
Teams line up at opposite ends of the pitch or playing area. Two balls are placed on a red and blue cone at the halfway point.

On the teacher's command, the first person to collect the ball and make the try at the other end of the pitch or playing area by placing the ball in the end zone gains one point for their team.

Key teaching points
- Speed – attack the space by travelling quickly.
- Always make the try whilst keeping both hands firmly on the ball.

Plenary
- What should we look for before receiving the ball?
- *What else can we think about before we receive the ball?*
- What shape do we need to make with our hands in order to catch the ball safely?

Cross-curricular links

Science: Teach pupils about the scientific names for various parts of the body, e.g. calf, hips, hip flexors, gluteus maximum, hamstrings, quadriceps, etc.
Science: Teach pupils why a low centre of gravity helps them to change direction quicker.
Science (biology): Teach pupils about the benefits of SAQs and improving speed, agility, and quickness. Discuss key ideas about the difference between these three key terms.

Lesson 3 Passing and moving in teams

Lesson objective: To develop fundamental footwork and passing skills within a small team, with a *passive defender so pupils improve decision-making skills*.

Key terms: "tag"; "awareness"; "passive defender"

Warm-up: Scarecrow tag (10 minutes)
Five pupils are nominated as 'taggers' and these pupils wear brightly coloured bibs. All pupils jog freely around the playing area with tag belts on their waist, responding to the instructions of the teacher, e.g.
- 'Up' – jump
- 'Down' – lunge or touch the floor
- 'Change' – pupils change direction by bending one knee and pushing off the back leg into a new direction
- 'Shuffle' – move the feet sideways quickly.

When the teacher calls 'Tag', the taggers begin ripping tags from the other pupils. If a pupil's tag has been taken, they must stand with their hands and legs apart until freed by another pupil who successfully runs underneath both of their arms. If a pupil is tagged twice, and has no more tag belts left on their waist, they must complete star jumps until the teacher calls 'Time' or signals for the game to stop. The game ends after a set amount of seconds. Reiterate the teaching points, choose new taggers and play the game again.

Tip
It is important that the teacher ensures that the pupils are confident and skilled at performing the tasks of the previous main lesson (see lesson 2) before progressing onto the more challenging tasks below. If the full learning objectives of lesson 2 have not been achieved to a high standard, the teacher should repeat main lesson 2 to ensure improved performance before making progress onto the main lesson below.

Key teaching points
- Show good awareness and stay clear of taggers.
- Demonstrate *quick* changes of direction.
- Bend low to win the tags – emphasise the need to keep a low centre of gravity.
- Teamwork in defence – the taggers work together as a team.
- Decision-making – pupils to make *intelligent decisions as to how to evade the taggers*, or how to restrict the space when tagging.

Main lesson: Pass off – chain reaction (20 minutes)
Pupils line up in groups of three, *four* or **five** side by side. On the teacher's command, the first line of five pupils set off jogging slowly forwards, starting on one end, passing the ball along the line, sideways or slightly backwards only. No forward passing is permitted. When they reach the end, the drill is repeated by the next group of pupils.

It is important to go through this exercise slowly, before developing the drill and encouraging pupils to travel faster. Rotate pupils clockwise (to the next position on their right) each round. This ensures that each person has a turn working from different start positions.

Differentiation
As pupils grow in confidence, ensure that pupils of similar levels are working together. Ask them to *increase their speed whilst travelling, setting target times for pupils to complete the challenge*.

Add a passive defender for WB pupils.

Progress to introducing an active defender.

Progression
Pupil 1 starts with the ball. Pupil 2 starts on one knee. Pupil 3 starts on both knees. Pupil 4 lies on their front. Pupil 5 lies on their back to create a fluent and sequential movement pattern while ensuring teammates time their runs to be able to receive the ball from behind the thrower.

Key teaching points
- Timing – pupils to get into position to receive the pass as *quickly* as possible.
- Always carry the ball in two hands.
- Pass the ball from the waist upwards – pupils to ensure that the hands travel in the direction they want the ball to go.
- Gentle passes *in front of the 'support player'*.
- Communication – pupils to call for the pass.
- *Time the run* – pupils shouldn't go too fast or too slow.

Match play (20 minutes)
Once children have gained the relevant skills from playing one vs one tag rugby, then the teacher can progress them onto *two vs two* or **three vs three** tag rugby as shown below. Create several mini pitches or playing areas to ensure maximum participation at all times.

Two vs two tag rugby: Split the playing area into four–six playing areas (the more the better) before making four teams for each section. At the halfway point of each side of each pitch, a red team lines up behind a red cone and a blue team lines up behind a blue cone. The cones should be no more than five metres apart.

Set up several mini pitches or playing areas. (up to 8 mini pitches approximately 10x20 yards if time and space allow). On each playing area has a red cone and a blue cone placed five yards apart near the half way point on the perimeter of the playing area, which marks the starting point for each pupil or team. At the corner and on the same side as the starting cones of each playing area is another tall cone which pupils must travel around before facing their opponent for the two vs two activity.

On one side of the playing area, the pupil behind the red cone passes to the pupils behind the blue cone, both of whom run around their opposing end cones. The two pupils at the front are joined by their teammates on the opposite end, thereby creating a two vs two situation. The blue players attempt to make the 'try' before being tagged by the red players.

After each person has had their turn, the roles are reversed and the red team becomes the attacking team.

Key teaching points
- Attack the space by travelling quickly into the pitch to gain an advantage on your opponent. Defenders attempt to close the open space whilst attackers attempt to attack the open space.
- The attacker without the ball should travel behind, not in front of their teammate. Can you use: diagonal runs/crossover runs/dummy passes/feints to evade the defenders?

Cool-down: Pass the buck and go! (10 minutes)
Divide the class into teams of five who stand in a circle. Pupils must pass the ball around their circle as fast as possible. On receiving the final pass (when the pupil who made the first pass receives the ball again), the pupil (we will refer to this person as the 'runner') sprints to a designated end line, places the ball down to make a try and returns to the circle.

Once the runner receives the final pass, all pupils in that team sit down and the runner joins them in sitting down when he/she returns. The fastest team to have all of their players sitting in their circle, with their hands on their heads after completing the task is the winning team of that round. Repeat the activity with a new runner for each round.

Key teaching points
- Pass the ball from the waist and follow through with the hands towards the receiving person (hands travel in a motion from 'hips to lips' ending at the height of the lips).
- Hands up in a 'W' shape ready to receive the ball.

Plenary
- How do we ensure good timing for our passes?
- How do we communicate for the pass?
- What are the key differences between tag rugby and other invasion games?

Cross-curricular links

English: Indicate that the lines as set out are in 'parallel lines' and ask pupils if they understand the meaning of parallel lines.

More lesson ideas and activities for tag rugby

Scarecrow tag (two team variation)
There are two teams for this game (e.g. blues vs reds). All pupils begin with two tags on their waists. Once a tag has been taken by someone from the other team, the pupil becomes a scarecrow and stands with their arms out until freed by a pupil from their own team who runs underneath their arms.

When the teacher blows the whistle or calls 'Time', the team with the most 'free' players wins.

Blow the whistle or call 'Time' at appropriate times in order to maintain a safe and fun environment.

Line games
For a class of 30 pupils, create ten lines (to minimise queuing time). Set out a cone for each line approximately 15 yards ahead.

Phase 1: The first pupil runs to the cone with the ball and runs around the cone once or twice then returns to the start and the next pupil in the line goes in relay fashion.

Phase 2: Introduce other tasks to do with the ball on reaching the cone, e.g.
* throw the ball in the air and catch it before returning to their line. Progress to *throwing the ball up and clapping once* or **several times** before catching it
* rotate the ball in a figure of eight between the legs before returning
* rotate the ball round the head or waist twice.

On the final round, pupils must complete all tasks at the end cone before returning to their team: throw the ball in the air, figure of eight through the legs head rotations and waist rotations then sprint back. The first team to complete the task and sit down sensibly wins.

Cat and dogs
Create a central line of blue cones, a parallel line of yellow cones at one end point, and a line of red cones at the opposite end. Divide the class into pairs – a cat and a dog. Pupils stand in their pairs facing each other, two to four yards apart. Cats stand on the left side of the central line of cones whilst dogs stand on right side of the cones.

All pupils jog on the spot and/or complete various activities such as: star jumps, sprinting on the spot, bounding on the spot, bounding side to side, etc. They follow the teacher's commands:
* When the teacher calls, 'Cats', the cats chase the dogs to their end line, attempting to catch them (in the form of a gentle touch or ripping of the tag).
* When the teacher calls, 'Dogs', the dogs chase the cats to their end line.

One point is awarded for each successful catch.

Train game
In small groups of five or less, pupils stand one yard away from each other holding onto the shoulders of the person in front of them, like a train.

Pupils must follow the leader of the train everywhere he/she goes without breaking the train.

When the teacher calls, 'Go', the pupil at the front of the line sprints to the back of the queue, maintaining the one yard rule. The teacher may also reverse this rule, so that the pupil at the back sprints to the front.

When the teacher blows the whistle or calls, 'Freeze', all pupils must freeze. The teams who have maintained their lines (with pupils one yard apart and with their hands on the shoulders of the pupil in front) gain a point.

Progression
1. Introduce a ball to the pupil at the front. On the teacher's command, pupils hand the ball over their left shoulder or *make a small pop pass* to the pupil behind.
2. The pupil at the front throws the ball to the player behind off the right shoulder. The teacher commands 'left' or 'right' rather than using the whistle. Discourage pupils from turning around completely before passing but encourage *quick passing by a quick glance over the shoulder*. Emphasise that pupils should not pass the ball without looking.

The chaser train game
This is a development of the train game above. Pupils firmly grip a piece of each player's clothing by the waist in their train.

Select one 'chaser', who stands at the front of the train with the ball and without touching or being touched by any other person. The chaser's aim is to tag the pupil at the back of the train with the ball by gently touching them with the ball. Pupils are not allowed to throw the ball for this activity.

Pupils in the train must attempt to shield the player at the back by moving left and right, to develop balance, co-ordination, communication and teamwork. This game must be played safely, and the teacher should be very firm on advising pupils on the rules, and ensuring that the rules are followed appropriately.

Give as many pupils as possible the opportunity to be the chaser (e.g. changes roles every five–ten seconds).

Free for all
All pupils have two tags, one on each hip. On the teacher's signal, all pupils attempt to steal each other's tags without having their own tag taken. When the teacher blows the whistle all pupils must freeze.

Each tag that has stayed on a pupil's waist is worth five points; each tag in the hand is worth two points. The pupil with the most points wins.

Repeat this game several times to give several different pupils the opportunity for success.

One vs one
Line the pupils up in single file in two rows on the side of the playing area in the centre. Have an end zone at each end of the playing area, marked on the left by a single blue cone and on the right by a single red cone. The pupil at the front on the left starts with the ball.

On the teachers' command, the pupil at the front on the left must sprint around the blue cone; the pupil at the front on the right must sprint around the red cone on their right before entering the playing area.

The pupil with the ball attempts to make a 'try' in the end zone without being tagged by their opponent.

One point is awarded for each try. Remind pupils that they must have two hands on the ball to successfully make the try.

Pupils may analyse the performances of their peers to assess how they can use various skills to help improve their performance and the performance of others. The teacher should swap attacking and defending roles after each player has had their turn. Ensure there are lots of mini-pitches to maximize playing time for each pupil.

Note: Pupils observing may be asked to write down key elements of the learning on their own mini whiteboards, e.g. what did the pupils do well? What could they do to improve their chances of success?

Progression
1. As skill level improves, introduce *two vs two or three vs three* and **up to seven vs seven games.
2. Encourage pupils to attack the space; discourage pupils from travelling backwards.

Unit 2: Gymnastics and athletics

14 Gymnastics

What do I need to know?

Gymnastics forms a strong foundation for physical development across all sports and activities, hence it is a core part of the PE curriculum. Teaching gymnastics in primary PE helps pupils to develop strength and awareness of the ABCs (agility, balance, co-ordination and core stability), posture and working in co-ordination with others.

Content over a typical six week half–term may include:

- warm-ups
- floor work
- paired floor work
- group floor work and sequences
- apparatus work
- paired apparatus work
- group apparatus work
- technical appraisals and group performances
- whole class performances.

By the end of this unit, pupils should be able to:

Gymnastics
a. Demonstrate simple actions including shapes at various levels *with control, precision and fluency*. *Demonstrate more complex sequences*, **with control, precision and accuracy.**
b. Link sequences, skills and techniques alone and in groups, *using a wide range of skills with control, precision and fluency*. **Use these skills to be creative and demonstrate their own sequences and performances.**
c. Describe their work and performance of others. *Describe how to refine, improve and modify sequences*, **and suggest ways to improve quality of performance**.
d. Demonstrate sections of warm-up activities and *demonstrate all round safe practice, consistently and effectively*. **Lead warm-ups on their own**.

Athletics
a. Demonstrate good technique for starting a sprint race and follow through towards the finish line *with pace* and **consistent running technique**.
b. Jump various distances *with control* and a safe landing.
c. Throw a javelin and or shot-put *with control* to the required distance as set by the teacher *and beyond with consistency*.

Key: Step 3 | *Step 4* | **Step 5**

Equipment required:

- 15 mats
- 6 benches, vaults and gymnastics apparatus
- tripod stands
- projector screen (desirable)
- 6 triangle boxes (desirable).

Safety

While delivering all activities, it is important to follow the safety guidelines set out below to ensure a safe and effective learning environment.

- Ensure the playing area is always safe and free of any hazards such as sharp objects, before use.
- Ensure pupils are wearing the appropriate attire and that any shoes with laces are sufficiently tightened.
- Check that equipment is not damaged or torn before each lesson.
- Inform and reinforce to pupils the importance of finding space and not bumping into others during warm-ups and other activities.
- Lay the equipment out before the start of the lesson, where possible, to ensure easy access to resources and a smoother transition between activities.
- Inform and remind pupils of the rules and expectations at the beginning of each lesson.
- When delivering line games or activities in which small queues exist, ensure pupils stand side by side so that you can always see them and they can see what is going on in front of them.
- Use verbal as well as visual signals to regain pupil focus and attention.
- To provide a high-quality level of pupil support and facilitate rapid progress, it is advisable that teachers attend a gymnastics course to develop confidence and technical understanding of the various moves and skills they are required to teach. A good gymnastics course will build confidence in supporting positions that will enable teachers to provide acute and professional support which help facilitate rapid pupil progress.
- When using apparatus, ask pupils to walk group by group to the next station. Remind pupils about the additional levels of safety required and the importance of not rushing around the room, notably when apparatus are laid out.

Rules

- No talking while the teacher is explaining something to the group or demonstrating a task.
- No talking whilst others are explaining something to the group or demonstrating a task.
- No touching other people or equipment without the teacher's permission.

Lesson 1 Gymnastics shapes

Lesson objective: To learn the four gymnastics floor shapes, be able to name the appropriate shapes and perform them with a *reasonable degree of accuracy*.

Key terms: "pike shape"; "tuck shape"; "dish shape"; "arch shape"; "timing"; "balance"

Warm-up: Mr Men game (10–15 minutes)

Say the name of one of the Mr Men characters. Pupils have to move like him, following a brief demonstration from the teacher, a pupil or both, e.g.

- Mr Slow – move slowly
- Mr Rush – move fast
- Mr Muddle – travel backwards
- Mr Bounce – bounce
- Mr Small – crouch and move
- Mr Big – ask pupils how big they can travel by spreading their arms and legs as wide as they can
- Mr Strong – flex muscles on the move
- Mr Tall – reach up on the balls of the feet
- Mr Short – crouch as low as possible.

Progression

Encourage independent learning and creative development by introducing other examples that the pupils suggest. When the teacher calls 'Mats', pupils jump onto one of the mats using:

a. tuck jump | b. star jump | c. pike jump

Key teaching points

- Explore the space effectively by staying clear of others and objects.
- Focus on clear variations between slow and fast, small and tall.
- Travel with poise – stomachs tucked in, chest out, pointed toes.

Main lesson: Low-level shapes (40 minutes)

Ask the pupils to move quickly and sit down, two pupils per mat. Give pupils five seconds to do this sensibly and safely. This activity introduces the four shapes: pike shape, tuck shape, dish shape and arch shape. Start with the pike shape. Demonstrate the shape then ask pupils to practise performing this shape on their mats, first by sitting down in the shape, then by performing the shape on their back. Explain to pupils that they are working at different heights. Ask pupils to hold the shape for ten seconds with their bottom on the floor, then ten seconds with their backs on the floor (*increase this time the stronger the pupils become*). Repeat the explanation, demonstration and rehearsal process above with the other three shapes.

Go through all of the shapes, ensuring that pupils adjust the shape according to the instructions, e.g. say 'Can you show me the dish shape, now hold your position, and hold your tummy in. Well done, now show me the arch shape.'

Ask pupils to *demonstrate a sequence of the four shapes with control, precision and fluency* for approximately 40–45 seconds, holding each shape for ten seconds **consistently and accurately**.

Next, ask pupils to work in pairs (two per mat) to *develop a sequence of four shapes*. Ask pupils to practise all four shapes with their partner and practise moving *fluently* from one shape to the other. If pupils have reached the desired expectations and show good demonstrations of each shape, introduce basic 'linking' – this is where children make contact with their partner whilst changing shapes (e.g. wrist to wrist contact or interlocking ankles). Explain that pupils *need to demonstrate two or three of the following points*:

- good posture
- good timing
- good balance
- *good co-ordination with their partner*
- *good sequencing (adjusting from one position to another)*
- *good fluency of movement from one position to another*.

Explain and demonstrate the following before pupils are required to create co-ordinated paired sequences:

- matching (same)
- mirroring (facing)
- contrasting (same but different heights)
- arabesque balance (balancing on one leg, whilst the other leg is behind the body, parallel to the floor)
- bunk beds balance – counter balances from *various heights and levels, using various patterns of movement and apparatus including kneeling, standing, on the bench etc.*.

Differentiation

Decrease the length of the hold for each position for WT pupils and increase it for WB pupils.

WB pupils may progress to working in pairs or performing the shapes on low-level apparatus, e.g. benches.

Key teaching points
- Learning the four shapes – pupils to show pointed toes, pointed fingers where appropriate, and straight backs.
- Balance and control – pupils to keep their stomachs tucked in, whilst holding the shape.
- Posture – pupils to point their toes and hands during the demonstration of each shape.
- Linking (working in pairs) – pupils to make positive contact with their partner during the performance with control, precision and fluency.
- Core strength and stability (stomach strengthening).
- Fluency of movement – pupils to move *fluently* from one shape to the other with consistency and a high degree of accuracy.

Cool-down: Dynamic stretching (10 minutes)
Pupils jog on the spot following teacher's instructions, e.g.
- down – sit down in the straddle position (legs wide apart with pointed toes)
- up – jump (in the straddle position – legs as wide apart as they can go)
- criss-cross – swap feet over back and forth in a criss-cross style
- walk on the spot
- jog on the spot
- hop on the spot
- skip on the spot.

Next, ask pupils to walk on the balls of their feet and reach up really tall, as high as they can reach. Remind pupils to breathe in on the way up and breathe out on the way down.

Repeat three or four times to develop pupils' basic breathing and relaxation techniques.

Key teaching points
- Reinforce what pupils have learned in the main lesson.

Plenary
- What four shapes did we learn and practise today?
- Why is it important to stretch our muscles?

Cross-curricular links

Science: Discuss key ideas about speed of movement, velocity and shape and how this affects the quality of movement and performance outcomes.
Mathematics: Question pupils about the number of body parts they are using to balance and co-ordinate during the activities. Ask pupils to multiply these numbers.

Lesson 2 Performing shapes at various levels

Lesson objective: To build upon prior learning performing the four basic floor shapes on a low level and on a medium level, and to introduce contrasting pairs, movement, strengthening and balancing skills required for future learning.

Key terms: "pike shape"; "tuck shape"; "dish shape"; "arch shape"; "balance"; "posture"; "fluency of movement"

Warm-up: Mr Men game (10–15 minutes)
Say the name of one of the Mr Men characters; and pupils have to move like him, following a brief demonstration from the teacher, a pupil or both, e.g.
- Mr Slow – move slowly
- Mr Rush – move fast
- Mr Muddle – travel backwards
- Mr Bounce – bounce
- Mr Small – crouch and move
- Mr Big – ask pupils how big they can travel by spreading their arms and legs as wide as they can
- Mr Strong – flex muscles on the move
- Mr Tall – reach up on the balls of the feet
- Mr Short – crouch as low as possible.

Progression
Encourage independent learning and creative development by introducing other examples that the pupils suggest. When the teacher calls 'Mats', pupils jump onto one of the mats using:

a. tuck jump | b. star jump | c. pike jump

Key teaching points
- Explore the space effectively by staying clear of others and objects.
- Focus on clear variations between slow and fast, small and tall.
- Travel with poise – stomachs tucked in, chest out, pointed toes.

Main lesson: Medium-level shapes (40 minutes)
Demonstrate each of the four shapes from lesson 1 in turn in an upright or standing position: pike shape, tuck shape, dish shape and arch shape. Ask pupils to practise each shape and to hold their shapes for 10–*15* seconds (increase the time the stronger they become).

Next, go through all the shapes, ensuring that pupils can adjust from one shape to another fluently following the teacher's instruction (dish shape to arch shape, arch shape to pike shape, pike shape to tuck shape, etc.).

Repeat the process in pairs (two pupils per mat), and introduce 'linking' – where children make contact with their partner whilst changing shapes.

Ask pupils to practise all four shapes with their partner and practise moving *fluently* from one shape to the other with their partner.

Differentiation

Ask WB pupils to form **contrasting shapes** – one partner performs the shape on a low level, whilst their partner demonstrates the shape on a medium level. Pupils hold each shape for ten seconds, before moving fluently into their next shape.

Introduce more complex sequences, using additional resources.

Progression

Pupils work in their pairs for two–three minutes to develop a gymnastics performance that includes both low-level shapes *and medium-level shapes*. Ask groups to demonstrate their performances to the class, ensuring good posture, timing, co-ordination with their partner and fluency. The performance should last 40, *60* or **80** seconds.

Key teaching points
- Learning the four shapes – revisiting the low-level shapes and introducing the medium-level shapes.
- Balance and control – pupils to keep their stomachs tucked in whilst holding the shape.
- Posture – pupils to point their toes and hands during the demonstration of each shape.
- Linking (working in pairs) – pupils to make positive contact with their partner during the performance *with control, precision and fluency*.
- Core strength (stomach strengthening).
- Fluency of movement – pupils to move fluently from one shape to the other. Introduce basic rolling, kicks, turns and twists as ways that pupils can travel and make transitions from one shape to the next.

Cool-down: Sit-ups (10 minutes)

Pupils work in pairs: one pupil lies on their back and their partner presses down on their feet by interlocking their hands. The pupil lying down completes five sit-ups. Increase the number with stronger groups and individuals to *10–15* or **20–30**. Then pupils should swap roles.

Explain to the pupils that these muscles will need to be strengthened for future learning when they perform the forward roll.

To complete the cool-down, ask pupils to: lie on their backs, point their toes forwards, stretch their hands and fingertips behind the head, close their eyes and concentrate and follow your instructions. Ask pupils to perform one half roll to the left or right or one complete roll to the left or right.

Key teaching points
- Hold the feet firmly to the ground by placing the hands in a 'W shape' over the feet.
- Hold your stomach firmly in towards your spine and use your stomach muscles to push your body up.
- Keep your head in a firm, fixed position.
- Keep your hands in a fixed, firm and comfortable position such as behind your head or across your chest.

Plenary
- What where the good parts of the performances?
- What do we need to work on to improve our performances?

Cross-curricular links

Science: Discuss key ideas about speed of movement, velocity and shape and how this affects the quality of movement and performance outcomes.

Mathematics: Teach pupils about different types of turn, e.g. half turn (180 degrees), quarter turn (90 degrees), complete turn (360 degrees).

Mathematics: Question pupils about the number of body parts they are using to balance and co-ordinate during the activities. Ask pupils to multiply these numbers.

Lesson 3 Forward roll

Lesson objective: To develop strength and co-ordination skills required for the forward roll and be able to perform a forward roll either with or *without support* by the end of the lesson.

Key terms: "box position"; "strength"; "hip flexors"

Warm-up: Tape deck game (10 minutes)
The teacher gives various commands to do with operating a DVD player and pupils follow the commands accordingly, e.g.
- 'play' – walk
- 'fast forward' – jog
- 'fast fast forward' – run faster
- 'pause' – static balance in your position (ask pupils to hold their balances for three seconds, *five seconds* or **eight seconds**)
- 'stop' – legs together, arms by your side (or above the head), neck and back straight
- 'rewind' – jog backwards
- 'eject' – jump up and down
- 'fast rewind' – run backwards
- 'skip' – skip
- 'change (DVD)' – change direction.

Key teaching points
- Demonstrate clear differences in speed of travel.
- Peripheral vision – always scan the area for spaces.
- When pupils hear 'eject', they should jump as high as they can using a 'pike jump', using their arms for leverage and toes pointed as they leave the ground.

Main lesson: Forward roll (40 minutes)
Phase 1: To increase strength in key areas for the tuck shape, forward rolls, jumping high, etc.

Begin with paired sit-ups – one pupil stands and their partner lies on their back with their knees bent and tucked together. Ask pupils what position they are in: 'pike' (standing) or 'tuck' (pupil lying down). The standing pupil stands on their partner's feet, holding their hands out in front and facing upwards towards the ceiling. The pupil in the lying down position performs the sit-ups: as they raise their upper body they reach for their partner's wrists. They must ensure that their hands are facing downwards as they grab hold of their partner's wrist. Repeat for a set amount of times before changing roles.

Progress this activity to the pupil on the floor moving to a standing position: they begin in the tuck position, raise the upper body and reach for their partner's wrist as before, but this time continue to a standing position; they then release their partner's wrist as they go back down. They repeat this five times. This helps to increase the strength in the gluteus maximum and the hip flexors.

Phase 2: Pupils work in their pairs to practise the forward roll:
- feet together
- bent knees for the tuck position
- hands and elbows slightly in front of the knees and shoulder-width apart
- chin tucked in
- push yourself forward come up in the tuck position and stand up
- straight jump to finish.

Pupils practise in their pairs one at a time, with one pupil supporting at the other end of the mat at the finish point. The supporting pupil offers their wrist (facing upwards), so that on completing the roll, pupils are offered support to move into a standing position.

Teaching tips
Ask the pupils if they can notice any of the floor shapes when a forward roll is performed? Can they see the tuck shape at the beginning and near the end? Can they notice the near pike shape and arch in the middle?

The teacher may provide support by asking the pupil if it is okay to hold them at the hips, using both hands to lift their bodies upwards, so that pupils roll and come down safely. However, it is strongly advised that teachers have received professional gymnastics training and guidance prior to providing such one-to-one support.

Differentiation
If WT pupils find it difficult to deliver the forward roll, ask them to perform the roll in one of the following ways, depending on where their weaknesses lie:
- log roll across the mat – if weakness lies in their posture and confidence of rolling
- roll off a higher platform such as a sloped soft box, or stack of mats – if weakness lies in propelling their body forwards
- front support crawl across the mat without the knees or legs touching the floor – if weakness lies in placing pressure on the hands
- frog leap across the mat – if weakness lies in standing at the end of the forward roll (weak hip flexors).

Teach WB pupils the backwards roll – same as forward roll but facing backwards and away from the mat. If time is limited, this can be introduced in future lessons.

Progression
Develop independent learning by asking pupils to hold a front support position (upright press-up position) for a set amount of time, e.g. five, *ten* or **twenty** seconds. Start with a low number, and then ask pupils to increase the length of the 'hold' until they feel they can no longer hold themselves up (up to a maximum of 45 seconds). The partner who is watching should identify any weaknesses in their partner's posture and ask them to correct it in accordance with best practice. Pupils swap roles after a set is completed.

Key teaching points

- *Balance and control* – pupils to keep knees and ankles together.
- Hand position – press hands firmly into the floor with fingers widely spaced.
- Core strength – pupils should hold stomachs in and follow a smooth breathing pattern.
- Release partner in a smooth, gentle fashion.
- Come down into the box position slowly and safely.
- Develop good breathing patterns.
- Improve core strength, and strength in the biceps, triceps (arms), quadriceps and hamstrings (legs).
- Supported positions – develop linking and co-ordination skills.
- Improve the performance of the forward roll (from tuck position to tuck position).

Cool-down: Small to large (10 minutes)

Ask pupils to make the smallest shape they can make with their body and then to grow from small to big, like a seed growing into a flower. Repeat this exercise three or four times to improve breathing technique, control of the body and balance.

Next, ask pupils to stand facing you with their legs shoulder-width apart (standing straddle position). All start wiggling their fingers with their hands between their legs. Continue to wiggle the fingers, whilst making a circular motion with their hands like a clock (hands move left, up, right and back to the starting point) and raising the hands gradually upwards. When the hands reach the top, above the head, the teacher says a simple phrase for the pupils to respond to, e.g. 'Hi class'.

Key teaching points

- Pupils develop good breathing patterns, reduce their heart rate and cool down for the next lesson.

Plenary

- How did you feel about delivering your forward rolls? Did you feel confident?
- Did your performance improve as the lesson went on?
- What can you improve upon for next time?

Cross–curricular links

Science: Discuss key ideas about speed of movement, velocity and shape and how this affects the quality of movement and performance outcomes.

Mathematics: Question pupils about the number of body parts they are using to balance and co-ordinate during the activities. Ask pupils to multiply these numbers.

Inter-curricular learning: Gymnastics warm-up games and creative ideas can also be widely used across various PE lessons topics and subjects for continual progress to be made, developing agility, balance, co-ordination, strength, speed, suppleness, stamina and an all-round healthy lifestyle.

More lesson ideas and activities for gymnastics

See **www.bloomsbury.com/BCB-Teaching-PE** for additional warm-up games and activities for KS2 gymnastics.

15 Athletics

What do I need to know?

Athletics is a key part of the National Curriculum for PE. The main reason that athletics forms such a core part of PE in schools is because it focuses on the fundamentals of movement that are referred to at the beginning of this book: ABCs – agility, balance, co-ordination and speed. Speed can be broken down into three further dimensions: speed, agility and quickness.

Athletics can comprise any core movement activities, including running, jumping and throwing and endurance.

Athletics games and activities include the following:

- standing long jump
- standing triple jump
- fitness (SAQ circuit)
- endurance activities, e.g. pupils perform a 20–*75* metre dash and walk back to the start point; they repeat this activity four or *seven* or **ten** times with appropriate recovery time
- hurdles running (up to 60m or ** over 75m**)
- sprinting games and activities (60m or **over 75 m**)
- discus throwing
- javelin throwing
- shot-put throwing
- cool-down: five 40 metre relaxed strides, reducing speed throughout.

Only use equipment that is safe and appropriate for the age group.

All stretches done within the warm-up should be dynamic stretches. Static stretches should take place at the end of a cool-down, when pupils' muscles are very warm, and can increase flexibility as a result.

Sport and PE can have a powerful influence on the lives and development of young people. Athletics can have a strong positive impact and can help young people to develop physically, socially, emotionally, and intellectually. It can help to shape their attitudes and values in many ways towards health, fitness, winning, losing and sportsmanship – in the way they respect and communicate with others.

Note: This unit is typically delivered in summer term 2 (athletics and/or cricket).

Key: Step 3 | *Step 4* | **Step 5**:

Equipment required:

- stack of cones
- 30 hoops
- 30 beanbags.

Safety

While delivering all activities, it is important to follow the safety guidelines set out below to ensure a safe and effective learning environment.

- Ensure the playing area is always safe and free of any hazards such as sharp objects, before use.
- Ensure pupils are wearing the appropriate attire and that any shoes with laces are sufficiently tightened.
- Check that equipment is not damaged or torn before each lesson.
- Inform and reinforce to pupils the importance of finding space and not bumping into others during warm-ups and other activities.
- Lay the equipment out before the start of the lesson, where possible, to ensure easy access to resources and a smoother transition between activities.
- Inform and remind pupils of the rules and expectations at the beginning of each lesson.
- When delivering line games or activities in which small queues exist, ensure pupils stand side by side so that you can always see them and they can see what is going on in front of them.
- Use verbal as well as visual signals to regain pupil focus and attention.
- Ensure all pupils complete a thorough warm-up.
- Organise pupils safely and ensure they maintain adequate space between each other.
- Supervise all pupils and maintain good class control.
- Comply with all safety guidance related to specific events.

Rules

- No talking while the teacher is explaining something to the group or demonstrating a task.
- No talking whilst others are explaining something to the group or demonstrating a task.
- No touching other people or equipment without the teacher's permission.

Lesson 1 Long jump

Lesson objective: To improve skills for jumping over distances which will prepare pupils for more advanced skills (triple jump) in the next lesson.

Key terms: "long jump"; "speed"

Warm-up: Classic warm-up (10 minutes)
Pupils jog around the playing area following the teacher's commands, e.g. jogging, jumping off two feet, hop on one leg, hop alternating legs, jumping from two legs to one leg, jumping from one leg to two legs, jogging backwards, skipping, jogging whilst rotating the arms, sidestepping, jogging backwards, etc.

Ask pupils to avoid bumping into others by showing good awareness of space.

Key teaching points
- Look for spaces.
- Travel with confidence and accuracy of movements.

Main lesson: Long jump (40 minutes)
Set out ten stations with three pupils per station. Pupils sit behind a green cone, which is the start of each station. Four red cones are placed approximately 10–12 yards ahead of each team and the four red cones are spaced approximately one yard apart.

Following a teacher demonstration, one at a time, pupils run up to the first red cone and jump from one leg to two legs, attempting to reach past the second cone.

Repeat the activity jumping from two legs to two legs, attempting to reach past the second cone.

Competition
The first team to complete the task of jumping over the fourth and final cone three times within their team is the winning team.

Differentiation
For WB pupils, add more cones to increase the distance of the jump or increase the distance between each of the red cones.

For WT pupils, decrease the distances between the cones.

Key teaching points
- Speed in approach – pupils to start low and drive the legs and arms as fast as possible *with good co-ordination*.
- Drive off the back leg and elevate the arms to gain height and momentum.
- Land safely with bent knees.

Cool-down: Jump relays (10 minutes)
Remaining in their teams of three, pupils complete a relay-style activity. Holding a baton (or soft ball), the first pupil in the team runs to the first red cone and performs bunny hops to go between each of the other red cones. They then turn and run back to their team and hand the baton (or soft ball) to the next person in the line, who then repeats the activity.

Key teaching points
- Travel as quickly as you can towards the cones using short, quick steps.
- Pump the arms in co-ordination with the legs.
- Slow down a little bit as you approach the cones.
- Travel on the balls of the feet between the cones and avoid landing on the heels.
- Safe and effective handover of the baton or ball.

Plenary
- How do we gather speed for our jump?
- Why do you think speed is so important for a good long jump?

Cross-curricular links

Science: Ask pupils about ways in which they can streamline their bodies in order to travel faster.
Science: *Ask pupils about how wind pressure can affect their speed, by linking key terms such as 'resistance' and 'force'.*

Lesson 2 Triple jump

Lesson objective: To develop the required skills for the triple jump, following the hop, skip, jump technique.

Key terms: "speed"; "co-ordination"

Warm-up: Foxes and rabbits (10 minutes)
A selected number of pupils are nominated as 'foxes' (taggers). All the other pupils are 'rabbits' and have bibs tucked neatly into their hips.

Pupils travel around the playing area following various instructions from the teacher, e.g. jog, jump, skip, jog backwards, sidesteps, hop, jog at various paces from gear one through to gear five. When the teacher calls, 'Foxes and rabbits', the foxes attempt to win as many rabbit tails (bibs) as possible from the other pupils.

A rabbit becomes 'injured' when his or her tail is lost, and can only hop or bounce on two feet like a kangaroo around the playing area to try to win a tail from another rabbit. If they win another tail, they can place it in their waist and revert to running as normal.

Health and safety

Ensure the bibs are on the side of the hips and not in front or behind.

Key teaching points

- Awareness of space – pupils to keep away from the foxes and injured rabbits.
- Speed – pupils to change speed to avoid oncoming foxes or injured rabbits.
- Co-ordination – pupils to show good co-ordination to win another tail if theirs is taken.

Main lesson: Hop, skip, jump (40 minutes)

Set out ten stations with three pupils per station. Pupils sit behind a green cone, each with a white cone (or throw down rope) in their hand. The green cone represents the start point for each station. Three red cones are placed approximately 10–12 yards ahead of each team and these are spaced evenly apart, followed by a green cone, placed a further 1 – 3 yards away.

One at a time, pupils run to the first red cone, before performing a hop, (from the first to the second red cone), a skip (form the second to the third red cone) and a jump (from the red cone to green cone.) Wherever they land, pupils place their white cone (or rope). The other pupils in the team repeat the process, attempting to jump further than their previous teammate.

Differentiation

Pupils work at their own pace and according to their own level. Decrease the run-up distance for WT pupils and increase it for WB pupils.

Key teaching points

- Hop off one leg.
- Bend the knee when hopping to secure good balance and spring.
- Elevate the arms when jumping, developing *good co-ordination throughout the exercise*.
- Run quickly to the jump spots, *without hesitation* and be confident in approach.
- **Perform all of the above skills consistently.**

Cool-down: Classic cool-down (10 minutes)

Pupils jog around the playing area at a slow and steady pace, following the teacher's commands, e.g. hopping, skipping, jumping (bounding), jogging backwards, with high knees, with heel flicks, doing star jumps, etc.

When the teacher calls a number, pupils must respond quickly by getting into a group of that number.

Variation

When the teacher calls out the name of a part of the body, all pupils must balance on that part of the body, e.g. two feet, knees, knee and elbow, bottoms, two hands and two feet, etc.

Key teaching points

- Re-inforce key teaching points from the main lesson emphasising good agility, balance and co-ordination.

Plenary
- What could they do better to improve their jumping skills?
- How many legs do we hop off of?
- What should we do with our arms when jumping to get leverage?

Describe to pupils why it is important to be active and develop a healthy lifestyle.

Cross-curricular links

Science: Ask pupils about ways in which they can streamline their bodies in order to travel faster.
Science: *Ask pupils about how wind pressure can affect their speed, by linking key terms such as 'resistance' and 'force'.*

Lesson 3 Sprinting

Lesson objective: To improve health and fitness whilst introducing the development skills for sprinting, which will be required for future lessons.

Key terms: "sprint"; "endurance"

Warm-up: Domes and dishes (10 minutes)
Phase 1: Divide the class into two teams to play this game. Spread out a rack of cones on the the floor, some of them being the right way up 'domes', and some of them being upside down, 'dishes'. One team turns the domes into dishes, and the other turns the dishes into domes. Each team cancels out the efforts of the other team to encourage prolonged running and bending of the knees to turn the cones over. Advise and remind pupils that they are not allowed to stand still for this activity.

Phase 2: Play the game again, this time each team goes one at a time. The playing area is set out as all dishes to start with. The first team turns the dishes into domes and the other team performs star jumps at the side whilst counting out loud together how long it takes them to complete the task. Once complete, the teams swap over, with the domes being turned back into dishes.

Variation
Classic warm-up: pupils travel around the space and respond to the teacher's instructions, including jogging, bounding, changing direction, jumping, touching the floor and sidesteps.

Key teaching points

- Travel quickly taking short, sharp steps to each cone.
- Bend your knees and get low to pick up the cone.
- Sprint off in a new direction by pushing off the back leg.
- Plan ahead as to where you will go to turn your next cone over.

Main lesson: Star relay (40 minutes)

Phase 1: Set out ten cones of various colours at one end of the playing area, and ten hoops of the same colour on the opposite end of the playing area. Place a pile of three or *six* beanbags in each hoop.

Divide the class into groups of three, each group starting next to one of the cones. One at a time, pupils sprint to their hoop and collect a beanbag. They sprint back their team, high five the next person in their team and place their beanbag by the cone.

The next person repeats the exercise until all beanbags are cleared from the hoops.

Phase 2: Divide the class into six teams, each with a different colour for their station. Sit each team at the same distance from the centre of the playing area and place 30 beanbags in the centre (five of each team's colour). On the teacher's signal, the first member of each team sprints into the middle, picks up a beanbag and sprints back to their team, before giving a high five to the next teammate who then repeats the process. The team who are first to collect all of their beanbags are the winning team.

Competition

Once all of the beanbags have been returned to their team, the pupils sit down with their arms folded to show that they have successfully completed the task.

Differentiation

Match children and groups appropriately according to their speed, so that all teams are fairly equal in terms of ability levels. One simple way of doing this is to put your WT pupils at the front of each line, followed by WO pupils, followed by WB pupils at the back of each team. This will ensure each pupils runs against somebody of a similar ability level to themselves.

Progression

1. Once pupils have collected their beanbag, they run backwards to their team.
2. Introduce two appropriately-sized small hurdles in between the beanbag and each team. Each pupil must jump over the two hurdles before collecting their beanbag.
3. Endurance run: each pupil collects one beanbag at a time from their hoop until they have collected them all. The second person in each team repeats the activity in reverse, by placing the beanbags back into the middle. This phase is for developing conditioning of each pupil and middle distance running.

Key teaching points

- Drive off and land on the *forefoot* (balls of the feet).
- Shoulders low and relaxed.

- Fast arms – *drive elbows back*.
- Drive from a *low position* to minimise wind resistance.
- **Perform all of the above skills consistently and help influence the team.**

Cool-down: Sharks in the water (10 minutes)
Set out a series of various hoops (at least one per participant) around the 'island' (playing area). Without touching anyone else, pupils must attempt to travel around the island, however, they can only travel by making strides into each hoop. Explain that in between the hoops is water, with sharks, so they must try to be in a hoop at all times.

Differentiation
For WT pupils, introduce more hoops and/or place the hoops closer together.

For WB pupils, use fewer hoops and/or place the hoops further away from each other.

Progression
Pupils are only allowed one foot on the floor at any given time. They may alternate feet for jumping from one hoop to another, but they are not allowed to place both feet on the floor at the same time. This progression develops good balance and control.

Key teaching points
- Take long strides between each hoop, and attempt to place only one foot in each hoop.
- Focus on good co-ordination and balance whilst holding the stomach muscles in.

Plenary
- What are the key teaching points for good sprinting?
- Why should we start from a low position? How does this help our speed?

Describe and discuss key ideas as to why it is important to be active and develop a healthy lifestyle.

Cross-curricular links

Science: Ask pupils about ways in which they can streamline their bodies in order to travel faster.
Science: *Ask pupils about how wind pressure can affect their speed, by linking key terms such as 'resistance' and 'force'.*

More lesson ideas and activities for athletics

Sprinters traffic lights
Pupils travel around the playing space looking out for and responding to the teacher's signals. The teacher raises different coloured cones:
- red cone – stop and go into sprint position
- orange cone – pupils practise fast feet sprinting on the spot
- green cone – pupils sprint in and out of each other as they travel around the space.

Sprinters tag
Five pupils are nominated as 'taggers', each with a soft ball or bib to tag others with. The taggers attempt to tag as many pupils as possible. Once tagged, children must go into in a 'sprint start' position and steadily count to seven before re-joining the game. The game ends after a set time and new taggers are selected.

Variation
Pair pupils up with someone of a similar speed and endurance and play a 'Tom and Jerry' style game in which one pupil attempts to tag the other. Once tagged, the pupil takes the bib or soft small ball and gives their partner three clear seconds to get away, before trying to tag them back. The aim of the game is to be the tagger for the least amount of time possible whilst developing speed and endurance.

60 metre sprints
Phase 1: Create ten teams, depending on the space available and fitness of the pupils, with three pupils in each team. One by one, pupils practise sprinting from their starting cone to a red cone, which is 10 metres away. Pupils work on the start of their sprint (the first 10 metres only).

Advise pupils to take short, quick steps over the first few paces in order to gain momentum. Remind pupils of prior learning 'quick feet' in football and tennis.

Phase 2: Introduce a new yellow cone, which is placed a further 10 metres away, thereby increasing the distance from start to end cone, to 20 metres. Following the same technique between the first two cones, pupils continue their sprint through to the yellow cone.

Phase 3: Introduce a third green cone a further 10 metres away, increasing the sprint distance to 30 metres. Pupils then practise running 30 metres, maintaining good form and smooth transitions between the red, yellow and green cone. Advise pupils to begin gathering full speed by lengthening their stride pattern by phase 3 (between the yellow and green cone, which is 20–30 metres).

Phase 4: Pupils practise the full 60 metre sprint. Keep the same cones in place where possible, so that pupils are aware of the different phases of their sprints.

Javelin throw

In pairs, one at a time, pupils run quickly towards the start cone before throwing their javelin as far as they can. Scoring zones are marked out by various colours, e.g.

- 10 yards – red zone (line of red cones) – 2 points
- 12 yards – yellow zone (line of yellow cones) – 4 points
- 14 yards – green zone (line of green cones) – 6 points
- 16 yards – blue zone (line of blue cones) – 8 points
- 18 yards – orange zone (line of orange cones) – 10 points.

Pupils gain points in accordance with the zone where their javelin landed. For example;

Web links

Please find below some useful web links athletics-based resources.

- **www.funtrivia.com** (Type in the year group (e.g. 'Year 6'), followed by 'sports quiz'.)
- **london2012.com**

Unit 3: Net/wall and striking/fielding games

16 Tennis

What do I need to know?

Tennis is a net and wall game that plays a unique role in developing hand-eye co-ordination, balance, agility, reflexes and speed. Pupils can progress at their own pace to develop the basic fundamentals before progressing to playing the game at a higher level and at a faster pace.

Note: *This unit is typically delivered in summer term 1.*

By the end of this unit, pupils should be able to:

a. Catch and throw the ball at *various heights and speeds with control and accuracy* **with consistency**.
b. Strike the ball *into various target areas* **with control, accuracy and consistency**.
c. Understand the tactics of the games and *use this knowledge effectively (i.e. playing various tactical shots and reacting to situations quickly)* **to strategically advise others**.
d. Understand why exercise is important for health, *the benefits of warming up and cooling down* and **can explain the short- and long-term effects of exercise**.

Key: Step 3 | *Step 4* | **Step 5**

Equipment required:

- 30 tennis racquets
- stack of 100 cones and/or spots and throw down lines
- bucket of 96 tennis balls
- six or more tennis nets (desirable).

Safety

While delivering all activities, it is important to follow the safety guidelines set out below to ensure a safe and effective learning environment.

- Ensure the playing area is always safe and free of any hazards such as sharp objects, before use.
- Ensure pupils are wearing the appropriate attire and that any shoes with laces are sufficiently tightened.
- Check that equipment is not damaged or torn before each lesson.

- Inform and reinforce to pupils the importance of finding space and not bumping into others during warm-ups and other activities.
- Lay the equipment out before the start of the lesson, where possible, to ensure easy access to resources and a smoother transition between activities.
- Inform and remind pupils of the rules and expectations at the beginning of each lesson.
- When delivering line games or activities in which small queues exist, ensure pupils stand side by side so that you can always see them and they can see what is going on in front of them.
- Use verbal as well as visual signals to regain pupil focus and attention.
- Ensure pupils place their tennis racquets on the floor whilst the teacher explains or demonstrates a task.
- Ensure pupils are adequately spaced when conducting tennis activities and where pupils have racquets in their possession.
- Use placemats and throw down lines as opposed to cones or disc markers where possible, to minimise the risk of pupils slipping over objects.

Rules

- No talking while the teacher is explaining something to the group or demonstrating a task.
- No talking whilst others are explaining something to the group or demonstrating a task.
- No touching other people or equipment without the teacher's permission.

Some of the key rules you will need to know for teaching primary school tennis include:

- The ball may only bounce once in order for play to continue, except in circumstances in which the teacher has conditioned the game to make it easier in practice and allows two bounces.
- The ball must travel over the net and in court for a point to be scored. If the ball is not returned over the net and into court, a point is awarded to the person who originally sent the ball.

Lesson 1 Bouncing and catching the ball

Lesson objective: To develop hand-eye co-ordination skills and good footwork with the tennis ball, whilst also ensuring pupils understand the 'ready position' and develop skills of stroking the ball along the floor.

Key terms: "hand-eye co-ordination"; "ready position"; "flight of the ball"

Warm-up: Bounce about (10 minutes)
Phase 1: Pupils begin by travelling around the playing area in various ways, as specified by the teacher, e.g. sidestepping, skipping, rotating the arms, bounding, jumping, hopping, and jogging at various paces (gear 1 = slow, gear 2 = medium pace, gear 3 = fast pace).

Phase 2 – Bounce about: Pupils jog around the playing area bouncing the ball in basketball style. Ask pupils to travel in different ways, e.g. walking, jogging, sidestepping and shuffling, walking or jogging backwards, skipping, sprinting, etc. Also instruct the pupils to bounce the ball in different ways, e.g.
- 'left' – bounce the ball using the left hand
- 'right' – bounce the ball using the right hand
- 'change' – change direction with the ball
- 'swap' – swap balls with a pupil nearby whilst *keeping control and not allowing the ball to bounce more than once*
- 'up' – pupils throw the ball into the air before catching it.

Numbers: When the teacher calls a number, pupils must get into a group of that number as soon as possible. Pupils who are last to respond may complete two star jumps (whilst the class count their jumps to increase pupil engagement) before re-joining the game.

Tip
On the command, 'Up', ensure pupils throw the ball no higher than their head.

Differentiation
If there are pupils who find this challenging (WT pupils), follow the 'bounce-catch' technique which is more slow and steady. WB pupils may increase the speed they are travelling. Pupils travel at their own pace.

WT pupils: Children place their ball on the floor. When the teacher calls 'pick up', pupils quickly seek to pick up a new tennis ball from the floor.

Layered differentiation:
- Pupils start with the bounce-catch technique.
- Once pupils have caught the ball successfully six times consecutively, pupils progress to a continuous bounce with the writing hand.
- Once pupils can bounce the ball consecutively with the writing hand ten times, pupils progress to using their non-writing hand.

Progression

1. Once pupils are capable of throwing the ball up level with their head, then progress to throwing it slightly *above the head*.
2. Where appropriate, progress to **throwing the ball 3 metres above the head**.

Key teaching points

*   Agility and co-ordination with the tennis ball.
*   Reacting quickly to instructions.
*   Throwing and catching skills – pupils to palm their two baby fingers together and their two thumbs up with their fingers spread to make a 'safe cage' for the ball to land in.
*   Teach pupils to 'suck' or 'draw' the ball into the body once they have caught it, in order to further protect the ball and ensure it doesn't fall from their hands (pupils will also need this skill for goalkeeping in football and fielding in cricket).

Main lesson: Catch tennis (20 minutes)

Divide the class into pairs; one pupil has a ball and the other a cone.

Each pair stands facing each other. The pupil with the ball throws it underarm, above head height and straight ahead to their partner who must be on the balls of his or her feet (jogging on the spot) all the time in order to react to the flight of the ball. That pupil lets the ball bounce and then catches it in their downturned cone. They throw the ball back to their partner and the process is repeated. Each pupil has six, *eight,* or **ten** turns before swapping roles.

Tip

Ensure that pupils are adequately spaced, according to their age group and ability level.

Competition

Pairs stand either side of a net. One pupil throws the ball underarm, over the net. The pupil on the other side attempts to catch the ball in their downturned cone after one bounce only. One point is awarded every time a pair makes a successful catch. The first team to complete ten successful catches sits down and place their hands on their head to demonstrate that they have successfully completed the task.

Pupils on the left hand side of the teacher rotate clockwise after each round. This means that all children have more chance of success by pairing with different children in the class.

Note: If there are no nets available, use a set of cones or a low bench to represent the net.

Differentiation

Decrease or increase the distance between partners for WT and WB pupils respectively. WT pupils work closer together and/or with a lower target number of catches. WB pupils work further apart and/or with and a higher target number of catches.

Key teaching points

*   Prepare for the 'ready position' – bent knees, hands out in front of the body.
*   *Accurate and speed-appropriate* throwing skills – pupils to throw from low to high ('from knees to trees').

- Judging and reacting to the 'flight of the ball' – pupils to get their body behind the ball as it bounces.
- *Quickness* – pupils to *anticipate and react quickly using side to side movements*.

Match play (20 minutes)
Play a game of floor tennis.

Two cones are placed in between each pair and spaced approximately one to two yards apart. These cones are known as 'gates'. Facing each other, pupils stand in between the cones before taking three big steps back away from the cones.

One pupil holds the racquet and the other rolls the ball along the floor.

Pupils rally the ball along the floor back and forth, trapping the ball and aiming the racquet first before gently striking the ball forwards.

Pupils are not allowed to use their hands or their feet to trap the ball, except if the teacher has specified such actions for a pair or group of WT pupils for whom the success criteria is that they need more practice at an easier task.

The first pair to reach 10, *15* or **20** successful racquets through the gate, sits down to signal that they have successfully completed the task.

Tips
The teacher may request that pupils rotate on their instruction, e.g. pupils to the left hand side of the teacher rotate in a clockwise direction. This means that children will have a greater chance of success and work with different classmates throughout the lesson.

The game floor tennis, can be delivered with several different variations and tactics, e.g. to develop pupils being able to hit the ball across the court, ask one pupil to always hit the ball diagonally and the other pupil to always hit the ball straight down the line. Then ask pupils to swap roles.

This game should be played several times with pupils before they make progress onto bouncing the ball.

Differentiation
WB pupils can focus on striking the ball through *smaller target zones* and/or **at various angles through the gates**, e.g. pupils pass the ball to each other along the floor through a red gate and blue gate alternately, thereby ensuring each pass is diagonal.

Progression
As soon as the teacher is satisfied with the skill level being delivered, progress to giving both pupils a tennis racquet.

Key teaching points

- Trap the ball by angling the racquet over the ball, ensuring the bottom of the racquet stays in contact with the floor, so as to avoid the ball rolling under the racquet.
- On contact with the ball, withdraw the racquet slightly to push the ball out in the direction of where you are about to make the pass. Make a small 'C' shape with the racquet as you strike it towards your partner.
- Follow through towards the target.

Cool-down: Switch (10 minutes)

Three pairs join together to form a team of six pupils. Each team faces two sets of five cones: five blue cones on the left, and five red cones on the right. All the tennis balls are on top of the blue cones.

Pupils must quickly collect the balls from the blue cones using their left hand and one by one, place them onto the red cones opposite, using their right hand.

Once the first person in each team has completed the task, they return to their team, give the next player in their team a high five and that person then sets off to repeat the exercise, but transferring the balls from the red cones, using their right hand, to the blue cones, using their left hand.

The first team to complete the exercise wins the round.

Variation

Sprint relays – pupils collect one ball from the end and bring it to the team, before the next person in the line goes and brings back another ball.

Key teaching points

- Bend your knees whilst travelling quickly from cone to cone.
- Can you collect the ball from the left side, using your left hand, and place it to your right with your right hand?
- Stay on the balls of your feet, taking short, quick steps between each of the cones.

Plenary

Ask the class questions about the learning, e.g.

- What part of the racquet did we use to trap the ball? What part of the racquet did we use to send the ball?
- What do we do if the ball is travelling to our right or left, or out of our reach?
- Why is it important to adjust our body position?

Lesson 2 Volley shots

Lesson objective: To develop footwork skills and to make progress from the previous lesson by tapping the ball up in a straight line with the racquet (to ensure a *smooth connection* with the centre of the racquet in preparation for the volley shot).

Key terms: "footwork"; "tap ups"

Warm-up: Footwork activities (10 minutes)
Phase 1: Complete the Classic warm-up (see Glossary) as an introduction to the next phase below. Finish by playing the numbers game, where pupils are asked to get into a group of three. Ask pupils to sit down in their small groups before demonstrating the next phase below and then assigning each team to a starting cone.

Phase 2: Set up ten footwork activity stations, including a starting cone and an end cone for each station. The starting and ending cone for each station should be the same colour for ease of reference. You may wish to set up stations that each have the same equipment and activity or use different equipment and incorporate a different activity at each station. If you are setting up different activities, every so often pause the activity, ask pupils to place their hands on their heads and team by team, ask pupils move to the next station to their left.

Starting behind the starting cone, pupils complete the given activity. The second pupil may only start travelling once the person ahead has reached the second cone or other appropriate distance as specified by the teacher. Below is an example of footwork skills that can be applied at each station in accordance with the learning objectives:
- sidesteps, side to side through three, *six* or **eight** cones
- six small jumps over mini hurdles (or larger cones)
- cross the river – jump over the throw down line or cones from two feet, landing on two feet
- run with 'quick feet' through a ladder followed by long strides through a set of three hoop, landing one foot in each hoop
- three moguls (jumps side to side) over a set of four, *six* or **eight** cones placed closely together
- hopping – placing one foot in between each cone
- sideways movements travelling to and touching each of the cones, which are laid out diagonally
- sideways movements as above, but *pupils to imitate a forehand shot at every cone*.

Differentiation
Decrease the level of intensity of the circuit or activity by adding fewer activity cones for WT pupils and increase the level of intensity for WB pupils by adding more activity cones.

Key teaching points
- ABC – agility, balance, co-ordination.
- Preparation for tennis-related movements, *good balance and footwork control*.
- Fitness and endurance.
- Timing – waiting until the person ahead has reached the second cone before proceeding.

Main lesson: Tap-ups tennis (20 minutes)

Phase 1: Ask pupils to carry the ball on the racquet, keeping the ball steady. Suggest pupils imagine the ball is an egg, and they cannot drop it, or it will crack.

Ask pupils to group up: when the teacher calls a number, pupils must group up into a group of that number as quickly as they can. The ball must remain on their racquet to help develop *good balance and control*.

If the ball falls to the floor at any time during the activity, pupils must complete three star jumps before continuing the activity.

The last number to be called before moving on to phase 2 should be 'two'. Once the class is in pairs, each pair is given a hoop or four cones to make a small square (one square yard).

Phase 2: With one ball between two pupils, pupils take turns tapping the ball gently upwards and into the mini square or hoop. Pupils stay on the outside of the mini square or hoop. Ask children to count how many successful tap-ups they and their partner complete in the mini square or hoop.

Repeat the exercise using tap tap-downs (tapping the ball down to the floor) as opposed to tap tap-ups.

Move the pupils round so that they play the game with a new partner.

Competition

Compete to see who can deliver the most tap-ups individually. The pupil who completes the most tap-ups without the ball falling to the floor demonstrates the skill to the class. As a class, discuss what the pupil did well and how they kept good control. Look for key teaching points within their answers such as those listed in the key teaching points below.

Differentiation

WT pupils may repeat the floor tennis exercises from lesson 1 (p72). WB pupils demonstrating excellent control and confidence may work together **switching between the forehand and the backhand**.

Layered differentiation: Pupils count to 15 whilst walking with the ball on the racquet. If the ball does not fall, progress to jogging with the ball on the racquet. Count to 15 whilst travelling, and if the ball does not fall, progress to walking with the ball on the racquet and tapping it up once, letting the ball bounce once, then catching it on the racquet.

Once pupils can complete this five times in a row, they should progress to tapping the ball up three times or *five times* or **ten times** consecutively before catching it on the racquet. Then, progress to pupils tapping the ball down using the centre of the racquet.

Keep pupils in a relatively small space to enhance their racquet control. Make sure the area is not too small, so as not to compromise safety.

Progression

After each tap-up into the hoop, pupils must *rotate positions with their partner*.

Key teaching points
- Racquet control – pupils to use the centre springs on the racquet.
- Quality footwork with the racquet – pupils to *keep their feet in a steady position in relation to the ball* whilst tapping the ball.
- Hand-eye co-ordination.
- Practising *gentle strokes with the racquet with accuracy*, *control* and **consistency**.

Match play (20 minutes)
Divide the class into six–eight groups and mini courts with one pupil per group being assigned the role of 'server'.

The server throws the ball underarm over the net to the oncoming pupil.

The pupil calls 'Volley shot' and volleys the ball over the net. Connection with the ball should be made *slightly above the head with the racquet across the face of the body. The right foot should come across the left foot for increased balance and control*.

Once a pupil has had his/her volley shot, they must return the ball to the basket and rejoin the back of the line.

Teams may compete for each round. The first team to ten successful volleys over the net is the winning team.

Progression
Introduce a *target square or a target hoop for each team*. A team will gain ten points for getting the ball in the target zone or five points for successfully volleying the ball over the net. The target area should be appropriate for the ability of the pupils using it.

The teacher may wish to select a team captain to count the score for their team. Pupils consistently scoring in the target zone are likely to be achieving step 5 progression.

Key teaching points
- Travel quickly towards the net and quickly get into the ready position.
- Keep your eyes on the ball.
- Place your left foot across your right foot as the ball is travelling.
- Position the racquet so that the ball hits the centre of the racquet.

Cool-down: Tennis relay races (10 minutes)
Small teams complete footwork relay races across short distances of 5 yards, *8 yards* or **12 yards**. The racquet may be used as a baton to increase the focus of the group and allow pupils to become used to sprinting with the racquet in their hand.

Key teaching points
- Pupils should concentrate on staying low to the floor and 'pushing off' the back leg when turning.

Plenary
- Why is good footwork important in tennis?
- What part of the racquet should we aim to make contact with the ball?
- What can we focus on to ensure the ball reaches the intended targets?

Lesson 3 On rack

Lesson objective: To develop footwork skills and hand-eye co-ordination on the move, and to develop tactical skills of always returning to the centre of the court.

Key terms: "speed"; "home base"

Warm-up: Low, middle, high (10 minutes)
Phase 1: The teacher may wish to introduce a gentle pulse-raising activity such as the Classic warm-up (see Glossary) before progressing to phase 2 below.

Phase 2 – Low, middle, high: Divide the class into pairs who stand facing each other six, *eight* or **ten** yards apart.

Pupils throw and catch the ball with their partner. They start by throwing the ball low along the floor. When this is confident they progress to throwing it a medium height – between the waist and neck. Finally, they practise throwing the ball high –*just above head height*.

Develop independent learning by asking pupils to decide whether they will throw the ball low, middle or high, so that their partner reacts quickly.

Differentiation
Decrease or increase the distance between partners for WT and WB pupils respectively.

Differentiate how much notice a pupil has for whether the throw will be low, middle or high by having the pupil throwing the ball saying, 'low', 'middle' or 'high' before they throw the ball or *as they throw the ball*, or **the receiver calling the relevant height before he or she catches the ball**.

Progression
After each throw and catch, pupils sidestep a couple of paces to the left or right before repeating the activity. *Ask pupils why and when they think these skills will be important for tennis.*

Key teaching points
- Development of catching skills – pupils to keep their eyes on the ball.
- Watching the flight of the ball – pupils to *get their body behind the ball in good time*.
- Adjusting to different heights of the moving ball.
- Bend the knees when catching the ball.
- Pupils to *cup their hands successfully to consistently catch the ball on the move* or **at various challenging speeds and heights** ensuring baby fingers are touching and thumbs are facing up, with fingers spread out when catching the ball. (Be sure to revisit the key teaching points from previous lessons in basketball, used in a different context.)
- Sideways movement and *quick footwork*.
- Communication between pairs – pupils to tell their partner 'low', 'middle', or 'high', when they are about to throw the ball.

Main lesson: Catch tennis (20 minutes)
Each pair should be allocated to an adequately-sized mini court (approximately six yards by six yards) with a cone or throw down line marking the 'home base' at the centre of the mini court.

One pupil throws the ball to different areas of the court for the other pupil to attempt to catch after one bounce or, if possible, whilst the ball is still in flight.

Each time that pupil catches the ball and returns it, he or she must *immediately* return to the home base. This encourages pupils to always return to the middle of the court, giving them increased chance of getting to either side quickly.

After ten throws, the pupils should swap roles.

Competition
The pupil throwing the ball attempts to get his or her partner out of the game by throwing the ball quickly. Please note that the ball must land 'in court' for the throwing pupil to be successful.

The pupil catching the ball counts how many times he or she has managed to catch the ball before it bounced twice in his or her side of the court. Tally up the total score after ten repetitions before swapping roles.

For enhanced game-play, progress to rotating pupils every round to ensure pupils get used to playing competitively with a range of other children.

Differentiation
WT pupils work in a smaller area or practise gold star throwing and catching skills whilst standing still.

WB pupils work together and *progress to playing this game with a racquet*.

Progression
Play the same game, but this time the pupil doing the catching uses a racquet to *volley the ball back to their partner's hands* as opposed to throwing it back.

The pupil doing the throwing continues to use their hands only.

Note: This progression should only be used where pupils are fully skilled with the racquet and can confidently complete the task.

Key teaching points
- Speed across the court – pupils to travel quickly to and from the 'home base'.
- *Increasing reaction speed, moving quickly* to get in line with the flight of the ball.
- Develops an *instinctive reaction* to return to the centre of the court after returning the ball (return to 'home base').
- Getting the body in line with the ball – this will result in increased power in a pupil's shot (in forehand) when they progress to using racquets.

Match play (20 minutes)
Working in pairs, one pupil serves the ball over the net, using an underarm throw. Their partner responds to the flight of the ball by getting his or her whole body behind the ball and catching the ball on the racquet (by holding the racquet with the right hand and catching the ball on the racquet with the left hand).

Pupils should *return to the middle* after each 'on rack'.

Pupils should call 'on rack' on each successful repetition. Swap roles after ten repetitions.

Differentiation
If WT pupils find this too challenging, revert to floor tennis and catching games as delivered in previous lessons. Increase the level of difficulty by ensuring both partners have a racquet and/or play in a larger playing area.

Key teaching points
- Start in the 'ready position', knees slightly bent, eyes on the ball and racquet out in front of the body.
- Watch the flight of the ball and try to get your body in line with the flight of the ball.
- Catch the ball on the centre strings of the racquet. (Commonly known as the 'sweet spot'.)
- The pupil serving the ball should throw underarm, holding the ball beside the knee and lending his/her arm forwards and upwards level with their shoulder.

Cool-down: Catch and tag (10 minutes)
Divide the class into teams of seven or eight, and for each team select one 'tagger'. *The tagger must attempt to intercept the ball, whilst the other pupils pass and move, using underarm throws (or rolling the ball on the floor).* Pupils cannot travel outside the boundaries of their own mini court.

Once the ball has been intercepted by the tagger, the pupil who last had possession of the ball now becomes the tagger.

If the ball falls to the floor, the pupil who dropped the ball immediately becomes the tagger.

Pupils are not allowed to hold onto the ball for more than two or three seconds. No touching of pupils is allowed at any point during this game.

Differentiation
Pupils stand in a circle and pass the ball to each other. No tagger or interceptor is involved in the game.

Alternatively, pupils could play the game as above but roll the ball along the ground to each other, as opposed to throwing. This adaptation can be played with a tagger (harder) or without (easier).

Key teaching points
- Throw/roll the ball quickly using the technique(s) as developed in previous learning.
- Keep moving to find and create space for yourself.
- Call for the pass if you are free, but don't be upset if you don't receive it since you working as a team and by calling for the pass you are contributing to your team by creating a distraction for the defender.

Plenary
- Where should we always return to after sending the ball?
- Why is this important in tennis?
- How do we shape our hands when receiving the ball? Why is this important?

Cross-curricular links

Science (forces): Teach pupils about the importance of the 'body position' in relation to the amount of force that can be generated for the shot, e.g. *if the body is too far away from the ball on contact, maximum power cannot be generated*.

More lesson ideas and activities for tennis

These games have many variations and should be adjusted according to the age group, ability and preferred earning styles of your pupils.

Airball
Using a shuttlecock or **tennis ball**, pupils work in twos or threes to take turns hitting the ball up into the air alternately. The aim of the game is not to let the shuttlecock or ball fall to the floor. See which team gets the most repetitions.

In or out?
In pairs, one pupil serves the ball and their partner returns it in court. Repeat five times and then swap roles. Pupils aim to get the ball 'in court' *consistently* and **whilst under pressure as the ball is thrown at various challenging heights, speeds and angles**. The server calls 'In' or 'Out' after each shot.

Depending on the ability level of the pupils, teachers may wish to play this game with no racquets (catching and throwing) or with *one pupil with a racquet* or **both pupils with a racquet**.

Cone targets
Set out cone grid target (a small triangle or square grid of cones) or hoop targets for pupils to strike the ball into. From the baseline, or starting point, pupils drop their ball from shoulder height and attempt to strike the ball over the net and into the target zone. Pupils will gain points for getting the ball *over the net consistently* and **consistently into the target area**.

One up, two down
Each pupil stands still with a tennis ball in their hand. When the teacher says, 'One up', pupils throw the ball slightly above head height and catch the ball after one bounce. If the teacher says, 'Two down', pupils drop the ball down from just above head height and catch after two bounces. The teacher calls any number, followed by 'up' or 'down' and pupils respond accordingly. Progress to performing these skills whilst on the move.

Enable leadership opportunities by selecting one pupil to call the commands for the class.

Making a pancake
Pupils jog around the court, rolling the ball on the racquet, maintaining stability and good balance. If the ball drops, the pupil must complete (three–*five*) full star jumps

before continuing the game. Start by walking before progressing to jogging, *running* and **sprinting**.

This game can also be delivered in the form of a race or a relay for competition purposes.

Caterpillar

Pupils line up in groups of four. The front pupil puts the ball on his or her racquet and travels by weaving in and out of the other three pupils towards the back of the line.

The next pupil repeats the process and so on until all four players have completed the exercise.

Add an element of competition by having groups racing against each other: the fastest team wins.

Two vs two tennis

This can be played as badminton or tennis. **The teacher sets up a game of doubles using a single net. This game is for advanced pupils.**

Ready Steady (warm-up game)

Pupils jog around the court in different directions. On the command, 'Ready', they jump into a split step position (legs apart, racquet in front of the body with two hands on the racquet). This is also known as the 'ready position'.

When the teacher calls, 'Line one', 'Line two' or 'Line three', pupils then sprint to the given line and balance in a particular way which has been selected by the teacher, e.g. in the ready position, on one leg, on one leg and one hand, on two legs and two hands.

This game may be played with or without racquets.

Cone ladders

The teacher sets up three–five teams. Pupils travel one at a time, in and out of the cone ladder towards the net.

When they reach the net, they jump into the ready position then return to the back of the line.

Variation

Perform various footwork exercises using the ladder, including one foot between each cone, bunny hops between each cone, hopping between each cone, etc. Use various footwork drills and exercises in order to develop various footwork skills.

Target throw

Pupils throw balls or beanbags over the net into a designated area, either a hoop or square of cones. Pupils may only pick up and throw one ball or beanbag at a time.

The team with the most balls or beanbags in their half of the court after 30 seconds is the winning team.

The teacher will award bonus points for any balls or beanbags that are in the designated target area.

React and volley

In teams of four, one pupil is the 'server' who throws the ball for a forehand or volley return to their other teammates one at a time. If the person returning the ball gets the ball over the net, he or she runs to the back of the line. If they fail to get the ball over the net, they must take a racquet and ball from another section of the playing area to complete ten tap-ups with the ball, before returning to the back of the line.

Variation

Pupils are asked to only serve a volley (a volley is easier to perform than a forehand shot) or **only serve a backhand**.

Pupils must sprint around the court regardless of success or failure to get the ball over the net.

17 Cricket

What do I need to know?

Cricket is a popular striking and fielding game that is typically delivered in the summer term. In teaching primary PE, teachers may opt to purchase soft play cricket balls, or to simply use mini tennis balls to deliver their cricket lessons. During cricket lessons, it is important to keep pupils as active as possible so as to avoid pupils becoming bored or otherwise easily distracted. For this reason, the match play scenarios in this chapter are small-sided games where all pupils have an active role throughout each lesson.

Note: *This unit is typically delivered in summer term 2 (cricket and/or athletics).*

By the end of this unit, pupils should be able to:

a. Successfully catch the moving ball at *various heights and speeds with control, accuracy* and ** a high degree of consistency**.
b. Strike the ball confidently into *various* target areas *with control, accuracy* and ** a high degree of consistency**.
c. Bowl the ball accurately in a straight line.
d. Understand basic tactics for the game, including fielding and anticipating where the ball is going to go.
e. Understand why exercise is important for health, *the benefits of warming up and cooling down* and ** can explain the short-term and long-term effects of exercise** (ongoing skills).

Key: Step 3 | *Step 4* | **Step 5**

Equipment required:

* 15 cricket bats
* 15 throw down lines
* bucket of 96 soft tennis-sized balls
* 8 coloured hoops.

Safety

While delivering all activities, it is important to follow the safety guidelines set out below to ensure a safe and effective learning environment.

* Ensure the playing area is always safe and free of any hazards such as sharp objects, before use.
* Ensure pupils are wearing the appropriate attire and that any shoes with laces are sufficiently tightened.

- Check that equipment is not damaged or torn before each lesson.
- Inform and reinforce to pupils the importance of finding space and not bumping into others during warm-ups and other activities.
- Lay the equipment out before the start of the lesson, where possible, to ensure easy access to resources and a smoother transition between activities.
- Inform and remind pupils of the rules and expectations at the beginning of each lesson.
- When delivering line games or activities in which small queues exist, ensure pupils stand side by side so that you can always see them and they can see what is going on in front of them.
- Use verbal as well as visual signals to regain pupil focus and attention.

Rules

- No talking while the teacher is explaining something to the group or demonstrating a task.
- No talking whilst others are explaining something to the group or demonstrating a task.
- No touching other people or equipment without the teacher's permission.

Some of the rules that teachers will need to know and understand in cricket are as follows:

A 'No ball' is declared if:
- the bowler bowls the ball from the wrong place.
- the bowl is declared dangerous (often when the ball is bowled too high or directly at the batters body).
- the ball bounces more than twice before reaching the batter.
- the fielders are in illegal positions.

- The batsperson can hit a no ball and score runs off it but cannot be out from a no ball except if they are run out, hit the ball twice, handle the ball or obstruct the field. The batsman gains any runs scored off the no ball for his shot while the team also gains one run for the no ball itself.
- A 'wide ball' is declared where the ball is bowled outside of the bowling lane or too wide of the stumps for the batter to reasonably be able to make contact with the ball.

Lesson 1 Catching the cricket ball

Lesson objective: Collecting the ball from the floor using correct fielding techniques, and to practise striking the ball from the floor using the correct 'hold' position for the bat.

Key terms: "right angle"; "side-on"; "underarm"; "overarm"

Warm-up: Cones and domes (10 minutes)

Divide the class into two teams. Each pupil is given a marker cone and asked to place the cone in an open space on the floor. One team places their cones the correct way up, as or 'cones'; the other team places their cones upside down, as or 'domes'.

On the teacher's command, one team turns all of the 'cones' into 'domes', whilst the other team attempts to turn all of the 'domes' into cones.

At the end of pre-determined time (e.g. 20–30 seconds), assess whether there are more 'hats' or 'bowls' on the floor to decide the winners of that round. Repeat the activity to raise the pulse rate and prepare pupils for the next activity.

Variation

Classic warm-up: Pupils travel around the space following the teacher's various instructions, including: 'Left hand' – pupils pretend to pick up the ball with their left hand – and 'Right hand' – pupils pretend to pick up the ball with their right hand.

Key teaching points

- ABCs – agility, balance, co-ordination, speed.
- Awareness – pupils to find the nearest cone.
- Teach pupils to keep 'bent knees' on collection of the cone – this becomes important when fielding a ball which is travelling on the floor.

Main lesson: Make the cage (20 minutes)

Asks pupils to quickly gather into groups of three. Pupils begin by linking hands in a triangle and then unlinking hands to take six, *eight* or **twelve** steps back, maintaining their triangle shape.

The first pupil bowls the ball along the ground to the second pupil, who then catches the ball and rolls the ball to the third pupil.

The aim of the game is to move the ball quickly along the floor without losing control of it.

Competition

The first group to complete 10 or *15* or **20** (depending on the ability of the group) catches within their group is the winning group.

Differentiation

Decrease the distance between each members of the team for WT pupils, and increase it for WB pupils.

Progression

Progress to following their pass after passing to their teammate, so that as soon as they pass the ball, they move to a new space, and all pupils in the team are constantly moving, which makes thee game more challenging.

Layered differentiation:

Give pupils the independence to decide themselves when to progress to the appropriate task level in accordance with their performance: once pupils have caught the ball successfully, and without having to chase after it, ten times consecutively progress to each pupil in the team taking three steps back to repeat the activity. Once they have completed ten consecutive successful catches, progress to *throwing the ball underarm*. After ten successful passes underarm, progress to **overarm throws**.

Key teaching points

- Bend the left knee at a right angle to the floor, keeping the right foot close to the heel of the left foot to form a barrier that prevents the ball travelling through it.
- Place both little fingers together with fingers spread to make a cage with the hands.
- When rolling the ball, *ensure the ball travels in a straight line* by following through towards the target person **consistently**.
- Pupils to *ensure correct weight of the roll* – not too fast and not too slow – and do this **consistently**.

Match play (20 minutes)

Divide the class into groups of three: one pupil is the batsperson, one is the bowler and the other is the fielder.

The bowler rolls the ball along the floor to the batsperson, who hits the ball in any direction for the fielder to collect and quickly return to the bowler. After a set period, e.g. every few minutes, pupils rotate roles.

Tips

The fielder stands in any position where they are anticipating the ball to travel so that they can return the ball to the bowler as quickly as possible.

Differentiation

WT pupils practise at a closer distance.

WB pupils practise at a greater distance or with an underarm bowl (with one bounce before the batsperson strikes the ball).

Key teaching points
- Roll the ball underarm – start by holding the ball on the outside of the right ankle (if right-handed and on the left side if left-handed) and follow through towards the target.
- Fielding – pupils to collect the ball *quickly and confidently* and return it to the bowler as quickly as possible.
- Striking the ball – focus on *good batting technique*; hold the non-writing hand above the right hand on the cricket bat, adopting a 'side-on' stance (there should be an imaginary straight line between both shoulders facing the bowler).
- **Pupils to perform all of the above skills accurately and consistently to positively impact others.**

Cool-down: Spin, swap, jump (10 minutes)
Divide the class into groups of two or three. Place one cone (or ball placed on top of a cone) between the three pupils.

All pupils move their feet quickly up and down on the spot ('quick feet') ready to follow the teacher's instructions, which must include, but not be limited to:
- spin – spin around 360 degrees
- swap – rotate positions of all three players avoiding collisions
- jump (or star jumps)
- shuffle – move the feet backwards and forwards quickly, or in a criss-cross fashion.

When the teacher calls, 'Cone' or 'Ball', the first person in each group to react quickly and gather the cone (or ball) from the ground gains a point.

Progression
Give pupils the opportunity to lead: ask one pupil to lead the group and call the appropriate commands.

Key teaching points
- Stay jogging on the balls of your feet, keeping your feet low to the ground, pumping your arms in co-ordination with your legs.
- Keep your knees slightly bent, to help you react quickly.

Plenary
- What do we need to do before we catch the ball?
- What technique do we use?
- What do we need to focus on to ensure the ball travels to our partner successfully?

Cross-curricular links

Mathematics (numbers and counting): Pupils count how many cones that they have as 'hats' and how many cones they have as 'bowls'. Challenge pupils with mental arithmetic questions to keep their brains stimulated, e.g. work out the difference between the numbers, multiply the numbers by 2, 3, 4 or 5 (up to multiples of 10 dependant on the age and ability of your pupils), or work out the percentage of hats and bowls.

Lesson 2 Sending and receiving the cricket ball

Lesson objective: To further develop basic team skills through games for batting, bowling and fielding.

Key terms: "conditioning"; "front foot batting"

Warm-up: Conditioning (10 minutes)
Phase 1: Introduce a classic warm-up: for a short time in which pupils are responding to the teacher's instructions, including: jogging, skipping, hopping, jogging backwards, jumping, etc. Pupils are completing dynamic stretches of the muscles whilst travelling in the ways listed above.

Play the numbers game to get pupils into groups of four. (When the teacher calls a number, pupils quickly get into a group of that number; the teacher finally calls the number four, so that pupils react quickly and get into a group of that number.)

Phase 2 – Conditioning: Set up seven or eight mini grids, approximately ten by ten yard square. Place four hoops in the middle of each grid, one for each pupil and one hoop in each of the corners, i.e. Pupil A in the red central hoop, faces the red hoop in the corner. Pupils B in the green central hoop faces the green hoop in the corner. Place four balls in the corner hoop of each square.

All pupils start in the middle of their own central hoop, completing an activity on the spot, e.g. star jumps, tuck jumps or jogging on the spot.

On the teachers' command, pupils run to their corner hoop, pick up a ball, run back to the centre and place the ball in their centre in their central hoop. They repeat this exercise until all the balls are returned to the centre.

The game ends when all pupils have returned all of their balls to their central hoop.

Progression
All pupils start in the middle of their grid *throwing and catching a ball whilst jogging on the spot*. Instead of four hoops in the middle, there is a stump.

The pupils complete the activity in pairs, with one pupil working as the fielder, the other as the keeper. The first fielder runs to a corner, picks up a ball and returns it to the keeper at the stump.

When all balls are in the centre, the keeper then returns each ball to the four corners, carrying only one ball at a time.

The other pair repeats the activity.

Variation

Instead of taking turns, each pupil starts with four balls in their own coloured hoop in the middle. There is a central stump where all four pupils start. On the teacher's command, all pupils take one ball from their middle hoop and place it in their corner hoop before sprinting back to the middle as quickly as they can to collect the next ball.

The activity pauses when pupils have returned all of their balls to the hoops in the corners. *Pupils have a few moments to recover before the teacher instructs them to repeat the task, this time collecting the balls from the corners and returning them to the middle.*

Note: The teacher may wish to group pupils according to their speed so that pupils can compete to be the fastest in their team.

Key teaching points
- Speed of collecting the ball (fielding).
- General positive conditioning.
- Teamwork – pupils to work together to achieve the best results.

Main lesson: Throw and go (20 minutes)

Divide the class into groups of three. Pupils begin by linking hands in a triangle and then unlinking hands to take six, *eight* or **twelve** steps back, maintaining their triangle shape.

The first pupil rolls the ball along the floor or a underarm throw with a bounce in between, or **overarm** to the second pupil, who catches it then rolls or **throws** the ball to the third pupil.

Competition

The first team to complete ten catches gains one point. Progress to 20 catches.

Differentiation

WT pupils practise rolling the ball along the floor or throwing from shorter distances.

WB pupils practise throwing the ball at various heights, or throwing from longer distances.

Ask WB pupils to **throw the ball overarm, ensuring you teach and demonstrate the correct technique for the overarm throw**.

Progression

After throwing the ball, the pupil follows the pass to the next point in the triangle, following their pass. All pupils continue to throw and go to a new space in the triangle.

Key teaching points
- Accurate throwing – start by holding the ball beside the knee.
- Hold the ball using 'snake fingers' – index and middle finger over the top of the ball, with the thumb underneath the ball. To help improve accuracy, pupils may find it useful to follow through by pointing their index finger to their target on releasing the ball.
- Catching the ball – Make a cage with the hands by placing the hands together with fingers widely spread apart.

Match play (20 minutes)

Use your space effectively to create several mini playing areas. Each playing area has a stump with a cricket bat a few paces in front of it. Place one cone either side of each bat to represent where the pupils must aim to bowl the ball in between. Lay out a cone or throw down line opposite the stumps to represent where the bowler will bowl from. A final cone is placed to the left of batsman and approximately six yards away from the stump.

Divide the class into teams of four or five and give each pupil a number (one–five). In each team, pupil 1 begins as the batter whilst pupil 5 begins as the bowler. Each team has one batter, one bowler and two or *three fielders*.

The batter begins the game with five points. The bowler bowls the ball and the batter strikes the ball as smoothly as they can and away from the fielders. After striking the ball, they run around their cone. The batter gains one point for each time they run around the cone but loses one *or two points* for each time they are bowled or caught out.

If the batter does not manage to strike the ball, he or she must still run around their cone, providing the ball is not bowled illegally or wide of the set markers.

Rotate the batting and fielding players every so often to ensure a smooth pace to the lesson.

Tips

Ensure pupils have developed the relevant skills from the match play in lesson 1 before progressing to the activity below. If pupils have not achieved the desired objectives of the previous lesson, then repeat the main lesson section from lesson 1.

Differentiation

Ask WT pupils to roll the ball along the floor as opposed to completing an underarm bowling action.

Variation

If space is too small (e.g. in a small hall), the teacher may find it more beneficial to play a game which is more relevant to the space, e. g. throwing and catching games or small-sided tournaments, where observers write down on their whiteboards positive points, and points to improve.

Key teaching points

- Front foot batting – pupils to *lead into the ball from the front foot*.
- Fielding – pupils to catch the ball *quickly* and get it back to the bowler.
- Bowling – pupils to bowl the ball *accurately, with consistent control, accuracy and speed* (underarm or **overarm**) towards the stump by following the skills learnt in previous lessons.

Cool-down: In-goal diving (10 minutes)

In groups of three, pupils stand in a line, one behind the other but keeping a six yard distance apart. The pupil in the middle has two cones on either side (which represents the 'goal', which are approximately two–*four* yards apart.

The pupils on either end both have cricket balls. They take it in turns to bowl the ball towards the goal where the pupil in the middle is standing.

The first bowler bowls the ball towards the goal. The person in the middle must sprint towards the ball, gather the ball and roll it back to the bowler, diving if necessary (if the surface is safe and appropriate), ensuring the ball does not go into the goal.

Once the ball has been returned, the middle pupil turns to face the other bowler to repeat the activity.

After a set amount of time (e.g. 20–45 seconds), the teacher should ask pupils to rotate positions.

Key teaching points
- Stay ready and on the balls of the feet.
- Bowl the ball accurately focusing on the techniques learnt earlier in the lesson and in previous lessons (e.g. snake fingers, throwing from the knee and moving the throwing arm up towards the shoulder level, etc.).
- React quickly and try to get your body behind the ball before returning it.

Plenary
- What technique(s) do we use to bowl the ball to the target?
- Should we lead off the front or back foot for front foot batting? Why is this important?

Lesson 3 Bowling to a target

Lesson objective: To improve skills for throwing the ball towards a target and for striking the ball *accurately* and **consistently** towards a target area.

Key terms: "snake hold"; "hold position"

Warm-up: Keep it up (10 minutes)

Phase 1: Start with the classic warm-up whereby pupils jog around the given playing area responding to the teacher's instructions, e.g. jogging, skipping, hopping, sidestepping, arm rotations, etc.

Then play the numbers game to get pupils into groups of the right size for phase 2 (when the teacher calls a number, pupils respond by getting into groups of that number as quickly as they can).

Phase 2: Give groups of three, *four* or **five** a tennis ball or soft while ball. Pupils must throw the ball underarm to different people in their group, while keeping on the move. Pupils must ensure good practice and work well together to ensure that their ball does not fall to the floor.

Pupils should aim to produce a quick turnover of passes. The teacher may progress to giving the group a target for a certain number of catches within a set amount of time, e.g. 20, *30* or **40** seconds.

Differentiation
WT pupils may complete the same game using rolling as the specified technique, as opposed to throwing the ball underarm.

Layered differentiation: Pupils start by rolling the ball to their partners. Once pupils have caught the ball ten times in a row without the ball going astray, pupils progress to throwing the ball to their peers at chest height. **If or when they make ten consecutive passes without the ball dropping, pupils progress to throwing the ball approximately tree metres above the head height of their peers.**

Note: Be sure to deliver a safe and effective demonstration of each stage, so that pupils have a clear visual demonstration of the expectation. Teachers may also wish to show videos on YouTube of this success criteria whilst pupils are getting changed or during the lesson.

Progression
For each ball that touches the floor, one pass is deducted from the total score.

Key teaching points
- Transferring the cricket ball – pupils to pass it *quickly and accurately* by following through towards the target person.
- Developing catching skills – pupils to make a cage (remind pupils of skills learnt in previous lessons).
- Warming up the muscles and preparing the mind for the more advanced elements of the lesson.
- **Pupils perform the above skills consistently to have a positive impact on the team.**

Main lesson: Target bowl (20 minutes)
In groups of three, pupils take turns to practise bowling the ball into a target zone or hoop before sprinting to collect their ball and returning to their group. Award ten points for each successful hit of the target. The team who scores the most points at the end of each round wins.

Repeat the game and challenge pupils to beat their previous score each time.

Differentiation
The teacher may wish to group pupils according to pupil ability and inform each group that they can bowl the ball in a way that is most comfortable for them. WT pupils may have a shorter distance to throw and/or larger targets to aim at. WB pupils may have a longer distance to throw and/or shorter targets to aim at.

WT pupils may wish to throw underarm or use beanbags as opposed to balls.

WB pupils may wish to use an **overarm bowl**.

Once pupils have reached 50 points, they move their starting cone or throw down line three paces further back and progress to bowling the ball from a longer distance.

Key teaching points
- Ensure pupils are using the *correct hold position* for the ball, enclosing the index and middle finger around the top of the ball, with the thumb aligned underneath. (This technique is also known as the 'snake hold'.)

Match play (20 minutes)
In groups of five, repeat the same layout and points system as for the match play in lesson 2. Provided that pupils have reached the target aims of lesson 2, this lesson the teacher shall introduce the target zone for the bowler, e.g. by placing *a hoop in front of the batter*. If only some pupils have achieved the target aims for lesson 2, then use the 'target zone' for only these pupils, as an extension activity only.

The bowler shall gain one point each time the ball lands in the target zone before the batter moves on to stroke the ball.

Key teaching points
- Remind pupils of the correct way to hold the cricket bat.
- Strike the ball accurately by following through the target.
- Run as fast as you can, once you have struck the ball.

Cool-down: Footwork ladder drills (10 minutes)
Three pupils begin on one side of each ladder and two pupils on the other side. Pupils start behind a cone, five yards away from the ladder.

The teacher informs and demonstrates the style in which pupils are to travel through the ladder for each round, e.g. sideways footsteps placing two feet in each space alternately, single leg hops (repeat leading with both the left and right leg), two-footed jumps, facing forwards and placing one foot in each space.

The first of the three pupils goes first. They carry a ball whilst doing the footwork drill up the ladder. On exiting the ladder, the pupil must roll the ball underarm to the teammate waiting at the front of the queue on the opposite side to where they started, before joining the back of that queue.

Progression
Pupils *throw the ball underarm to the next person*.

Key teaching points
- Keep on the balls of your feet.
- Keep your stomach muscles tight.
- Pump the arms in co-ordination with the legs.

Plenary
- What technique(s) do we use to bowl the ball to a target?
- Why do we need to follow through towards the target?
- How do we develop *accuracy* and **speed** in our bowling?

Cross-curricular links

Mathematics: When practising the appropriate stance for batting, ask pupils to draw an imaginary parallel line through the shoulder to the bowler, and teach pupils the meaning of key terms such as parallel.

Science (physics): Discuss the angles and weight of transfer with the pupils, thereby developing their understanding of why the ball travels faster or slower depending on the *weight of the roll* and the **speed of transfer**.

More lesson ideas and activities for cricket

Continuous catch cricket

Separate the class into ten teams of three pupils per team. Each 'batter' starts with five points. In small teams of three, the bowler throws the ball towards the 'batter'. The batter attempts to catch the ball, before throwing it out to the field and running around the cone, which is placed to the side of the wicket (approximately six–*twelve yards* away). The batter has to run, whether the fielders catch the ball or not and return to his/her 'batting' position.

The batter loses a point when:
- the bowler hits the stump with the ball. If the batter is in front of the wicket, this must be done by throwing the ball to the stump, from the bowling position
- one of the fielders catches the ball before it bounces.

Batters gain points each time they run around the cone without being bowled or caught out.

After three bowls, pupils change the batter and bowler. Once all batters and bowlers have had their turn, pupils tally their scores.

Skittles bowling

Working as individuals or in small teams of three, pupils start at the red cone, run forwards towards the green cone and bowl the ball towards the stumps or skittles (three large cones) in front of them.

Differentiation: Mark out a green cone which is closest to the skittles, an orange cone which is a little bit further away and a yellow cone, even further still, from the skittles. Once pupils have hit the skittles from the green cone twice, they progress to bowling from the orange cone. Once they have hit the skittles from the orange cone twice, they attempt to bowl from the yellow cones.

Throw and Go

In pairs, pupils practice throwing and catching the ball to each other. Immediately after throwing the ball, the pupils move to a new space. Develop the activity by:
- introducing different types of bowl (e.g. underarm, overarm).
- varying the height at which the pupils must throw and catch the ball. Pupils must throw the ball at least three metres above their head for their partner to catch it. Progress to five metres, eight metres and so on. Teachers can challenge pupils further by insisting that the catcher catches the ball above their head.

- changing the distance between the thrower and the catcher. To begin, pupils throw the ball when their partner is approximately three metres away. Progress to five metres, *seven metres*, **twelve metres** and so on.

Relay bowl

Group pupils into small teams of up to three pupils and set out a large cone a set distance ahead of each team. Ask the pupils in each team to form a queue; the first pupil in each line sprints to the cone and bowls the ball at a target. On releasing the ball, the pupil sprints to collect his/her ball before returning to their team. The next person in the line repeats the activity, as soon as the person ahead has picked up their ball.

Scoring method a.

The first team to hit the stump three times is the winning team. Repeat the game a few times as appropriate.

Scoring method b.

Play for a set amount of time, e.g. two minutes. Pupils gain one point for each time they hit the stump and collate their team scores at the end of the round.

To challenge pupils further, the teacher may wish to set out a second and third cone, further away from the stump and inform pupils that if they hit the target from the second cone, they gain two points, and if they hit the stump from the third cone, they gain three points.

Catch and count

Pupils work in pairs and stand approximately three–five or *six–eight* or **ten–twelve yards** apart. Pupils count how many catches they have made out loud. The game ends after a set amount of time, e.g. 30 seconds. Check the pupils' progress by asking them how many times they were able to catch the ball.

Batting rotation

Create teams of up to five pupils per team. The fielding team sets up in the usual way, however the batting team line up, side-by-side, six yards away from the batter. The batting team always starts the game with five runs.

As the bowler bowls the ball, the batter attempts to strike it, before running behind the bowler and joining the end of the batting line. As soon as the ball is bowled, the next batter in line steps forward ahead of the stump, a new bowler quickly comes into place at the 'bowling spot'. The batting team loses points when:
- the bowler hits the stump
- a fielder cathes the ball (after the batter strikes it, but before it bounces).

The batting team gains one run for each time they hit the ball without getting bowled or caught out as above. Play for a set amount of time, e.g. three minutes, before rotating the batting and fielding team. The teacher may also wish to run this as a tournament, so that different teams play against different opponents.

Glossary

Arch shape: A gymnastics position that can be performed on the floor, on apparatus or in the air whereby the core of the body is arched/curved slightly in the shape of a arch, e.g. if lying on the floor, facing downwards towards the floor, the legs would be together and a few inches off the floor, and the chest would also be a few inches off the floor, using the hips and lower abdominals as the balancing point.

Bounce pass: Passing the ball from the chest. Start with the ball in front of the chest and elbows out before stepping forwards towards the receiver, extend the arms forward towards the receiver. Throw the fingers outwards to the side or downwards, with the thumbs pointing down. The ball should bounce at approximately two thirds of the way to the receiver and should typically arrive above the receiver's waist area.

Bounding: Jumping continuously off two feet with the feet close together.

Chest pass: Passing the ball from the chest. Start with the ball in front of the chest and elbows out before stepping forwards towards the receiver, extend the arms forward towards the receiver. Throw the fingers outwards to the side or downwards, with the thumbs pointing down. The ball should arrive at around the intended receiver's chest area.

Classic warm-up: In a coned off area in the playground or hall, pupils travel around the given area in various directions looking for space. You should either inform pupils of the selected way in which they should travel or ask them if they can think of any alternative methods of travel. Warm-ups should be progressive in their intensity in order to ensure the key criteria are successfully met, i.e. walking progresses to skipping, then to jogging and so on.

Dish shape: A gymnastics position that can be performed on the floor, on apparatus or in the air whereby the core of the body is arched/curved slightly in the shape of a dish, e.g. if lying on the floor facing up towards the ceiling, the legs would be together and a few inches off the floor, and the back would also be a few inches off the floor, using the bottom and lower back as the balancing point.

Double dribble: This is where a pupil receives the basketball, dribbles it, catches it and then dribbles again.

Gates: Two cones of the same colour are spaced one to two yards apart to represent a form of 'goal' or target zone for various pupil practices.

Hip flexors: The joints at the top of the legs, above the quadriceps. These need to be strong and supple for bounding, jumping, rolling and various other sports related movements.

Jump stop: When a pupil receives the basketball with two feet on the ground. Children are often taught to jump and land in this position, to emphasise the technique.

Layered differentiation: Explain and demonstrate the key progressive phases of the activity before it begins, setting clear targets that pupils must meet before moving to the next phase, enabling pupils to self-evaluate when they are able to progress to the next phase and challenge themselves further.

Linking: Pupils make contact with their partner in gymnastics whilst changing shape.

Lob pass: An overhead pass used in netball and basketball, where the ball travels upwards usually over an opponent or object.

Peripheral vision: Scanning the whole playing area to ensure you a aware of where others are in relation to ones self.

Pike shape: A gymnastics position that can be performed on the floor, on apparatus or in the air whereby the legs are straight out in front, with pointed toes.

Pivot: Pupils keep one foot in place whilst the other foot is moving. Pivoting is used in basketball and netball to avoid travelling and double dribble, often whilst screening the ball from opponents and/or looking for a teammate or before shooting for the hoop.

Pop pass: a short pass to a teammate which is often also disguised.

Reverse stick: Involves a changing of the grip to reverse the hockey stick from the open side to the reverse side, meaning the ball and the stick are on the non-writing hand side of the body.

SAQ (Speed, Agility, Quickness):

Speed: The pace at which it takes to travel from one position to another.

Agility: The speed and fluency of movement, e.g. the pace at which and fluency of how a pupil can lift their leg over a hurdle.

Quickness: The pace at which a pupil can change direction or activity, e.g. the pace at which a pupil transitions from receiving a ball to passing a ball.

Shadow: To follow the actions and movements of the teacher or another pupil or person.

Shoulder pass: A single handed pass from the shoulder, typically aiming for or reaching the shoulder area or chest area of a teammate.

STEP principle: Increases or decreases the level of challenge according to pupils' needs:

Space – make the space smaller or larger.
Tasks – alter the main task or activity.
Equipment – change the equipment used.
People – arrange for pupils to work in larger or smaller groups and/or with more advanced or less advanced peers. The lesson plans assume (in most cases) that there are 30 children in each lesson, so adjust the numbers or teams accordingly to suit the needs of your pupils or group.

Trap: To control the ball by stopping its motion (or slowing it down significantly).

Travelling: A violation of the rules where a pupil receives the ball and takes more than one step (not including the landing foot), with the ball without bouncing the ball in a continuous motion.

Tuck shape: A gymnastics position that can be performed on the floor, on apparatus or in the air whereby the knees are close together and tucked in towards the chest.

W shape: Showing two hands up in the form of a 'W shape'; open hands and fingers in front of the chest with the thumbs touching or almost touching.

WB pupils: Pupils who are 'working beyond' the relevant success criteria and need to be challenged further.

WO pupils: Majority of pupils who are 'working on' the relevant success criteria in accordance with the required expectations.

WT pupils: Pupils who are 'working towards' the relevant success criteria and require further support.